BRAZILIAN FICTION

BRAZILIAN FICTION

*Aspects and Evolution
of the Contemporary Narrative*

Robert E. DiAntonio

THE UNIVERSITY OF ARKANSAS PRESS
Fayetteville   London   1989

Copyright © 1989 by Robert DiAntonio
Manufactured in the United States of America
93 92 91 90 89   5 4 3 2 1

DESIGNER: Brenda J. Zodrow
TYPEFACE: Linotron 202 Sabon
TYPESETTER: G&S Typesetters, Inc.
PRINTER: Edwards Brothers, Inc.
BINDER: Edwards Brothers, Inc.

The paper used in this publication meets the minimum requirements of the American
National Standard for Permanence of Paper for Printed Library Materials Z39.48-
1984. ∞

LIBRARY OF CONGRESS CATALOGING-IN-PUBLICATION DATA

DiAntonio, Robert E., 1941—
    Brazilian fiction : aspects and evolution of the contemporary narrative / Robert E.
DiAntonio
        p.   cm.
    Bibliography: p.
    Includes index.
    IBSN 1-55728-056-8 (alk. paper). ISBN 1-55728-057-6 (pbk. : alk. paper)
    1. Brazilian fiction--20th century--History and criticism.
I Title.
PQ9603.D5 1989
869.3--dc19   *T* _155728056*8*_   88-19882
                                                                    CIP

Esqueci de dizer que tudo o que estou agora escrevendo é acompanhado pelo ruflar enfático de um tambor batido por um soldado. No instante mesmo em que eu começar a história—de súbito cessará o tambor.

(I forgot to mention that everything I am now writing is accompanied by the emphatic ruffle of a military drum. The moment I start to tell my story—the noise of the drum will suddenly cease.)

Clarice Lispector (1977)

CONTENTS

CONTENTS

PREFACE

Neste romance inesquecível, ele proporciona ao leitor uma experiência enriquecedora, um mergulho num Brasil que é "o nosso", o de todos, o Brasil do nosso inconsciente coletivo, mitológico, misterioso, vibrante, escondido . . . mais de três séculos de uma anti-História do Brasil.
(This unforgettable novel brings to the reader an enriching experience, an exploration of a Brazil that is "ours," everyone's, the Brazil of our collective unconscious, mythological, mysterious, vibrant, hidden . . . more than three centuries of an anti-history of Brazil.)

Viva o povo brasileiro
Editora Nova Fronteira

While underscoring the tension that has evolved between the mythic and anti-mythic world views, this effusive cover quote encapsulates many important concerns of the contemporary Brazilian narrative. In essence, it brings into sharp focus the almost obsessive nature that various Brazilian fiction writers express regarding a need to reshape the national consciousness. One can think of few other world literatures that exhibit such a passion for introspection and the refocusing of national ideals and myths. It is also interesting that the term anti-history is subjoined to the patriotic title *Viva o povo brasileiro* (*Long Live the Brazilian People*). This seems to imply that by the mid-1980s the demythification of Brazilian history, cultural ideals, and myths had become acceptably mainstream. This was not always the case with the generation of writers who emerged after the military coup of April 1, 1964, and whose writings were greatly affected by the sociopolitical turmoil of the ensuing years.

The evolutionary passage from the poetics of myth, "o Brasil do nosso inconsciente coletivo" (the Brazil of our collective unconscious), to the present day poetics of anti-myth is to be the framework within which the following essays are conceived.

Referring to the past four centuries of Brazilian writing, Earl E. Fitz has stated that they form part of one of the world's "most neglected national literatures."[1] David William Foster considers this same body of literature "unquestionably the equal of any Western artistic production."[2] In comparison to the boom years of Spanish American literature when academic critics constructed a veritable panoply of interpretive readings for all but the most minor works, excellent examples of innovative Brazilian writings still remain steeped in obscurity.

Contemporary Brazil has contributed to the world many important developments in the fields of architecture, film, music, and art. In the field of literature, only a select few works and writers are known outside their home country. The guiding principle of the following studies of this vibrant body of literature is to provide a helpful introduction to several important authors and to delineate the major characteristics of their writings. The books selected to be commented upon are all readily available in translation and are easily accessible in their Portuguese originals.

Within the United States and Europe publishing houses are beginning to bring to light excellent examples of Brazilian writings from the award winning novels of Márcio Souza to the most avant-garde works of Ignácio de Loyola Brandão. Presently there exists a generation of critics who are in the initial stages of focusing upon this vast literature. The standard is being established whereby the literary text itself takes precedence over the erudition, politics, and critical theories of the reviewer.

An overview of contemporary Brazilian fiction is a vast undertaking. The consequence of such an endeavor easily could result in the anatomizing of small bits and passages of literary works, yielding poorly substantiated generalities. Often this approach evolves as an encyclopedic and confusing compilation of data. For this reason, the central focus of this book is to be the presentation and analysis of several representative works of fiction, highlighting their integrity as narrative works of art.

To make this presentation meaningful, the text begins with an introductory sociopolitical chapter on Brazil. Here the stage will be set for social and political tie-ins with the various novels to be studied. Each of the ensuing chapters will concentrate upon and reflect important "aspects of the novel," and in its totality, the book will be representative of the modern Brazilian novel. Each aspect of the novel, each chapter, will evolve from the general to the specific, with a brief overview followed by one or two works explicated in depth. In the manner of Ivan Ângelo's *A festa* (*The Celebration*), this book is purposefully structured to allow the chapters to exist as separate entities with the specific studies in each chapter also existing independently.

Since most modern fiction is comprised of varying formal, thematic, and narrative techniques, it is felt that each text can be rendered more comprehensible by a combination of critical approaches. While the texts will be reviewed primarily from a sociopolitical and archetypal perspective, absurdist, reader-response, and psychological approaches will be liberally employed. The opting for a variety of theoretical approaches is dictated to a great extent by the strongly ideological nature of the period and by the fact that the differing texts are rendered more accessible from a specific and determined perspective.

To this end, France's Marc Chénetier in *Critical Angles: European Views of Contemporary American Literature* (1986) puzzles "over the more or less faddish and more often than not blundering vogue of 'structuralism,' 'poststructuralism,' and 'deconstruction' in the United States."[3] He states that the "most important practitioners of the disciplines roughly confused with or subsumed under these terms never dreamed themselves of endowing them with such sledgehammer power."[4] Brazil's preeminent poet Carlos Drummond de Andrade's now famous work "Exorcismo," "Exorcism," expresses an impatient disdain for the excesses of this criticism. "De Zolkiewski, Jakobson, Barthes, Derrida, Todorov/ De Greimas, Fodor, Chao, Lacan et caterva/ Libera nos, Domine"[5] ("From Zolkiewski, Jakobson, Barthes, Derrida, Todorov/ From Greimas, Fodor, Chao, Lacan 'et' the rest of the gang/ Libera nos, Domine") The dean of Brazilian literary critics, Wilson Martins, states that Drummond is reacting to a critical methodology that "tinha atingido proporções epidêmicas"[6] ("has reached epidemic proportions"). The following studies propose to eschew the "jargão, pretensamente científico"[7] ("alleged scientific jargon") and place in primary focus, in Drummond's words, "o tempo presente, os homens presentes, / a vida presente"[8] ("present time, present life, present man"). Chénetier goes on to observe that theoretical explorations "are meant to feed literary reflection rather than to dictate recipes for the shaping of its practical output . . . (and that) the text cannot be fodder for critical theories, which must at all times retain their ancillary quality."[9] He believes that microanalysis and "an eagerness to tackle the texts at hand"[10] is always preferable to forcing a particular theory upon an unreceptive work. Terry Eagleton mirrors Chénetier's view. "Literary criticism does not usually dictate any particular reading as long as it is 'literary critical.'"[11] He underscores the subjective nature of both the critic's and reader's roles. "Most of us recognize that no reading is innocent or without presuppositions . . . there is no such thing as a purely 'literary' response: all such responses, not least those to literary *form*, to the aspects of a work which are sometimes jealously reserved to the 'aesthetic,' are deeply imbricated with the kind of social and historical individuals we are."[12]

The following studies represent the diversity and vitality of an important segment of contemporary Brazilian fiction. These studies are designed to turn the attention of today's reader to an important period in Brazilian literary history, providing a sense of how and why these writers are both innovators and perpetuators of longstanding literary traditions. Brazilian writing has been coming of age, and it is hoped that the following observations will contribute to a further understanding of the individual vision and concern of each author and the literary and cultural assumptions upon which they are based.

NOTES

The epigraph to the preface is from the anonymous cover quote that accompanies the novel. João Ubaldo Ribeiro, *Viva o povo brasileiro* (Rio de Janeiro: Nova Fronteira, 1985). Unless otherwise indicated, this and all other English translations are my own. However, every effort has been made to use previously published translations.

1. Earl E. Fitz, *Clarice Lispector* (Boston: Twayne, 1985), p.vii.
2. David William Foster, "Major Figures in the Brazilian Short Story,"

The Latin American Short Story, edited by Margaret Sayers Peden (Boston: G. K. Hall, 1983), p. 34.

3. Marc Chénetier, *Critical Angles: European Views of Contemporary American Literature* (Edwardsville and Carbondale: Southern Illinois University Press, 1986), p. xxiii.

4. Chénetier, p. xxiii.

5. Carlos Drummond de Andrade, "Exorcismo," *Jornal do Brasil* 12 April 1975.

6. Wilson Martins, *A crítica literária no Brasil*, Vol II (Rio de Janeiro: Francisco Alves, 1983), p. 791.

7. Martins, p. 791.

8. Drummond's well known *ars poetica* is featured as an epigram in Ivan Ângelo's *A festa*—the subject of the following chapter—(São Paulo: Summus, 1978), p. 11. The work was published in English as *The Celebration*, trans. Thomas Colchie (New York: Avon Books, 1982), p. 6. For a futher discussion of this important poem see also, Robert DiAntonio, "The Confessional Mode as a Liberating Force in the Poetics of Carlos Drummond de Andrade," *Quaderni Ibero-Americani*, Turin, forthcoming.

9. Chénetier, p. xxiii.

10. Chénetier, p. xxii.

11. Terry Eagleton, *Literary Theory* (Minneapolis: Univ. of Minnesota Press, 1983), p. 89.

12. Eagleton, p. 89.

ACKNOWLEDGMENTS

I would like to express my sincere appreciation to the following editors and journals where earlier versions of studies have appeared: Brian Dendle, *Romance Quarterly*; Saad Elkhadem, *The International Fiction Review*; Ivar Ivask, *World Literature Today*; Ted Lyon, *Chasqui*; Theodore Sackett, *Hispania*; and William Stafford, *Modern Fiction Studies*. I would also like to thank Clarence Olson of the St. Louis *Post-Dispatch*, Ernest Weiss of *Judaica Book News*, Larry Mintz of *Midstream*, Steve Paul of the Kansas City *Star*, and Trude Weiss-Rosmarin of the *Jewish Spectator* for allowing me to work out ideas in the form of features and reviews.

I am especially indebted to Suzana Amaral, Aaron, Adam, and Joan DiAntonio, David William Foster, Paul Guenther, Clifford Landers, Beatriz Carmem Wrath Raymann and Acir Raymann, Marcos Rey, Plínio Santos Filho, the faculty and students of Southern Illinois University at Edwardsville, and Camille Storts for their suggestions and encouragement.

BRAZILIAN FICTION

THE SOCIAL
AND POLITICAL
NATURE
OF RECENT
BRAZILIAN
FICTION

In the 1960s Fábio Lucas in his essay "Aspectos culturais da literatura brasileira" ("Cultural Aspects of Brazilian Literature") theorized, "Pergunta-se freqüentamente se o Brasil apresenta uma literatura autônoma, de características próprias . . . o que representa perguntar se temos uma cultura independente." ("It has frequently been asked whether Brazil has produced an autonomous literature with characteristics all its own, . . . this is another way of questioning whether we, as an independent nation, have created an autonomous culture.")[1] Lucas in his exploration of this significant and open-ended question concludes that "a autônomia *está-se formando*, é um processo em curso" ("this autonomy is in formation, it is an evolutionary process").[2] While Lucas's query, like most polemical questions, is open to a wide range of interpretations, it can be concluded at the very least that the new fiction which the following studies highlight forms part of an affirmative movement toward both literary and cultural autonomy. Many contemporary works, much like Lucas's questioning, evolve as an assiduous exploration of Brazilian reality. Taken in their totality, they attempt to define national myths and character. These writings address a distinctly Brazilian sociopolitical actuality by means of narrative strategies that are highly diversified and universal.

Recent Brazilian authors have created an important body of literature by seizing the meaning of the sociopolitical present, recasting it from a universal philosophical perspective, and incorporating transnationalized literary techniques. Literary historians may eventually come to regard this era as the time when there occurred a blending of aesthetic achievement, a truly national focus, and the production of literary genres that were of international merit and interest.

※ ※ ※

Much of recent Brazilian history reads like a novel. Many of the real life figures and events that dominated the politics of their time have captured the popular and artistic imagination. One characteristic of modern Brazilian fiction is that political figures and occurrences are incorporated into, discussed, and mythologized as part of the literary consciousness. The violent exploits of the bandit chieftain Virgulino Lampião, the "Long March" of the Prestes Column, the siege and fall of the city of Canudos, and a long succession of military dictators have all passed over from the historical to the literary realm. Renato Tapajós's *Em câmara lenta* (1975; *In Slow Motion*), a novel partially written while the author was imprisoned, directly integrates political figures and events into the flow of his work. Tapajós's narrative underscores the failure and futility of the Brazilian guerrilla movement during the height of the "ditadura."

Another case in point is the legendary and enigmatic life of the politician, Getúlio Vargas. Vargas ruled Brazil in what has been described as a "loose dictatorship" called the "Estado Novo," the New State (1937–1945). He was a charismatic and beloved leader from the southern state of Rio Grande do Sul, ruling as a paternal dictator whose failures and accomplishments are still discussed and disputed today. Vargas's regime spent a great deal of energy cultivating a sense of national pride. His propaganda machine extolled sports, soccer in particular, and folklore. All radio stations were compelled to present a compulsory "Brazilian Hour."[3] The yearly carnival and all popular music were organized to create a favorable state image. As historian Francis Lambert wryly observes: "This effort was largely nullified by

2

the Brazilian talent for ridicule. . . ."[4] The popular cynicism that is reported here in a historical context will later be paralleled in the reaction of the Absurdist novelists of the 1970s to the excesses of a succession of dictatorial regimes. Vargas was later duly elected in 1950 and supposedly committed suicide in 1954—an event that is still much discussed. Today novelists, dramatists, and composers like Dias Gomes, Chico Buarque, and Marcos Rey are still writing about Getúlio Vargas. Rey's *Ópera de sabão* (1982; *Soap Opera*) fictionalizes the days and events of Vargas's suicide and their effect on an Italo-Brazilian family, the Manfredis. Also, hundreds of examples of folk poetry, "literatura de cordel"—versed stories sold in the open-air marketplaces of Brazil—continue to mythify Vargas's exploits. Orígenes Lessa has collected and underscored the importance of this curious expression of popular feeling in *Getúlio Vargas na literatura de cordel* (1973).

After Vargas, Brazil then passed through a period of national and democratic rebirth with leaders like Juscelino Kubitschek, Jânio Quadros, and João Goulart. At that time the capital city of Brasilia was conceived and constructed, evolving as a symbol of national hope and pride. Brazil moved ahead to try to achieve fifty years of progress in five. However, on April 1st, 1964, the military moved in to close off the democratic process and impose a longstanding dictatorship that lasted until 1979. A succession of military governments took control of the economic and social life of the country and did not relinquish their power to elected civilian officials until 1985. They were repressive governments that did not receive the kind of international attention for their harsh measures that their Argentine neighbors did, but they were just as brutally totalitarian. "The patterns of torture and the rationale of the torturers in Brazil, especially during the period 1969–73, were surprisingly similar to those in Argentina. In both countries, the military torturers assumed that there were no legal nor moral constraints in what they viewed as an all-out war to terminate their enemies."[5]

Given this background, it is little wonder that a new generation of writers has focused upon their country's loss of freedom and in doing so, have constructed a literature of response. In *Sangue de Coca-Cola* (1981; *Coca-Cola Blood*), Roberto Drummond alludes to this recent history. "Aquele mesmo aviso que sentiu antes de Getúlio Vargas dar um tiro no peito, um tiro que ecoa no Brasil até hoje . . . o mesmo aviso do dia 1.o de Abril de 1964 . . . Sente medo: o Brasil está feliz, é um mau agouro, olha o céu luminoso e fala alto. —Meu Deus, o que

3

acontecerá com o Brasil hoje?"⁶ ("That same warning that he felt before Getúlio Vargas shot himself in the chest, a shot that still echoes throughout Brazil today . . . the same warning of the first of April, 1964, . . . He is afraid: Brazil is joyful, it's a bad omen, he looks at the bright sky and shouts: My God, what will happen to Brazil today?")

In response to a longstanding political reality, Spanish American literature has evolved a multifaceted genre, the novel of the dictator. This continuous tradition includes masterworks by García Márquez, Aguilera-Malta, and Miguel Ángel Asturias. Recent Brazilian fiction has addressed this same political reality by calling attention to the governmental repression that existed from 1964 to the "abertura," 1979, the opening. In the contemporary Brazilian novel, the chthonian vision of innocent victims braving graphically depicted torture is a pervasive one. George A. Panichas in *The Politics of Twentieth-Century Novelists* observes that, "The modern artist has come to see his [or her] role as one not of entertainment but rather of the expression of meaning, the communication of insight into some aspects of reality and human experience, the questioning and the redefining of life values."⁷

It is again Roberto Drummond in an interview with Granville Ponce who underscores the importance of this responsive anti-establishment writing, citing its firm link to the politics of the times. "—Tá acontecendo no Brasil uma revolução literária ou antiliterária tão importante como os dois maiores movimentos literários que já houve aqui: o movimento de 22 e o do romance nordestino. . . . E é uma literatura realmente de briga, em todos os sentidos."⁸ ("There's occurring in Brazil a literary revolution or anti-literary revolution as important as the two greatest literary movements that have already occurred here: the movement of 1922 and the Northeastern novel. . . . It's a militant literature in all senses.")

The sociopolitical failings of the 1960s and 1970s are documented and aesthetically transformed by many current Brazilian novelists. Contemporary Brazilian writers strongly reflect the thinking of Richard Hoggart, who states that literature "has to do with language exploring human experience, in all its flux and complexity. It is therefore always in an active relation with its age, and some students of literature—many more students of literature than at present—ought to try to understand these relationships better."⁹

※ ※ ※

During the last two decades in Brazil as elsewhere, the traditional novel as genre fell into disfavor, and writers freely experimented with

4

new forms of expression. While there existed varying degrees of experimentation with regard to the formal and structural aspects of the narrative, there also was present a unifying ironic vision among many of the new novelists. This ironic world-view underscored a common aim: to demythify the conception of a romanticized and stereotypical Brazil. Novelists dramatized the tension created between the national myths and the existing political and social reality. Even now, after the "abertura," the practice continues unabated, for a nation passing out of a time of repression seeks to understand itself in both sociological and artistic terms.

Brazilian status quo literature was just one of the many institutions which the writings of the past twenty years challenge. It was José Ortega y Gasset who stated, "In the 'today,' in every 'today,' various generations coexist and the relations which are established between them, . . . represent the dynamic system of attractions and repulsion, of agreement and controversy which at any given moment makes up the reality of historic life." [10] The sense of generational antagonism, especially during the volatile sixties and early seventies, created a counterculture that flourished in Brazilian university and literary circles. Add to this ambiance the alienation of an entire generation that reached maturity with its sense of freedom severely limited by an ultraconservative and nationalist political system.

Tied to the social alienation of this Brazilian generation of writers was a strong commitment to a literature of engagement. Generally these writers shared a politicized collective conscience that manifested itself not only in a desire to find new forms of expression, but also to explore themes that had previously been taboo. These writers demonstrated a willingness to deal with themes like homosexuality, rape, deviant sex, impotence, and drug use with a new openness. They dealt with these themes not from a judgmental perspective but as a reflection of their alienated world. These subjects were at times developed as part of the Brazilian refugee experience. Some of the writings of this generation are set in the exile communities of cities like Paris, Berlin, or New York.

Márcio Souza's *A condolência* (1984; *The Condolence*) takes the reader on a tour of the Parisian lives of the expatriots who are unable to escape the political intrigues of their homeland. Silviano Santiago's 1985 novel *Stella Manhattan* telescopes the concerns and ideological differences of recent political events into an imaginative work, a dark vision of the tensions and intrigues of the Brazilian diplomatic and exile communities in New York. The narrative evolves as an assiduous exploration of the varying ideological stances that comprise the political history of the "ditadura." Santiago focuses upon Eduardo da Costa e Silva and his transvestite alter-ego, Stella Manhattan. The author has created a unique personage who becomes the ideal vehicle for exploring the nature and consequences of political commitment and apathy. Stella is representative of a dramatic and escapist aspect of the Brazilian national character that wishes to eschew politics. However, Stella is directly drawn into the events of her homeland, and her life is destroyed by them. *O beijo não vem da boca* (1985; *The Kiss Doesn't Come from the Mouth*) by Ignácio de Loyola Brandão also explores the Brazilian exile experience, this time in Berlin and from the perspective of one man's mid-life reminiscences.

※　※　※

The absurdist vision is an important element of the post-1964 writers. The narrative heroes and anti-heroes of this generation are depicted as insignificant within the larger scheme of existence. The negative or absurdist world-view of the writers of this time demanded a negative myth and the destruction of older myths. The optimistic Brazilian myth of state and the attendant era of patriotic nationalism that accompanied the Kubitschek era was demythified in an attempt, through anti-official writing, to portray Brazilian history in more realistic terms.

Authors like João Ubaldo Ribeiro conceive of grotesque parodies that distort the accepted myth of state, the acceptable historical version of the national experience. Ribeiro's *Viva o povo brasileiro* is simultaneously brutal, frank, and wildly satiric. His anti-history evolves as an affirmative deterrent against the reoccurrence of political tyranny and unrealistic national myths. He delves below the surface of official history to examine its darker aspects. His cynical vision of Brazil is not aimed merely at demythification, but at rendering a more creditable, and at times scathingly humorous, portrayal of historical reality. "Você veja que os únicos lugares em que há algum progresso no Brasil são exatamente onde entrou o sangue estrangeiro, o alemão, o italiano, o japonês. Aqui na Bahia, o que é que nós temos? Os negros e o rebotalho da Europa, portugueses e espanhóis, e é isso que se vê. O Nordeste inteiro é assim. . . . Se tivéssemos sido colonizados pelos holandeses. . . . —Pelos ingleses, pelo ingleses! —Ou pelos ingleses! Tivemos o infortúnio de ser colonizados por Portugal, que inclusive só mandava bandidos para aqui."[11] ("You can see that here in Brazil the only places that have shown any sign of progress are those where there has been an infusion of foreign blood, German, Italian, Japanese. Here in Bahia, what have we got? The blacks and the crap of Europe: the Portuguese and Spaniards. That's all you see. The entire Northeast is like this. . . . If only we had been colonized by the Dutch. . . . —By the English, by the English! —OK by the English! We had the misfortune to be colonized by Portugal and it only sent over a bunch of thieves.")

The writers of this period created a literature that had to test the limits of both public and governmental acceptability. The political controls on writers were strong. Thus, to try to create a literature aimed at correcting social injustice within the political constraints of the times was a difficult task. Márcio Souza's *Galvez, Imperador do Acre* (1976; *The Emperor of the Amazon*) succeeded by drawing a thinly veiled analogy between the status quo government and Luiz Galvez's absurdly inept and self-serving empire. Other writers of the sixties and seventies not only were responding to their own failed national and political myths, but against the overly stylized foreign perceptions that have long existed regarding their country. Hollywood, on more than one occasion, has depicted Brazil as a land of joyous samba dancers, sun-worshipping playboys, and even Spanish-speaking natives. Movies like *Orfeu do carnaval* (1959; *Black Orpheus*), for all its fine points, perpetuates myths and racial stereotypes such as the poor but contented "favela" resident. Romanticizing poverty and confusing Brazil with the rest of Latin America are only half of the issue. Within Brazil itself, magazines and literary supplements abound with articles detailing what is fashionable and "happening" in New York and Paris. Writers attacked with equal ferocity those Brazilians who appeared to have turned their backs on their country's social problems. In summation, these authors evolved a responsive literature that shared a commonality of purpose. It was a literary awakening that bonded an entire generation of writers.

※ ※ ※

In an effort to call attention to specific novels that have influenced this generation, two forceful narratives by Antônio Callado should be mentioned: *Quarup* (1967) and *Bar Don Juan* (1972). The first of these works deals with the existential crisis of Padre Nando, a young Catholic priest. At the onset of the work he symbolically emerges from the catacombs of his monastery and sets out on a journey of discovery. Both of Callado's novels deal directly with moral and political questions. His writing explores the social milieu of the times: guerrilla movements, drug use, sexual freedom, political repression, the plight of Brazil's indigenous population, and governmental corruption.

Through Nando's wanderings Callado's book unearths the underlying sense of alienation that will characterize this new generation. *Bar Don Juan* is based upon an analysis of political commitment, and as such the zoological metaphor becomes a component of the work's structure. Callado uses an animal analogy to symbolize a political interrogator's bestial nature, underscoring his ape-like being. "Mas tinha a fronte baixa, simiesca, observou João corrigindo uma impressão inicial: era mais como se as sobrancelhas tivessem sido destacadas do cabelo, que começava pouco acima delas, que da região do bigode." ("But his forehead was low and simian, and João's first impression had been wrong: His eyebrows seemed to have been detached from his hair, which began only a little way above them, not from his mustache, after all.")[12] The novel opens forcefully with a philosophical observation regarding the relationship between torturer and victim. "A ligação entre torturador e torturado é ao mesmo tempo totalmente violenta e totalmente impessoal, pensou João, mas no caso de Laurinha, não, não foi. O sujeito tinha ido além das suas ordens. Passado para o pessoal." ("The connection between torturer and victim was totally violent yet totally impersonal, thought João; but not in Laurinha's case. The man had gone beyond his orders into the realm of the personal.")[13] As a direct result of her suffering on the "pau-de-arara," the parrot perch, Laurinha's commitment to the revolution is born. In this way both João and Laurinha are impelled to political action by the simianesque Salvador who is the incarnation of the military dictatorship of 1964. There is present within *Bar Don Juan* a powerful philosophical current that views human behavior in subhuman terms. Callado's novels chronicle a generation's disillusionment and give impetus to a new era of politicized writing. "Sempre entendera que torturas são aplicadas em nome de ferozes convicções. O Brasil iria partir das turturas para extrair delas as convicções que não possuía?" ("He had always understood that torture was applied in the name of fierce convictions. Was Brazil lacking convictions . . . resorting to torture to extort the convictions that the nation lacked?")[14] "—Me ajude Padre Nando—disse Levindo. —O que eu quero dizer ao Leslie é que precisamos criar dentro do brasileiro a ajuda ao Brasil. Temos de fabricar os mitos." ("'Help me, Father Nando,' Levindo said. 'What I'm trying to tell Leslie is that help for Brazil ought to come from Brazilians. We need to invent some new myths.'")[15]

Ignácio de Loyola Brandão's *Zero* (1974) also utilizes a zooidal metaphor, that of a rodent running a maze. The novel expresses a human teleology offering not the slightest conviction that man has evolved beyond his animal state. Thus, Loyola's dystopian visions are not only viewed as a metaphor for the political failings of the Brazilian present, but also as a paradigmatic representation of contemporary man's meaningless existential situation. *Zero's* acrid satire and absurdist existential aspects highlight the immediacy of its environmental and sociopolitical concerns. "Veja, a nossa imagem não é nada boa no exterior. Dizem que somos ditadores, que o regime é de terror. Olhe só a lista de torturas e torturados" ("Look, our image abroad isn't very pretty. They say we're dictators, that this is a terrorist regime. Just look at this list of interrogation methods and people tortured or missing.")[16] Loyola's novel reveals the corruption of a political and social system winding down toward total disorder. The nineteenth-century physicist James Clerk Maxwell's postulates in *Theory of Heat*, 1871, have been passed over to the field of literature to aid in defining the absurdist and dystopian aesthetics of the past two decades. Critic Charles B. Harris states, "Entropy refers to the gradual leveling of energy in the universe. In any isolated system . . . entropy . . . tends to increase. As entropy increases, the system draws closer to chaos, its most probable state."[17] This continual movement toward disorder is expressed not only in *Zero's* thematic content, but also in the narrative structure that shapes its vision. The book laments the decadence of all systems, especially portraying an impotent governmental system sustaining itself in a "dirty war" against its own people. *Zero* exposes a society slowly winding down to the ultimate "Zero," to its true entropic state: chaos.

Novelists like Loyola, Drummond, Souza, and Callado confront and deal with all contemporary myths, but they most forcefully deny the myth of historical progress, the myth of societal evolution. Callado sets this tone in a more traditional format in *Quarup*. "Eu pergunto: vale a pena fazer um novo *país* no mundo, mais uma *nação*? Não estão os homens repetindo e repetindo o mesmo erro?" ("I ask you is it worthwhile creating a new *country* in the world? Another *nation*? Wouldn't we be repeating the same mistake all over again?")[18] The postmodern absurdist vision that pervades Márcio Souza's novels, Loyola Brandão's dystopian fiction, and the irreverent "pop fantasies" of Roberto Drummond catalogues the irrationality that is perceived as inherent in modern society.

※ ※ ※

Other novelists of this period choose different forms of expression and narrative techniques, but they too explore these same societal and political questions. Lygia Fagundes Telles's *As meninas* (1973; *The Girl in the Photograph*) was an instant editorial success. The fact that it received such a wide popular acceptance has, in part, kept it from receiving the type of in-depth critical attention it deserves. The critical establishment often equates success with mediocrity. The themes of modern relationships, politics, sexuality, drug abuse, and gender roles are frankly and openly dealt with. The book presents the tension of the contemporary Brazilian female as both incorporating and rejecting the images that have been imposed on her for generations. Three women, each in her own way, aspire to achieve a new awareness of selfhood. Telles's prose style is dense with dialogue, a dialogue that captures the desperate and colloquial rhythms of this generation. Through its imaginative narrative focus, *As meninas* is able to question the traditionalism of the Brazilian woman's place in modern society. Thus, it opens the way for a new generation of women writers to explore eternal existential questions within a contemporary historical and social system that has been, at best, indifferent to them for centuries. This new, post-Lispector generation includes Márcia Denser, Lya Luft, Ruth Bueno, Sônia Coutinho, and Anna Maria Martins.[19]

In 1976 Antônio Torres's third novel *Essa terra* (*The Land*) established his reputation as one of the finest writers of this period. In this work he tells of the harshness of life in the impoverished Northeastern village of Junco, Bahia. The narrative is comprised of four distinct focuses. All four visions underscore the desperation of the people and the extreme poverty of the land. *Essa terra* employs themes and motifs that have been dealt with previously by other Brazilian authors; however, Torres's narrative converts them into an original and moving expression of human frailty and suffering.

A family's eldest son returns from the south where he had gone to try to find work. He was the family's hope, and he returns a failed man only to commit suicide in their presence. Through a multiperspective presentation each family member's life is then highlighted. Each new perspective adds a deeper layer of understanding to the events that lead up to the son's, Nelo's, suicide and the tragic aftermath of his death. Here Torres updates an earlier Jamesian method of storytelling, an approach that is absent in most post-modern narratives. Through this shifting view Torres takes up the cause of Brazil's sociopolitical inequities, allowing each reader to experience first hand the abject poverty and ingrained desperation of the people of the backlands.

The book's vision of life in the "sertão," the dry hinterlands, is indeed bleak. At work's end the cycle of poverty and suffering continues unbroken as the youngest son—in imitation of his brother—also sets off to the southern capital of São Paulo. The reader is left to decide whether the boy, Totonhim, will escape from the land that his father describes as loved by no one. "—Ninguém gosta daqui. Ninguém tem amor a esta terra." ("'Nobody likes it here. Nobody has any love for this land.'")[20] To the bitterness of the father's words Torres then subjoins the boy's insightful wisdom. "Ele tinha, eu sabia, todos sabiam." ("He did—I knew, everyone knew.")[21]

The book combines various forms of narration to inventively piece together this tragically simple tale: songs, poems, folk literature, fantasies, and prayers. Even God is magically brought into this fictional world and portrayed with more than a touch of black humor. "—Então você existe? —Me visto de sol e de lua, me adorno de estrelas e tenho um raio em cada braço. Quer saber a verdade mesmo? Sou o campeão nacional de qualquer concurso de fantasia. Deve ser por isso que dizem que Eu Sou Brasileiro." ("'So you do exist?' 'I clothe myself with the sun and moon, I adorn myself with stars and wear a lightning shaft on each arm. Do you want the truth? I'm the national champion of all fancy-dress competitions, like Carnival, that's why they say I am Brazilian.'")[22] In an era dominated by minimalist writings, Torres's novel is richly imbued with emotion, a meaningful storyline, and a sense of commitment to social ideals. The work is both an ideological stance and an artistic creation that values originality. Out of the barren lives of the people of Junco, Antônio Torres—while drawing upon the concerns of an earlier generation of writers—has fashioned an inventively contemporary novel. *Essa terra* is an impressive work that reflects the innovation and creativity of the Brazilian narrative of this era.

Luiz Vilela's *Entre amigos* (1983; *Among Friends*) is a novel that portrays, through the artifice of dialogue recreation, the hopes, fears, and prejudices of a group of middle class and middle-aged friends. Vilela highlights and burlesques the intimacy that can only occur when we are "entre amigos." This short novel's dialogic structure consists of repeated philosophizing over the state of the country, its politics, its people, and literature. The banality of the friends' conversations is underscored, and this banality is even recognized by the characters themselves. "Banal, né? Extremamente banal."[23] ("Banal, isn't it? Extremely banal.") Vilela's book depicts the vapid complacency of the Brazilian intelligentsia. Theirs is a conversation that leads nowhere. It is perceived as conversation that is as impotent as it is insipid.

Moacyr Scliar's *A festa no castelo* (1980; *The Celebration in the*

Castle) deals with the effects of political repression on the lives of individuals. His novella is created as an extended ideological allegory. The work dramatizes the events of the military coup of 1964 by utilizing an aging Italian immigrant, Nicola Colletti, as the embodiment of idealistic and doctrinaire socialism. Scliar creates an allegorical story in which Nicola is characterized as passing from being a poor but socially committed shoemaker to being a wealthy factory owner who eschews his ideals for life's pleasures. Ironically, Nicola repents on the eve of the military takeover. His lifelong beliefs and ideals compel him to turn his factory into a microcosmic socialist state. Scliar, the eternal ironist, then allows the reader to decide the old immigrant's fate. Does he become a martyr for his ideals, or does he live out his life as a bourgeois capitalist? "Nicola desapareceu. Dos que o conheciam, uns diziam que tinha morrido na prisão, outros que fora extraditado; e também havia quem sustentasse que não ficara preso mais que dois dias, e que agora morava em São Paulo, onde era dono de uma grande sapataria." [24] ("Nicola disappeared. Of those who knew him some said that he died in jail and others that he was extradited, and still others maintained that he was only imprisoned a couple of days, and that he's now living in São Paulo, where he's the owner of a large shoe store.")

Emir Rodríguez Monegal draws a sharp distinction between the writings and intentions of established authors like Osman Lins, Dalton Trevisan, Autran Dourado, Nelida Piñon, and this present generation of writers. These authors had already defined their aesthesia and objectives well before the 1964 military takeover. Their writings tend to continue in a less socially committed direction. Rodríguez Monegal postulates:

> Very different is the case of those writers who at the time of the army coup were still in their twenties. For them, writing in a society in which every thought, where even the least political subject (sex, for instance) became political because of the repression, was an experience which prevented them from handling the novel in purely literary terms, as a fictional artifact. They were (or became) committed novelists not because they wanted to change society but because writing novels was in their society at that time a committed activity, almost a subversive one. [25]

※ ※ ※

The following study proceeds to a more detailed discussion of one of the most important novels of this period, Ivan Ângelo's *A festa* (1976; *The Celebration*). This work will be approached from the perspective of its artistic blending of sociopolitical, mythic, and narrative elements. Ângelo underscores the vagaries of political repression by portraying the individual lives and everyday events that evoke an era and define true history. His work well exemplifies the social concerns of the writers of this era. It remains as one of the contemporary novels that successfully manages to present its thesis using innovative temporal perceptions that reflect the international post-modern novel.

The Confluence
of Mythic, Historical,
and Narrative Impulses
in Ivan Ângelo's *A festa*

*It was the yearning for Paradise, which haunted
the minds of Isaiah and of Virgil . . .*

Mircea Eliade

*As primeiras levas de retirantes chegaram às
capitais do Nordeste, com a repetição dos fatos
que marcam a seca.*

*(The first waves of refugees have already
reached the major Northeastern capitals, with
the same repetition of dismal facts that
characterize every drought.)*

O Estado de São Paulo

*Os latino-americanos estão escrevendo até sobre
coisa nenhuma, são homens do mundo, e vocês
aqui, no Curral d'el Rey, querendo explicar a
situação brasileira. O saco. (P. 122)*

> *(Other Latin Americans write about anything*
> *they damn well please, at least they're*
> *sophisticated writers, and you people here, [at]*
> *the left end of nowhere, you want to explain the*
> *Brazilian condition. . . . Bullshit.) (P. 133)*
>
> Ivan Ângelo

In his highly original and controversial critique of the literary-cultural avant-garde, Charles Newman in *The Post-Modern Aura* (1985) observes:

> History is not intelligible without an extra-historical essence as a matter of principle. Therefore, fiction presumes an epistemologically *privileged* position as a matter of course. It operates as a distinct and whole addition to reality; in this sense, fiction *always* challenges conventional reality.[1]

Ivan Ângelo, one of contemporary Brazil's foremost writers, published his most important novel, *A festa (The Celebration)*, in 1976. Ângelo's novel reflects the tension created between the individual lives of history's victims and the broader historical context in which they live. *A festa*, through its skillful use of mythic and narrative impulses, portrays the underlying quotidian realities that evoke and define true history. Many times the modern novelist is able to lend history the human dimension that the historian is unable to convey.

The Brazilian critic and teacher Janete Gaspar Machado, in evaluating Ângelo's affect on recent Brazilian writing, concludes, "*A festa* é tido como um romance importante para a produção literária levada a efeito pelos escritores que passaram a obter reconhecimento na década de 70."[2] ("*The Celebration* is an important contribution to the literary output that has been achieved by those writers who gained recognition during the decade of the '70s.") The following study is a critical exploration of Ângelo's synthesis of aesthetic and mythic elements and their application to *A festa*'s central question of human suffering, responsibility, and culpability.

I

Ivan Ângelo worked as a reporter and managing editor for the *Jornal da Tarde*, a major São Paulo newspaper, before turning to literature.

His novel combines the art of the fiction writer with the investigative skills of the journalist. It explores the consequences of a specific historical event—a tragic and avoidable riot—that is viewed from the dual perspective of the journalist's need to clarify facts and the novelist's ability to evoke emotional responses.

A *festa* is conceived with a free-floating narrative focus, a Cortázarian openness. It is a novel that invites and even demands reader participation in the work's flow and interpretation. Ângelo refers to 1970 as the "ano da desgraça," (p. 191) "the year of Misfortune" (p. 219). His novel searches below historical events to concentrate upon societal and personal struggles. The conventional historical account of this period reads as follows: "After 1969 the military ruled without much consultation of the civilian politicians; the press was severely censured and the guerrilla movements ruthlessly crushed." [3] Ângelo's work personalizes this history, presenting its human drama from a multidimensional perspective. Upon the novel's publication Ivan Ângelo stated, "I hope to make the reader an accomplice not only in shaping the actual text, but in determining its significance, since my intention has been to provide wider participation in the terrible problems we face at the moment, in Brazil." [4]

A *festa*'s structure obscures the distinction between short fiction, novel, newspaper account, and historical writing. Each small vision of a central event can be laid out into an ever changing mosaic, one whose totality is designed to recreate the "ano da desgraça." The work's plot line is not revealed chronologically. The overall configuration of the novel is an imaginative schema that consists of several short pieces of independently existing fiction and six or seven autonomous microtexts. There is even a supposedly expendable section of the novel which, in fact, holds the key to the work's many mysteries. In a mock-serious gamelike presentation, the section is described and the reader is offered the following evaluations: "necessárias? surpreendentes? valiosas? complementares? desnecessárias? inúteis?" (p. 135). ("necessary? surprising? useful? corroborate? unnecessary? useless?" [p. 149].) The novel is an intense process, a narrative conundrum in which Ângelo's controlling metaphor is the symbolic search for a "New Eden." A group of eight-hundred refugees flee the wasteland of the Northeast, searching for a symbolic lost paradise in the city of Belo Horizonte.

Ivan Ângelo's artistic vision focuses upon two simultaneous occurrences: a riot and a birthday celebration. In his use of mythological prefigurations, Ângelo characterizes a modern day Moses figure, Mar-

16

cionílio de Mattos, as both victim-hero and activist-hero, always in very human terms. It is not the actions of this messiah figure that are central to Ivan Ângelo's fictional canon, it is the power that the work generates as a call to consciousness in the mind of the reader. Newman's observation regarding the participatory nature of modern fiction correlates with Ângelo's conception of *A festa*. "The reader is not a passive participant in this enterprise, any more than the narrator is a passive observer of reality."[5]

In this initial section "Documentário" (pp. 15–27) (A Short Documentary [pp. 9–26]), Marcionílio is portrayed as the New Moses leading his people to the Promised Land. This section of the book fashions together historical accounts that bridge well over a hundred years of political unrest. These factual accounts are interspersed with narrative renderings of the life of Mattos and the wanderings of this most recent group of Northeasterners. The impoverished migrants are barely delineated. They exist narratively as a monolithic representation of poverty. Only their leader's life is placed in high relief.

The refugees' train is met by the police, and they are reboarded to be returned North. However, unexplained fires break out on the exterior of the locked wooden passenger cars. The refugees march on the police, led by Mattos and a reporter, and then disperse throughout the city. The event is labeled a riot and several people die. What follows is a narrative piecing together of the story.

Marcionílio de Mattos, who has been involved in a series of reform movements over the course of his life, is now accused of inciting this riot. Ângelo includes newspaper reports from three months later that affirm that Mattos was killed trying to escape from the Department of Political and Social Order (DOPS). The mysteries and questions are then laid out for the reader. Were there accomplices? Was there an informant? Was Mattos murdered? Who lit the fires? What were the roles of the student Bicalho, Mattos, and the reporter Samuel Aparecido Fereszin?

In *A festa* the Biblical motif of the Exodus is viewed as truncated or failed. John J. White's statements regarding recent attitudes towards myth most closely approximate Ângelo's use of this mythological motif. "Attitudes to myths, inside and outside literature, may have changed in recent times, with a certain anti-mythic reaction setting in. . . . At most, they have been more often used in a pejorative way. Such prefigurations appear to have remained part of a standard method of telling a story and commenting on it at the same time from a different perspective."[6]

17

II

In the Old Testament the imposing figure of Moses, like that of Marcionílio de Mattos, dominates the Exodus story. Like the ancient Jews of Egypt, the "flagelados," the drought victims (the Portuguese noun seems to imply a greater sense of physical suffering than its corresponding English translation) leave an inhospitable land where they have been treated like slaves for hundreds of years:

> "Nas terras dos grandes proprietários, eles não gozam de direito algum político, porque não têm opinião livre; para eles, o grande proprietário é a polícia, os tribunais, a administração, numa palavra, tudo. . . . e então sua sorte é quase a do antigo servo da gleba. (P. 17)

> (Inside the boundaries of properties of the great landowners there are no political rights, because freedom of opinion is nonexistent. For the peasants, the landowners *are* the police, the courts, the government itself—in a word, everything. . . . And their lot is more or less equivalent to that of the ancient serfs of the glebe. (P. 13)

The edenic Paradise for which this group of drought victims longs is characterized later in the work as a place that is as morally and spiritually impoverished as the lands that they just left.

The prefiguration of Moses leading his people is periodically interrupted by a narrative shift in focus to a police investigation of Marcionílio. From this perspective, Marcionílio is viewed as a dangerous subversive who has acted in a calculating manner to challenge the present government. The reader becomes conscious of the continual overlay of star chamber proceedings that are in operation, condemning the peasant leader without a fair trial. "Sabe-se já que Marcionílio, preso incomunicável no DOPS, é subversivo e participou das Ligas Camponesas do ex-deputado Franciso Julião" (p. 26). ("It has already been established, for example, that Mattos—currently being held incommunicado at the DOPS—was a known subversive who participated in the Peasant Leagues of ex-Congressman Francisco Julião" [p. 24].) Ângelo uses a variety of different forms of discourse—recollections, narration, oral depositions, oral accounts, and newspaper reports—as a dramatic device to shift the burden of interpretation to his reader. Thus, the reader is made to function as the final arbiter in the novel's presentation of the facts of Marcionílio's life.

In an innovative accommodation of Biblical resonances, Ângelo's novel inverts Moses's promulgation of the Decalogue, the later ethical and more prophetic set of laws (20:2–17). In "Anotação do escritor" (pp. 131–32) ("Author's note") (pp. 145–146) Marcionílio expresses a lyrical wisdom, a promulgation of comments and precepts that transcend the views of a mere peasant leader. In contemporary Brazil he speaks to his followers, not of the laws of God, but of the laws of man, the laws of political survival, and of human compassion:

> Ouvimos falar da fome ("Meu pai contou que na grande seca de 87 foram mortos dois bandidos assaltantes e comidos pelo povo em Jacaré dos Homens.")
> da felicidade "Aquila dona que ali está, dona Lália, está feliz e aliviada porque vendeu a filha de 14 anos, nessa viagem mesmo, a um fazendeiro do Sul da Bahia. A filha agora tem onde comer e dormir, melhor do que nós.")
> de revolta ("Quando o vento sopra, o capim abaixa; quando o capim pega fogo, queima a mata toda.")
> de religião
> de coragem
> da morte (Pp. 131–132)

> (We listened to him, as he spoke of famine ["My father told me how, back in the great drought of '87, two bank robbers were killed and eaten by the people of Jacaré dos Homens."]
> of happiness ["That woman over there, her name is Lália, and she's happy now, thankful to have sold her fourteen-year-old daughter, . . . At least the daughter has a place to eat and to sleep now, which is more than we got."]
> of rebellion ["When a big wind blows, the grass'll bend; but let that grass catch fire and it'll burn a whole damn countryside."]
> of property . . .
> of religion . . .
> of courage . . .
> of death . . .) (P. 146)

In our anti-mythic, post-existential age, the new Moses rebels even against the existence of his creator.

> de religião ("Deus? Eu nunca ouvi falar de coisa boa que ele fez, garantido que foi ele, a não ser muito antigamente.") (of religion ["God? I never heard of one good thing he done, guaranteed to be his doing—except what maybe happened a long, long time ago."]) (P. 131, p. 146 trans.)

III

A *festa*'s implicit social criticism is achieved by the reader's reaction to the violence and repression that pervade every level of society. The novel continues by presenting a panoramic tableau of life behind the walls of Eden. The work now focuses on the lives of the beautiful partygoers, the efforts of the local newspaper to cover the story, and the machinations at the Department of Labor and the DOPS. All three are united by the events at the train station. The cast of people involved is large, and their lives all intersect. There is a vapid but sympathetic, androgynous society writer, a socially conscious journalist, a student activist, a self-important young lawyer, a married couple who made a strange suicide pact thirty years earlier, a working-class couple whose lives are ruined by fate, the continual musings of the intellectual and artistic community at the New Moon Bar, and finally Roberto Miranda, a homosexual artist from an influential family whose birthday the group is to celebrate.

Ângelo's book describes the morally bankrupt life of Jorge Paulo Fernandez, a lawyer whose superficial existence is contrasted to the concern and social involvement of Samuel Aparecido Fereszin, a reporter, and Carlos Bicalho, the ex-student leader. Fernandez is so self-involved that he is oblivious to reports of others' hunger and suffering. He is a paradigmatic representation of that section of the Brazilian populace who refuses to recognize the existence of poverty or political repression. "Porra, seis anos já. Parece que foi ontem. Leu a notícia sobre a seca no Nordeste. 50 mil retirantes? Ah, isso é exagero de jornal. Meio Maracanã.—Essa não" (p. 79). ("Christ, six years since the revolution. Seems like yesterday. Read about the droughts up in the Northeast. Fifty thousand refugees? Agh, damn papers are always exaggerating. That's half of Maracanã Stadium, for Christ's sake. —No way" [p. 81].)

Ataide and Cremilda are the working class couple whose sexual and emotional life has been shattered by the secret police's sexual coercion of the wife and the physical maiming of the husband. "Disseram: se você for boazinha conosco, hoje não batemos nele. Podemos fazer um trato. Só sacaneamos ele no dia que você nos sacanear" (pp. 160–161) ("They told her: if you're nice to us today, we won't beat him. Let's make a pact: we'll only give him a hard time on days you give us one" [p. 181].) "O terceiro medo, ter relações aleijado com Cremilda belíssima, nunca foi vencido. Nunca se acostumaram, os dois, àquela mão seca. Evitava tocar em Cremilda com aquela mão" (p. 189). ("The third fear, his intimacies as a cripple with his lovely Cremilda, he never overcame. Because they never got used to it, either one of them—to that cold hand. He avoided touching Cremilda with that hand" [p. 217].)

20

Repercussions from the events of the train station spread out over all levels of society and government. The minister at the Department of Labor and Social Services, Otávio Ernâni, Carlos's boss, attends the birthday celebration while the events at the train station occur. He is later dismissed from his job. Ironically, as his political and social life fall apart, he now feels strangely expiated of the guilt he has borne for years of being a mere pawn in a political end-game. Also, in a cynical application of the absurdist code, the police commissioner at the Department of Political and Social Order (despite its Orwellian resonance, the DOPS did in fact exist), grotesquely dies in 1982. "Morreu de rir, literalmente, em 1982. A estranha doença, certamente de origem nervosa, no mínimo psicológica, manifestou-se pela primeira vez em 1978. . . . Morreu rindo fragilmente sua gargalhada terrível" (p. 140). ("He died of laughter, literally, in 1982. The strange illness—certainly of neurotic origin, at the very least psychological—manifested itself for the first time in 1978. . . . He passed away weakly laughing his grim cackle" [pp. 154–155].)

Even the party-goers whose lives are insulated by wealth, power, and political influence are affected by the Department of Political and Social Order's investigation and the actions of the secret police. The following year at Roberto Miranda's next birthday celebration, "Um grupo de trinta rapazes armados com longos cacetes de madeira invadiu a festa de aniversário de Roberto em 1971. A porta foi aberta com estrondo de pontapé e os rapazes, de cabelos muito curtos, civis, entraram correndo, atropelando, batendo, gritando" (p. 193). ("A gang of thirty youths armed with long wooden sticks suddenly crashed Roberto's birthday party in 1971. The door opened with a splintering thud and the youths, with their hair cropped and wearing civilian clothes, entered on the run, yelling, beating, trampling" [p. 223].)

IV

As one of the work's epigrams by poet Carlos Drummond de Andrade states, "O tempo é a minha matéria, o tempo presente, os homens presentes, / a vida presente" (p. 9). ("The subject is time, present time, present life, present man" [p. 7].) This present is also analyzed from a future perspective. A *festa* tells of the life of former student activist Carlos Bicalho in 1979. (The novel was published in 1976.) He is in a bar in Recife discussing the March 30, 1970, events that destroyed his life. Due to his involvement, he now is left without wife or child or a chance for a meaningful job:

>—Acho que naquela eu fui o único que se fodeu.
>—Como único? Morreu gente, não morreu?
>—Morreu está morto. Se fodeu que eu digo é com cadeia, escola, família. Eu queria naquela época estudar economia, trabalhar em pesquisa. Me fodi. (P. 186)

>(—I think I was the one who got fucked the most by that whole mess.
>—What do you mean? Some people died, didn't they?
>—The dead are dead. Getting fucked has to do with jail, school, family. I wanted to study economics back then, do research, get a doctorate. I fucked it all. Or it fucked me.) (P. 213)

From this narrative perspective, Ângelo is better able to underscore the curtailment of freedoms that affected Carlos's past and now define his future.

>—Não deixaram. Decreto 477. Entrei na Justiça, claro. Ficou aquele chove-não-molha uns dois anos, sabe, como é esse negócio de Justiça. Bom, aí fui para São Paulo. Também não pude estudar, não me deram transferência. (P. 187)

>(They didn't let me. Decree 477. I couldn't even find a job. I went to court, naturally. It just sat at a complete standstill for two years, you know how the courts work. So, I went off to São Paulo. Couldn't study there either; they wouldn't let me transfer.) (P. 215)

However, it is Carlos who will carry on the mission of Marcionílio de Mattos. The new Moses, Carlos, is in the Northeast completing an age old messianic cycle: from the leadership of Antônio Conselheiro, the religious zealot, to Lampião, the bandit, to Mattos, and now Carlos, the unlikely Moses.

>Estava meio perdidão em São Paulo quando encontrei uns antigos companheiros dos tempos de estudante e fui me ajustando, compreendendo as coisas, deixando a revolta pessoal de lado, analisando a situação mais em profundidade, me politizando. Me arrumaram emprego e agora estou ai, quase cinco anos nesse batidão político.
>—Você vai gostar do Nordeste.
>—Acho que vou sim. Também se não gostar . . .
>—Isso é. Trabalho é trabalho. (Pp. 187–188)

>(—I was just about a total loss there in São Paulo, when I met up with some old friends from my student days and began to get myself together again, began to understand some things a little better, setting aside my personal hang-ups, analyzing my situation a little more

closely, politicizing myself. Well, they finally arranged some work for me. And so now, here I am: almost five long years in this political struggle.
—I think you'll like the Northeast.
—Yes, I think I might. But even if I don't . . .
—Right, a job is a job.) (P. 215)

Carlos's present life as a Moses figure is then ironically juxtaposed to Ângelo's acerbic vision of Esdras, the Hermetic, the cafe intellectual. This is yet another example of Biblical resonances, since Ângelo relates this character to the Books of Esdras, suggesting—as with all apocalyptic writing—that meaning is made manifest through the use of intricate and opaque symbology. Esdras is also representative of those Brazilian authors who are still writing a purist, dehumanized literature, and who retreat intellectually from the intense historical context in which they live:

> É um ser desiludido, intelectualmente rigoroso (o livro que ele escreve e reescreve em segredo nunca o satisfaz, não alcança a perfeição desejada—e não nasce). . . . Não acredita que a arte tenha algum valor hoje em dia, mas é a única coisa de que realmente gosta. Só a usa em casa, como um agasalho velho, fora de moda. . . . E a poesia de Esdras fechou-se sobre si mesma, perfeita. (P. 177)

> (He's a disillusioned soul, intellectually rigorous [the book he writes and rewrites in secret never really satisfies him, never really reaches the desired level of perfection—and is never really born]. . . . He doesn't believe that art has any value today, but it's still the only thing he prizes. He merely uses it at home anyway: like an old wrap; out of fashion. . . . So the poetry of Esdras closed in upon itself: perfect.) (Pp. 202–03)

V

The book's vision is panoramic in scope, tracing past histories and even projecting a futurist's rendering of the consequences of the events of March 30th. Interestingly enough, Ângelo's novel focuses on the past and the future, but the actual party itself is not described in the body of the text. This is even discussed in the intra-narrative situation. "Depois da Festa seria o inferno do tríptico. Mas então, como eu ia dizendo: falta a festa" (p. 167). ("'After the Celebration' was to have been the inferno of the triptych. But then, as I was saying: the celebration, the party itself is missing" [p. 190].)

23

Ângelo's narrator freely discusses the creative process and, to a great extent, burlesques the pretense and opacity of other writers. The book even concerns the reader in the work's organization and editing process. These following examples of narrative playfulness give the illusion of greater reader involvement in the creation of the literary work: "Que não dá mais pé. (Lendo.) 'Dele guardou ressentimento e uma fotografia 3x4".' Esse tipo de enumeração até o Machado de Assis já esgotou: o amor durou nove meses e onze contos de réis.—Faz uma cruzinha aí. Isso. Que mais?" (p. 172). ("You can't get away with this. [Reading.] 'She held onto her resentment, and a three-by-four photograph of him.' That kind of enumeration went out with Machado de Assis: love lasted nine months and fifty-five-hundred cruzeiros. — Cross it out. There. What else?" [p. 195].) "O escritor sou eu mesmo, claro, como eu hoje, neste 74, acho que seria em 1970 aquele intelectualzinho de 1960 (disse o escritor insistindo naquela auto-depreciação de ultimamente . . .)" (p. 173). ("The author, obviously, is me, but the way I think—today, in 1974—that the little intellectual of 1960 would have behaved in 1970 [said the author, insisting on that self-deprecation . . .]") (p. 196–197).

The sections "Anotação do escritor" ("Author's note") are filled with cynical black humor and mordant observations. The metafictional and self-reflective nature of the work is placed in high relief as the narrator discusses the genesis and configuration of the very novel he is presently writing, the very one the reader is now reading. Ironically, Ângelo's acerbic humor even turns on the writer's role. "O jogo dava-lhes a ilusão de serem, ao mesmo tempo, participantes-do-problema-social-brasileiro e/ou escritores-impedidos-de-escrever-porque-o-Brasil-não-estava-precisando-disso-agora" (p. 114). ("The game provided them the illusion of being at one and the same time, activists-with-respect-to-the-social-problems-of-Brazil and/or writers-kept-from-writing-because-Brazil-had-no-need-for-that-sort-of-thing-right-now" [p. 123].)

Like many postmodern anti-novels (here the term refers to the universal contemporary connotation, not to the Brazilian Modernist movement of 1922), there is a strong absurdist element throughout *A festa*. Ângelo as social critic is able to parody the hypocrisy, sterility, and inertia of the lives of the majority of Brazil's middle-class cafe intellectuals. "Palavras desconhecidas, inquietantes, atravessavam a mesa do bar, ricocheteavam nas garrafas e em Andrea: infraestrutura, pop-art, fenomenologia, estruturas bilaterais do verso decassílabo . . .

Uns dois da Polop (que seria isso?) passavam palavras de ordem no meio da conversa de botequim" (p. 57). ("Alarmingly incomprehensible words shot across cafe tables, ricocheting against bottles, glasses, and Andrea: infrastructure, pop art, phenomenology, bilateral patterns of decasyllabic verse, . . . A few members of Radical Action relayed plans across the barroom prattle" [p. 57].) "Aprendia também frases como: a mulher não pode ficar marginalizada. Em 62, era uma das suas frases preferidas" (p. 58). ("Andrea also picked up certain phrases like: 'Women must no longer accept marginal status.' In '62 this was one of her favorite phrases" [p. 58].)

At times the playful authorial tone turns didactic, as the narrator points to the inequities that factually separate the drought victims from the party-goers. "Isto é, que quase novecentos mil brasileiros ganharam em 1970 uma quantia maior do que a que perceberam 72 milhões de brasileiros; portanto, a renda de 1 por cento de brasileiros é maior do que a soma da renda de 80 por cento" (p. 129). ("Which is to say, nearly nine hundred thousand Brazilians, in 1970, earned a sum greater than what was amassed by seventy-two million Brazilians; or put still another way, the income of the top 1 percent exceeds the sum of all income from the bottom 80 percent" [p. 143].)

VI

Ângelo's fragmented and multidimensional presentation of historical experience engenders a meaningful vehicle for liberating both the reader's aesthetic appreciation and sense of social and moral consciousness. The work brings to bear disparate perspectives of the same reality, allowing the reader to fashion his or her private truth. Within the intricacies of the work's structure, the reader then is asked to discover the basic unity that bonds and supersedes the fragmented presentation.

A formulation of this technique is included in the novel itself as a suggestion for an experimental play. "Um homem sozinho. Gravadores, vozes, slides, cinema, discos, jornais, televisão. Ele contracena com os meios de comunicação. . . . É um cara muito pequeno (papel para um anão?) em comparação com o material em cena. Obrigado a optar a todo instante, a partir dos dados dos meios de comunicação, mas as informações não são nada seguras, são até contraditórias"

(p. 110). ("A man all by himself. Tape recorders, voices, slides, projections, recordings, newspapers, TV monitors. He plays opposite all the means of communication. . . . He looks like a little squirt [a role for a midget?] in comparison with the material he enacts. Obliged to make choices every moment, based upon facts provided by the various means of communication, but the information is never totally reliable, at times even contradictory" [p. 118].)

The work's totality conveys a sense of fidelity to experience; the distinction between fact and fiction, illusion and reality, is many times blurred. Ângelo's aesthetics transcend self-conscious technical innovation for its own sake. Thus, it is for each individual member of society, each reader, to make value judgements. A *festa*'s technical artifice has a discernible design and purpose: greater reader involvement in the problems of the times. In his discussion of "stories of reading" and the "reader's experience," Jonathan D. Culler's theories illuminate Ângelo's approach to his craft. Culler states, "These stories reinstate the text as an agent with definite qualities or properties, since this yields more precise and dramatic narratives as well as creating a possibility of learning that lets one celebrate great works. The value of a work is related to the efficacy granted it in these stories—an ability to produce stimulating, unsettling, moving, and reflective experiences." [7]

Out of the human drama of modern Brazil, Ivan Ângelo created a responsive novel that is at once nationally oriented and, at the same time, a prophetic and universal warning. A *festa* has evolved as the thesis novel of its generation. It truly encapsulates the thematic concerns and aesthetic preoccupations of an age. It was Jacques Ehrmann who stated, "The power of words over history, of history over words, such is the problem of our time." [8]

There have been many excellent novels by this present generation of modern Brazilian writers; however, A *festa* through its coalescence of historical, mythic, and narrative impulses is able to summarize in an inventively aesthetic fashion the cultural failings of an entire era of political repression. It is both an ideologic stance and a masterfully conceived work of art. Ivan Ângelo's narrative preoccupation with questions of social morality and culpability reflect his desire to reshape national consciousness. A *festa* is a work of fiction that, while not indifferent to historical perspectives, maintains a consistent and original aesthetic posture. [9]

NOTES

[1] Fábio Lucas, "Aspectos culturais da literatura brasileira" *O caráter social da literatura brasileira* (Rio de Janeiro: Paz e Terra, 1970), p. 23. The English translation is by Alexandrino E. Severino, *TriQuarterly*, ed. José Donoso 13/14 Fall/Winter, 1968/69, p. 33.

[2] Lucas, 23.

[3] Francis Lambert, "Latin America since Independence," *The Cambridge Encyclopedia of Latin America*, ed. Simon Colleir (Cambridge: Cambridge University Press, 1985), p. 271.

[4] Lambert, 271.

[5] Alfred Stepan, "War on the People," *New York Times* 23 Nov. 1986, natl. ed.: 20–23.

[6] Roberto Drummond, *Sangue de Coca-Cola* (Rio de Janeiro: Nova Fronteira, 1985), p. 13.

[7] George A. Panichas, ed., *The Politics of Twentieth-Century Novelists* (New York: Hawthorn Books, Inc., 1971) p. xiv.

[8] Roberto Drummond, *A morte de D. J. em Paris* (São Paulo: Ática, 1983), pp. 5–6.

[9] Richard Hoggart, *Speaking to Each Other*, Vol II: *About Literature* (New York: Chatto & Windus, 1970), p. 259.

[10] José Ortega y Gasset, *Man and Crisis*, trans. Mildred Adams (London: Allen & Unwin, 1959), p. 45.

[11] João Ubaldo Ribeiro, *Viva o povo brasileiro* (Rio de Janeiro: Nova Fronteira, 1985), p. 624.

[12] Antônio Callado, *Bar Don Juan* (Rio de Janeiro: Civilização Brasileira, 1982), pp. 7–8. The English edition is *Don Juan's Bar*, trans. Barbara Shelby (New York: Alfred Knopf, 1972), p. 9.

[13] Callado, p. 4. Shelby, p. 4.

[14] Callado, p. 6. Shelby, p. 7.

[15] Antônio Callado, *Quarup* (Rio de Janeiro: Civilização Brasileira, 1982), p. 23. The English edition is *Quarup*, trans. Barbara Shelby (New York: Alfred Knopf, 1970), p. 25.

[16] Ignácio de Loyola Brandão, *Zero* (Rio de Janeiro: Codecri, 1982), p. 263. The English edition is *Zero*, trans. Ellen Watson (New York: Avon, 1979), pp. 290–1.

[17] Charles B. Harris, *Contemporary American Novelists of the Absurd* (New Haven: College and University Press, 1971), p. 77.

[18] Callado, *Quarup*, p. 19, trans. Shelby, p. 21.

[19] Concerning the issue of power and powerlessness in Brazilian women's fiction of this period, see Elizabeth Lowe "Cries and Whispers: Answers to the Politics of Repression in Contemporary Brazilian Women's Fiction," *Oc-*

casional Papers in Women's Studies (Miami: Florida International University Press, 1986), and Luiza Lobo, "Women Writers in Brazil Today," *World Literature Today* 61 (1986): 49–54.

[20] Antônio Torres, *Essa terra* (São Paulo: Ática, 1987), p. 108. Published in English as *The Land*, trans. Margaret Neves (London: Readers International, 1987), p. 135.

[21] Torres, p. 108. English translation 135.

[22] Torres, p. 105. English translation 131.

[23] Luiz Vilela, *Entre amigos* (São Paulo: Ática, 1983), p. 80.

[24] Moacyr Scliar, *A festa no castelo* (Porto Alegre: L & PM Editores, 1982), p. 98.

[25] Emir Rodríguez Monegal, *World Literature Today*, 53, no. 1 (1979): 19–22.

Ângelo Study

The first epigraph to the study is from Mircea Eliade, "The Yearning for Paradise in Primitive Tradition," *Myth and Mythmaking*, ed. Henry A. Murray (Boston: Beacon, 1960), p. 74.

The second epigraph is as cited in Ivan Ângelo's, *A festa* (São Paulo: Summus, 1978), p. 23. The work was published in English as *The Celebration*, trans. Thomas Colchie (New York: Avon Books, 1982), p. 20. Further citations will be from both these editions, and page numbers will be directly entered in the text.

[1] Charles Newman, *The Post-Modern Aura: The Art of Fiction in an Age of Inflation* (Evanston, IL: Northwestern University Press, 1985), pp. 63–4.

[2] Janete Gaspar Machado, *Constantes ficcionais em romances dos anos 70* (Florianópolis: Ed. da USSC, 1981), p. 50.

[3] Francis Lambert, "Latin America since Independence," *The Cambridge Encyclopedia of Latin America*, ed. Simon Colleir (Cambridge: Cambridge University Press, 1985), pp. 274–5.

[4] Ângelo's undocumented quote is taken from publisher's notes on the back page of the Avon edition of *A festa* cited above.

[5] Newman, p. 63f.

[6] John J. White, *Mythology in the Modern Novel* (Princeton: Princeton University Press, 1971), p. 240. In the later section of *A festa*, "O retirante Viriato" (pp. 191–92) ("The Refugee, Viriato") (pp. 9–22), the migrants themselves, like the reader, recognize the dualistic nature of this Moses figure. Here the line between messiah and political agitator is blurred. The migrants' trek is called by the biblical term exodus and their later life, diaspora. Their view of reality is colored by a continual spiritual struggle between God

and the Devil. Their understanding of their present situation is interpreted by a biblical mind set, a battle between good and evil. Marcionilio is even referred to here as Asmodeus, one of the demons from Jewish mythology (the apocryphal *Book of Tobit*).

[7] Jonathan D. Culler, *On Deconstruction* (Ithaca, New York: Cornell University Press, 1982), p. 82.

[8] Jacques Ehrmann, *Literature and Revolution* (Boston: Beacon Press, 1967), p. 5.

[9] As this book was being written, an article by Michael Kepp appeared entitled "Armed Clashes Mark Brazil's Land Reform: Wealthy Landowners Hire Private Armies of Guards," *The St. Louis Post-Dispatch* 5 July 1986, p. B–1. According to the article, "The rich, rolling farmland surrounding the northern city of Imperatriz was, by mid June, so besieged by bloody clashes between big landowners and landless peasants that President José Sarney, preceded by 250 federal policemen, went there to restore peace."

MYTHIC
ASPECTS
OF THE
BRAZILIAN
NARRATIVE

In general terms in the field of Brazilian literature, critical studies from a mythological perspective have been rare. There has been a continuing tendency within the country itself to employ a philosophical approach to literature, seeking broad affinities between literary works and universal philosophical tenets. This trend applies to a national literature's ideals and judgments that are extraneous to that literature. It tends to analyze and evaluate a uniquely created body of writing—some of it orally inspired and in the African story telling tradition—by ideas and standards that are generally European in origin.

However, the recent appearance of four important books can attest to a growing awareness of the archetypal nature of much of Brazilian fiction, especially that fiction produced prior to the military putsch of sixty-four. David Haberly's *Three Sad Races* (1983) sheds new light on Brazilian racial myths as they relate to the fiction of this past century. His work points out the anguished search for a racial identity that has been such an integral part of the Brazilian literary experience. Elizabeth Lowe's study of the myth of the city in recent Brazilian fiction has unearthed valuable insights and important conclusions regarding the urban nature of this literature. Her work entitled *The City in Brazilian Literature* was published in 1982. Daphne Patai has written an in-depth presentation of the ideological implications and historical background of myth in modern literature. Her 1983 book *Myth and Ideology in Contemporary Brazilian Fiction* analyzes six important Brazilian novels. Finally, Regina Zilberman of the Catholic University of Rio Grande do Sul writes from a structuralist perspective. Her book, *Do mito ao romance* (1977; *From Myth to the Novel*), principally deals with Guimarães Rosa's novel *Grande Sertão: Veredas* (1956; *The Devil to Pay in the Backlands*). To the present moment, however, there exists little material of a critical nature that explores the mythical structure of Clarice Lispector's internationally acclaimed book *Laços de família* (1960; *Family Ties*). A loose textual examination of these stories reveals the mythic framework that is such an important, yet critically neglected, component of Lispector's narrative artistry. *Laços de família* has been called "one of the best short story collections in modern Latin American literature"[1] and one of "the most important works by a woman author in Latin American literature."[2]

These enigmatic narratives explore the philosophical aspects of alienation in a highly original manner. Of late, Lispector's writings have become prime ground in a search to explore and comment on the condition of being female. Her originality and narrative force are rooted in the intuitive resolutions that she affords the reader of very private worlds and moments. In the short story genre where she is most noted, her use of myth is recognized as an important part of her prose fiction style. One can think of few other modern writers of Brazilian fiction who have commanded such respect and critical attention.

I

It is an existential conflict that Clarice Lispector elaborates in her much anthologized short story "O crime do professor de matemática," "The Crime of the Mathematics Professor." While the corpus of Lispector's writings has received an overwhelming amount of critical attention, this one piece of short fiction—one of her best known and most enigmatic—has been somewhat overlooked from the standpoint of a detailed analysis of the work's structural and thematic content. There has been a general trend to discuss this esoteric narrative in broad terms that serve to exemplify the writer's adhesion to an existential world-view. In this classic of Brazilian literature, Clarice Lispector does not resort to the conventional existential scenario of portraying modern man's anguish as he confronts an oppressive and chaotic universe. She opts instead to dramatize the subtle psychological relationship between a man and his pet. She draws a distinction between a natural and primitive state of existence, as exemplified by a simple domestic animal, and a more involved intellectual being, as personified by the mathematics professor.

The relationship that exists between the man and his dog borders on a psychic consciousness of each other's ego. The dog's presence reveals to the man a sense of personal guilt based on his own self-betrayal. In this short narrative, Lispector portrays the mathematics professor resorting to primitive rituals in an attempt to purge his guilt and to find a new sense of identity. At work's end, the professor returns to society to live out his life within the "seio de sua família"[3] ("bosom of his family"). The final narrative pronouncement is more a sentence of punishment than a simple statement of fact. This parable-like narrative explores the complexities of human psychology by portraying primal events and emotions.

II

The first of the following studies analyzes in a longer format Clarice Lispector's use of mythic and primal elements in another of *Laços de família*'s more challenging stories: "Mistério em São Cristóvão," ("Mystery in São Cristóvão"). In this work, Lispector employs mythological correspondences and prefigurations in her ritualistic function as mythmaker. Richard Ellmann explains the pervasive influence of mythical forms in modern fiction: "The modern return to mythical forms is in part an attempt to reconstitute the value-laden natural environment that physical science has tended to discredit. Myths are public and communicable, but they express mental patterns that come close to the compulsive drives of the unconscious."[4]

Another very different use of myth in this period is employed by João Ubaldo Ribeiro. His novel *Sargento Getúlio* (1971; *Sergeant Getúlio*) utilizes mythological elements within a sociopolitical and ideological context to explore what Djelal Kadir calls an "allegory of dehumanization."[5] Ribeiro's novel was written at the height of the military dictatorship, and its highly charged mythic language and structures form part of a forceful call for social and political change.

Sargento Getúlio explores the interplay between victim and oppressor. The reader is drawn to the plight of an innocent prisoner and experiences his dehumanization through the mind of his captor. The work is one of the cornerstones of the "Romance Novo," "The New Novel,"[6] engaging the reader on many levels of consciousness. The sergeant's efforts to deliver his prisoner are elevated mythically to heroic proportions. The work transcends categorization, exploring an aberrant facet of human behavior. Ribeiro's book is a study of a violent mentality, an aesthetic and mythic transformation of evil.

This is one of the most accomplished Brazilian novels to date. Ribeiro, by reducing the novel's composition to the bare forms of language, is able to create an open-ended narrative that is simultaneously interpretable from various perspectives. With this novel a new form of social narrative is born. The work evolves as a multi-level reflection on the character of Getúlio from a grotesque of nature to a mythically heroic embodiment of the Brazilian national will. Much of the novel's richness is derived from its minimalist nature, allowing an active readership to participate and express its concerns and interpretations. This text exhibits the extremes of the transference process that are such an integral part of the reader-response theory of literary criticism.

The following two studies are included to demonstrate the strongly archetypal nature of the Brazilian narrative. The focus of these studies will be on two distinct uses of myth, one ahistorical, the other sociopolitical; one written prior to the coup, the other during its apogee.

Mythological Correspondences and Prefigurative Techniques in "Mistério em São Cristóvão"

> *The man who speaks with primordial images*
> *speaks with a thousand tongues; . . . he raises*
> *the idea he is trying to express above the*
> *occasional . . . into the sphere of the everlasting.*
> *This is the secret of effective art.*
>
> Carl Gustav Jung

    The structural principles of literature exhibit a strong heuristic aspect, that is to say, an invitation to the reader to view parallels and correspondences among divergent literary forms and periods. In the *Ordeal by Labyrinth*, Mircea Eliade characterizes his lifelong research as ". . . an attempt to rediscover the forgotten sources of literary inspiration. . . . It is well known that literature, oral or written, is the offspring of mythology and that it inherits its parent's function, narrating adventures, naming the 'significant' things that have happened in the world."[1]

    Contemporary Brazilian fiction writers, like their primitive counterparts, are the creators and perpetuators of the history, myths, and attitudes of the present age. Their writings reflect a mode of consciousness that is, and always has been, comprised of a confluence of sociological, mythic, and artistic elements.

A critical consideration of Clarice Lispector's conscious presentation of mythological correspondences and her artistic use of prefigurative techniques to structure "Mistério em São Cristóvão" is to be the central focus of this study.

I

In Fábio Lucas's aforementioned essay "Cultural Aspects of Brazilian Literature," he expresses one of the highest compliments that can be paid an author. "Clarice Lispector, cujo mundo mágico, encerrado em romances e contos, vem a ser a manifestação de surpreendente poder criador, um desafio permanente para a crítica." ("Clarice Lispector's magic world enclosed in her novels and short stories is the manifestation of an extraordinary creative talent—a permanent challenge to literary criticism.")[2] Lispector's publication of *Lacos de família* in 1960 set forth a flood of interpretative analysis and praise that has not abated to this day. This "permanent challenge to critics," this "magic world" was at first the object of a somewhat inordinate amount of critical attention, relating Lispector's works to a strict existentialist world view.[3] At the present moment this large body of criticism encompasses a wide spectrum of approaches aimed at an understanding of the beauty and mystery of her innovative writing style.[4] For over twenty-five years *Laços de família* has indeed been a challenge to critics due in part to its minimalist style, the open-endedness of the stories, and Lispector's fine sense of language and its use.

However, one facet of Lispector's writing that surprisingly has received very little critical attention is that of her role as a modern-day mythmaker. This aspect of her art has never been the object of a detailed literary analysis and is seldom if ever brought into a general discussion of her work.

This study deals specifically with Lispector's application of the Paradise and Hyacinthus myths to structure one of the most enigmatic stories from *Laços de família*, "Mistério em São Cristóvão." Lucas has singled out this particular story for special praise. "'Mistério em São Cristóvão'... vem a ser uma das mais notáveis composições de gênero na literatura brasileira."[5] ("'Mystery in São Cristóvão' is one of the most outstanding compositions of the short story genre in all of Brazilian literature.") This masterpiece of short fiction writing affords an excellent example of Lispector's ability to use patterns of correspondence and mythic prefigurations. In this work is found a strong sense of mythic primitivism that exists as an artful projection by this contemporary writer.

II

"Mistério em São Cristóvão" is structured on a coherent series of polarities: order-disorder, youth-age, innocence-evil, and light-darkness, all of which mirror the more universal Manichean polarity. "Numa noite de maio—os jacintos rigídos perto da vidraça—a sala de jantar de uma casa estava iluminada e tranquila." ("On an autumn evening, with tall, erect hyacinths beside the windowpane, the dining room of a house was lit up and peaceful.")[6] The narrative begins by focusing upon the security and intimacy of the family unit. "O sereno perfumado de São Cristóvão não era perigoso mas o modo como as pessoas se agrupavam no interior da casa tornava arriscado o que não fosse o seio de uma família numa noite fresca de maio" (p. 129). ("The cool perfumed night air of São Cristovão was in no sense dangerous, but the way in which the members of the household were grouped inside the house precluded everything except an intimate family circle on such a cool May, evening" [p. 133].) It must be remembered that the "jacintos," hyacinths, are an integral part of the opening scene. The family's existence is presented as moving through a series of events that indicate a "progression towards perfection."[7] The warmth of their now comfortable life is shared by all members of this close-knit family unit. "O que tornava particularmente abastada a cena, e tão desabrochado o rosto de cada pessoa, é que depois de muitos anos quase se apalpava afinal o progresso nessa família: . . . Sem se dar conta, a família fitava a sala feliz, vigiando o raro instante de maio e sua abundância" (p. 129). ("What made the scene so particularly complete and the expression of everyone there so relaxed, was the fact that after many years one could almost feel, at long last, the progress of this family. . . . Without realizing it, the family gazed upon that room with deep satisfaction, watching the rare moment of May and its abundance" [pp. 133–34].)

Lispector's conscious use of mythic topoi and symbology is germane to an understanding of her narrative art. In this work's presentation of prefigurative techniques is found a key to Lispector's mastery of style. John J. White's observations in this regard are relevant: "A myth introduced by a modern novelist in his work can prefigure and hence anticipate the plot in a number of ways. Although an awareness of sources is declining, the ideal reader can still be expected to be familiar with most prefigurations beforehand, just as the novelist himself was when he wrote this work." [8]

At this juncture of the story Lispector shifts the focus of the narrative to the family's garden, which is presented as walled off from the rest of the town. Animistically the garden comes alive as the family's alter ego. The paradisal landscape suggests the "locus amoenus" of a holy Garden of Eden. Again the heart of the scene is the pure white hyacinth. "A mocinha, na sua camisola de algodão, abriu a janela do quarto e respirou todo o jardim com insatisfação e felicidade. Perturbada pela umidade cheirosa, deitou-se prometendo-se para o dia seguinte uma atitude inteiramente nova que abalasse os jacintos e fizesse as frutas estremecerem nos ramos . . . o silêncio piscava nos vagalumes . . ." (p. 130). (The young girl in her cotton nightgown opened her window and inhaled the whole garden, restless yet happy. Disturbed by the fragrant humidity, she lay down, promising herself a completely new outlook tomorrow which would shake the hyacinths and make the fruits tremble on the branches . . . the silence twinkled in the glow of fireflies" [p. 134].) Commenting on specific mythic correspondences, Eliade observes:

> We encounter the "paradise myth" all over the world in more or less complex forms . . . in describing the primordial situation the myths reveal its paradisial quality by the fact that "in illo tempore" Heaven is said to have been very near Earth, or that it was easy to reach it by means of a tree, a vine. . . . When Heaven was rudely "separated" from Earth, when it became "distant" as it is today, when the tree or the vine leading from Earth to Heaven was cut . . . the paradisal state was over and humanity arrived at its present state. [9]

The existential conception of the Other is portrayed by the intruders who are now introduced into the story. "Um era alto e tinha a cabeça de um galo. Outro era gordo e vestira-se de touro. E o terceiro, mais novo, por falta de idéias, disfarçara-se em cavalheiro antigo e pusera máscara de demônio, através da qual surgiam seus olhos cândidos. Os três mascarados atravessaram a rua em silêncio" (p. 130). ("The first was tall and wore the head mask of a rooster. The second was fat and was dressed up as a bull. And the third, who was younger, for want of a better idea, had disguised himself as an ancient knight and wore a demon's mask, through which appeared two innocent eyes. The three masqueraders crossed the road in silence" [p. 135].) It is to be noted that the "mascarados" are out of sync with chronological events. "Os três cavalheiros mascarados, que por idéia funesta do galo pretendiam fazer uma surpresa num baile tão longe do carnaval . . ." (p. 133). (The three masked gentlemen who, at the rooster's fatal suggestion, aimed to cause some surprise at a ball in a season so remote from Carnival . . ." [p. 137].) The story moves on two interrelated planes as the masqueraders are symbolically depicted as the embodiment of virile and sexual forces: "cabeça de um galo," the "gordo" who "vestira-se de touro," and the "cavalheiro antigo" who "pusera máscara de demônio." However, Lispector brings the reader to a simultaneous realization of the innocents beneath the masks. "Os três aguardarem assustados: sem respirar, o galo, o touro e o cavalheiro do diabo perscrutaram o escuro" (p. 131). ("Too frightened to breathe, the rooster, the bull, and the demon knight scrutinized the darkness" [p. 135].) ". . . através da qual surgiam seus olhos cândidos" (p. 130). ("Through which appeared two innocent eyes" [p. 134].)

According to Joseph Campbell, "In the primitive world, where clues to the origin of myth must be sought, gods and demons are not conceived in the way of hard and fast, positive realities. The phenomenon of the primitive mask, for example, is a case in point. The mask is revered as an apparition of the mythical being that it represents, yet everyone knows that the man made the mask and that a man wears it." [10]

Here the reader is made aware of the dichotomy between mythic prefiguration and the reality of the youths as innocents in a commonplace drama. Again the focus is on the hyacinths, as animistically they are portrayed as oblivious to danger, just as the young girl is still cloaked in youthful innocence. "E, no jardim sufocado de perfume, os jacintos estremeciam imunes" (p. 131). ("And in the garden, suffused with perfume, the hyacinths trembled unconcerned" [p. 135].)

It is universally held that Clarice Lispector's prose is among the most polished of any modern writer. Assis Brasil observes, "A procura de uma nova linguagem para o romance, camina paralelamente a Grillet. . . ." ("In search of a new language . . . Lispector parallels Robbe-Grillet. . . .") [11] Thus, it seems highly unlikely that word selection or the choice of a title would be left to chance. That is precisely why this story's title serves as a specific example of her artistic use of mythological correspondences. São Cristóvão is never particularized within the narrative, existing mainly for its nominal symbology. Bella Jozef observes, "Clarice Lispector demuestra que la escena literaria es, por definición, ficcional, que su universo se construye en lo imaginario." [12] ("Clarice Lispector shows that the literary scene is, by definition, fictional, that her universe is constructed in the imagination.") If one views this work on its deeper, more mythologically symbolic level, then one is led to believe that Lispector is using São Cristóvão as a prefiguration. This is a masterfully placed authorial suggestion alluding to the St. Christopher legend and iconography which in the Iberian peninsula have considerable pagan connotations of male potency and priapism. [13] Witness these three male characters and their menacing youthful sexuality.

Much of the dramatic force of this work is rooted in the fact that the order-disorder polarity is so skillfully presented. Inexpressible and intangible fears are given a sensorial form which is reflected in nature. "Cada planta úmida, cada seixo, os sapos roucos aproveitavam a silenciosa confusão para se disporem em melhor lugar—todo no escuro era muda aproximação. . . . Os jacintos cada vez mais brancos na escuridão. . . . Os quatro, vindos da realidade, haviam caído nas possibilidades que tem uma noite de maio em São Cristóvão" (p. 132). ("Each humid plant, each pebble, the hoarse toads—all of them exploiting the silent chaos in order to arrange themselves in a better spot—everything in that darkness silently approached. . . . The hyacinths gradually seemed to become whiter in the darkness. . . . These four, having come from reality, had become subject to the possibilities an autumn evening possesses in São Cristóvão" [p. 136].) The young girl at the window and the three masked youths are caught in a moment frozen out of time. Paralyzed with fear, they hold each other's glance and then withdraw in silence. "A simples aproximação de quatro máscaras na noite de maio parecia ter percutido ocos recintos, e mais outros, e mais outros que, sem o instante no jardim, ficariam para sempre nesse perfume que há no ar e na imanência de quatro naturezas que o acaso indicara, assinalando hora e lugar—o mesmo acaso preciso de uma estrela cadente" (p. 132). ("The simple encounter of four masks on that autumn evening seemed to have touched deep recesses, then others, and still others which, had it not been for the moment in the garden, would have remained forever with this perfume which is in the air and in the immanence of those four natures which fate had designated, assigning the hour and place—the same precise fate of a falling star" [p. 136].) The previously unmentioned fourth mask is the mask of the girl's own innocence. After this fearful stand-off, animistic description is again employed to add a cosmic dimension to the confrontation. The "grande lua de maio" presides over the scene as the four youths are portrayed as "de asas abertas," in a scene more Lorquian that Sartrean. "Caídos na cilada, eles se olhavam aterrori-zados: fora saltada a natureza das coisas e as quatro figuras se espia-vam de asas abertas. Um galo, um touro, o demônio e um rosto de moça haviam desatado a maravilha do jardim. . . . Foi quando a grande lua de maio apareceu" (p. 132). ("Having fallen into the am-bush, they looked at each other in fear: the nature of things had been surpassed and the four figures spied each other with open wings. The rooster, the bull, the demon, and the girl's face had unraveled the mar-vels of the garden. That was when the great May moon appeared" [p. 136].) The confrontation has cosmic repercussions. It is commu-nicated as an anthropomorphic clash affecting all levels of existence, the human, the cosmic, and the natural world. "Era um toque perigoso para as quatro imagens. Tão arriscado que, sem um som, quatro mu-das visões recuaram sem se desfitarem . . ." (p. 132). ("It was a dan-gerous moment for the four images. So fraught with danger that, with-out a murmur, the four mute apparitions retreated without taking their eyes off each other . . ." [p. 136].) "Mal, porém, se quebrara o círculo mágico de quatro, livres da vigilância mútua, a constelação se desfez com terror . . ." (p. 133). ("No sooner, however, had the magic circle of the four been broken, liberated from their mutual vigilance, than the stars dissolved in terror" [p. 137].)

As the reader is brought to a realization of the overwhelming role of mythic primitivism in the short story, the following assumption by Robert Alter regarding modern fiction aids in illuminating Lispector's presentation of this Manichean confrontation. "It will be observed that there is a Manichean split here between the unalterable forces of boundless evil and the residual nostalgia of goodness, truth, and love. . . . Such dualism in itself implies an avoidance of real his-tory. . . ." [14] Youthful innocence has been symbolically violated. "Mas na imagem rejuvenescida de mais de uma época, para o horror da família, um fio branco aparecera entre os cabelos da fronte" (p. 134). ("But in her rejuvenated image, to the horror of the family, a white strand had appeared among the hairs on her forehead" [p. 137].) The paradisal setting has also been violated as symbolized by the harm done the tallest, most perfect hyacinth. "Finalmente a velha, boa con-hecedora dos canteiros, apontou o único sinal visível no jardim que se esquivava: o jacinto ainda vivo quebrado no talo . . ." (p. 134).

("Finally, the old lady, long familiar with the flowerbeds, pointed to the only visible sign in the garden that shunned discovery: the hyacinth—still alive but with its stalk broken . . ." [p. 138].) The moments of lifelong plenitude, the familial harmony, the "laços de família" were all shattered by a single undefined act.[15] Ironically, innocence has been violated by innocents. Family "ties" have been unable to insulate the young girl whose purity was reflected in the hyacinth. The sanctity of the family distrubed, the elders turn on all the house lights in a vain attempt to hold back the night, as the Manichean polarity is brought into play for the final time.

However, from within this same intimate family scene is born Lispector's vision of a yearning for paradise anew. Man lives with hope, as the story's final image is of the family warding off the night, eternally vigilant, awaiting "a brisa da abastança," a return to plenitude, a renewed yearning for paradise. "Voltaram, iluminaram a casa toda e passaram o resto da noite a esperar" (p. 134). ("They returned indoors, put on all the lights in the house, and spent the rest of the night—waiting" [p. 138].) Lispector leaves the reader with this minimal sense of hope much in the same way as T. S. Eliot's "The Waste Land" concedingly allows for the rite of renewal. "April is the cruellest month, breeding / Lilacs out of the dead land. . . ."[16] "Toda a casa parecendo esperar que mais uma vez a brisa da abastança soprasse depois de um jantar. O que sucederia talvez noutra noite de maio" (p. 135). ("The whole house appearing to lie in wait for that breeze of plenitude to blow once more after dinner. Perhaps it would happen some other autumn evening" [p. 138].)

III

Lispector's conscious use of primitivist impulses is central to her art. The confrontation of the four youths forms the narrative matrix of this story, a story whose mythic underpinnings accommodate both the paradisal and the Hyacinthus motifs. In discussing the symbology of the hyacinth, Gertrude Jobes reveals that the "hyacinth in Christian tradition typifies a desire for heaven, peace of mind and prudence. . . ."[17] as is its function in the expository section of the story. "Poderia colher o jacinto que estava à sua mão. Os maiores, porém, que se erguiam perto de uma janela—altos, duros, frágeis—cintilavam chamando-o" (p. 131). ("He could pick the hyacinth that was within his reach. The larger flowers, however, which grew beside a window—tall, brittle, fragile—stood glittering and beckoned to him" [p. 135].)

However, after the violation-of-the-garden scene, the symbol of the hyacinth functions as a paradigm for "hope as symbolic of resurrection,"[18] its message showing the possibility, centrality, and efficacy of human love.

Edith Hamilton's reading of this myth mirrors this observation. The friends "were only playing a game." As Apollo held his dearest companion Hyacinthus, "he tried to staunch the wound. But it was too late. While he held him the boy's head fell back as a flower does when its stem is broken." From the blood-stained grass "there bloomed forth a wondrous flower that was to make the lad's name known forever." This myth "tells of a flowery resurrection . . . born from youthful and inadvertent tragedy . . . the flowers were his very self, changed and yet living again."[19]

This archetype of redemptive suffering moves beyond the "figura" of Hyacinthus to form part of Lispector's existential vision of our present moment. *Laços de família, Family Ties* is Lispector's statement of the universality of the human experience. This experience, predominately tragic in nature, is viewed in this narrative as a source of man's consolation. Lispector suggests as does Jung, "In the final count, every individual life is at the same time also the life of the eons of the species."[20]

Fiction is never a pure view of the universe, but rather it is a means used to convey a writer's subjective vision. In a very real sense, Clarice Lispector's modification of classical archetypes is the unifying structure through which she expresses her particularized conception of existence. This seemingly simple tale, this poetized allegory of human history, evolves existentially as a beautifully told contemporary parable of man's dialogue with a silent God. The impenetrable fear that characterizes the surface level of this narrative is endured heroically by Lispector's Everyman family. Much like her primitive counterparts, Lispector as modern-day mythmaker struggles to make man's experience intelligible, as the tragedy of the family is given a cosmic identification and explanation.[21]

Lispector's style reduces characterization to a type of mythic shorthand through her terse, densely written prose. She postulates that the family unit's analgesic for existential conflict does exist in the love, warmth, and solace found in the well-lighted places of the human heart. Lispector is asking the reader to go beyond the work to gain from her writings a heightened sense of loyalty to a humanistic ethic.

As Charles I. Glicksberg observes, "The fundamental conflict fought out in the . . . literature . . . of our age is not between man and society but between nihilism and the nostalgia for the absolute. . . ."[22]

Short fiction from Machado de Assis to Luiz Vilela has always been one of the strongest components of Brazilian literature. Clarice Lispector's "Mistério em São Cristóvão" is universally recognized as one of the undisputed masterpieces of this dynamic literature, owing in large part to the author's original use of prefigurative techniques as a unifying force to explain and interpret atemporal sentiments common to all men in all cultures.

Chthonian Visions
and Mythic Redemption
in João Ubaldo Ribeiro's
Sargento Getúlio

*Arrojou-se sozinho, de machado em punho,
sobre a tropa que avançava contra a trincheira,
inteiramente exposto, numa atitude de heróica
beleza.*

*(A solitary figure wielding an ax, he rushed
headlong, against an entire troop . . . mercilessly
endangering himself in a gesture of heroic
proportions.)*

Lourenço Moreira Lima
(Secretary to the Prestes Column)

*Through the sacrifice of ourselves we gain
ourselves. . . .*

Carl Gustav Jung

*vi todo o drama do Nordeste . . . Vi a paisagem
árida . . . a inclemência dos homens e do tempo.*

45

> *(I have witnessed the total drama of the*
> *Northeast . . . I saw the parched landscape, . . .*
> *I saw . . . the mercilessness of man and of*
> *weather.)*
>
> General Garrastazu Médici

Many modern novelists attempt to discover basic cultural patterns that, through the narrative process, acquire mythic proportions within their particular society and epoch. In *Sargento Getúlio* (1971), (*Sergeant Getúlio*, 1977), João Ubaldo Ribeiro utilizes epic formulae and mythological correspondences to posit a chthonian vision of the modern world. While the contemporary Brazilian novel is as variegated in substance and narrative technique as that of any national literature, there exist intriguing thematic parallels throughout many works of that country's most respected writers. The grotesque motif born of the tension of innocent victims confronting torture is pandemic.[1] Often history relies on the novelist to aid in documenting in palpable and human terms the political failings of an era. George A. Panichas has stated: "To a large degree history, not literary aesthetic, dictates sensibility and belief in twentieth-century literature."[2] Ribeiro's novel fuses very real sociopolitical concerns, the aesthetic experience, and his role as modern-day mythmaker. It is truly a protean masterpiece, an elegantly wrought study which is, on balance, one of the most distinguished pieces of modern Brazilian fiction. Peter S. Prescott calls the work a "splendid novel,"[3] and writer-critic Érico Veríssimo observes: "É algo de novo. Não tem nada a ver com nenhum outro livro. . . . na minha opinião, vai ficar como um marco na nossa literatura."[4] ("It is something unique. It derives nothing from any other book. . . . In my opinion the book will remain as one of the benchmarks of our literature.") The supreme compliment comes from the internationally acclaimed novelist Jorge Amado: "Among the works of fiction published in Brazil in the last decade, few have been as important as João Ubaldo Ribeiro's *Sergeant Getúlio*. . . ."[5]

This analysis focuses upon *Sergeant Getúlio*'s inherent artistic integrity, its accommodation of mythic topoi, and the cogency of its vision of one man's journey to redemption.

I

Charles I. Glicksberg, in analyzing the zoological metaphor in modern literature, observes that this metaphorical metamorphosis "drives home the absurdity of investing human life with a divine purpose or any purpose at all; it reinforces the suspicion that the emergence of consciousness is in the service of instinct, an emanation of the blind energy of nature."[6] There exists no character in contemporary fiction that has so incarnated this "blind energy of Nature" as has Ribeiro's Sergeant Getúlio. No other work of modern fiction so strongly concentrates on analyzing this "consciousness in the service of instinct." This work stands in marked contrast to the narrative innovations and authorial playfulness that form such an integral part of the contemporary Brazilian novel. Ribeiro's style and focus could well be termed neo-Dostoyevskian. His novel's central consciousness is a modern day underground man, an ex-militia sergeant working for a local political boss. Ribeiro's narrator, Getúlio, in the fashion of Dostoyevsky's unnamed civil servant in *Notes from Underground*, offers his jaundiced views on life, from manhood to hair cream to sex and torture, all within the context of an extended monologue, a protracted soliloquy that acquires mythic and anthropomorphic dimensions. Jon S. Vincent's reading of *Grande Sertão: Veredas* illustrates the interplay between the "autobiographical account . . . of the narrator" and the non-registered speech of "the interlocutor."[7] An analogous narrative structure exists in *Sergeant Getúlio* with Amaro, his driver, being his silent sounding board.

The epic dimensions of this book can be measured from the Odyssean journey that Getúlio embarks upon, becoming a symbolic Grail Quest.[8] There are present many prefigurations of traditional epic formulae: the journey itself, the hyperbolic nature of Getúlio's feats of violence, the larger than life aspect of the hero's being, the threshold crossing, the legendary quality of his reputation, his trials against overwhelming odds, and the continual use of his name as an incantation. "Meu nome é um verso: Getúlio Santos Bezerra . . ." (p. 136). ("My name is a verse: Getúlio Santos Bezerra . . ." [p. 118].) "Eu sou o Dragão Manjaléu, Comedor de Coração" (p. 132). ("I am the Bogey Dragon. Eater of hearts" [p. 115].) "Seu nome é um verso, disse Luzinete, e você nunca que vai morrer" (p. 136). ("'Your name is a verse,' Luzinete said, 'and you are never going to die'" [p. 118].)

The work's many mythic and epic correspondences strongly suggest that the novel is archetypically rich, transcending a purely sociological reading. Ribeiro has created a unique epic hero who is not the embodiment of a nation's hopes and ideals, but one who is a hellish emanation of will, the violent will of the "sertão," the backlands. As such, the novel's vision can be considered socio-mythic, perhaps reacting to a political reality that needed to be addressed in aesthetic terms.

The plot line, in its simplicity, is expressed immediately by the author: "Nesta história, o Sargento Getúlio leva um preso de Paulo Afonso a Barra dos Coqueiros" (p. 7). ("In this story Sergeant Getúlio takes a prisoner from Paulo Afonso to Barra dos Coqueiros" [p. 7].) Then the flat value judgement is added: "É uma história de aretê" (p. 7). ("It is a tale of virtue" [p. 7].) Getúlio is hired to bring back a political enemy of one of the local politicians. He captures the man and they cross Sergipe province in an old bullet-ridden Hudson, driven by Amaro. Throughout the journey Getúlio freely offers his inverted sense of morality and his puerile views of politics and life. "Profissão é profissão. Não gosto de médico. Nunca atirei num médico. Ou já atirei? Não me lembro. . . . Coveiro, profissão miserável. Todo paraibano é conveiro. Paraíba é Brasil" (pp. 22–3). ("A profession is a profession. I don't like doctors. I never shot a doctor. Or did I? I can't remember. . . . Gravedigging, what a miserable profession. All men from Paraíba are gravediggers. Paraíba is Brazil" [p. 20].) "Eu e Amaro fomos ajudar a segurar para dar umas porradas nela. Merecia. Mulher que viu homem nessas condições é rapariga. Ou vai ser. Punitivos é bom" (p. 55). ("Amaro and I went over to help hold the girl, so that he could hit her once or twice. She deserved it. A woman who has seen a man in such a state is a whore. Or will be. Punishment does good" [p. 49].)

II

In broad terms *Sargento Getúlio* can be seen as an allegory of confrontation between civilization and the last stages of Brazilian barbarism. However, this work is more a multilayered confrontation which, on the first level of meaning, dramatizes the tension between victim and oppressor. This novel's victim is the true innocent. The prisoner is totally dehumanized by Getúlio. He is verbally, physically, and mentally debased. Getúlio fixates upon this sacrificial lamb and projects all his hatred upon this "creature," this "pox." He pulls out his teeth, ties him to trees, and berates him constantly. "O trem amordaçado atrás, gemendo por causa da dor do lenço nas gengivas, que o alicate não era mesmo para tirar dente e tinha ferruge e deslizava, de maneiras que a extraição foi puxada e desvaziou gengiva que não foi graça . . ." (p. 61). ("The creature was gagged behind us groaning because of the pain on his gums, since the pliers were not the kind specifically for pulling out teeth and they were rusty and slippery, so that the extraction was delayed and the gums almost came off with the teeth . . ." [p. 55].) "Me ajude a atar esse peste num pé de pau. Suas necessidades faça amarrado mesmo" (p. 28). ("Help me tie this thing to a tree. We're not going to untie him for his needs" [p. 25].) The victim is dragged across the "sertão" like a package to be delivered. Only the village priest has any compassion for the man. However, he is impotent to stop the Sergeant's cruelty or his mission; he can only momentarily alleviate the prisoner's suffering by placing a compress dipped in holy water on his bloody mouth.

Symbolically, the victim is the true innocent at the mercy of a ruthless political system that is as unfathomable as it is unjust. From this perspective, the prisoner's life can be viewed in Kafkaesque terms as an absurd nightmare. The prisoner is the quintessential Job figure with punishment after punishment heaped upon him by an irrational captor. "Vosmecê sabe o termo bonito para arrancar dente? Vosmecê não quer abrir logo essa bonquinha de bunina? Ôi peste, ôi peste! Aí inverti a arma encarquei duas vezes no beiço do alguém e arranquei quatro dentes de alicate. E deixei" (p. 60). ("'Do you happen to know a fancy word for pulling out teeth? Would you be so kind as to open your little daisy of a mouth quick? Dammit, damn you!' Then I turned my weapon around, pounded twice on the creature's lips and pulled out four teeth with the pliers, and stopped" [p. 53].) As Getúlio, Amaro, and the prisoner continue on their journey, government soldiers led by a young lieutenant come to cancel the mission. Getúlio is bound by his personal code of honor to deliver the "pox." It seems it is now politically expedient even for Getúlio's boss to rescind his vendetta. This Getúlio refuses to do:

> Depois, o chefe me mandou buscar isso aí e eu fui, peguei, truxe, amansei, e vou levar porque mesmo que o chefe agora não possa me sustentar, eu levei o homem, chego lá entrego. É preciso entregar o bicho. Entrego e digo: ordem cumprida. . . . eu levo esse lixo de

qualquer jeito, chego lá e entrego. Nem que eu estupore. Quero ver
esse bom em Aracaju que me diz que eu não posso, porque eu sou
Getúlio Santos Bezerra e igual a mim ainda não nasceu. (P. 84)

(Besides, the chief told me to go look for this creature and I went, I
caught him, brought him along, broke him and I am going to take
him, even if the chief can no longer support me I will have taken the
man and delivered him. It is necessary to deliver the animal. I deliver
him and I say: Mission accomplished. . . . I will take this trash with
me no matter what, I will get there and deliver him. Even if I burst. I
want to see who is man enough in Aracaju to tell me I can't do it,
because I am Getúlio Santos Bezerra and my equal has not yet been
born.) (P. 74)

His sense of mission cannot be influenced, and it is against these government soldiers that Getúlio's most violent act is committed. In a
mythological accommodation of Perseus's beheading of Medusa, Getúlio coldly cuts off the lieutenant's head:

Impossível cortar a cabeça de uma jia sem cortar o resto do corpo todo, por falta de pescoço, mas o tenente, assim que decepei,
pude amarrar a cabeça num pedaço de corda e rodar por cima da
cabeça . . . olhe a cabeça dele, olhe a cabeça dele, quem permanecer
vai acabar assim também e dei um safanão na corda e joguei lá no
meio da força. . . . (P. 77)

(It's impossible to cut off a frog's head without cutting the whole rest
of the body for lack of a neck, but as for the lieutenant, as soon as I
had finished the beheading I was able to tie his head to the end of a
piece of rope and swirl it around my own head . . . , "Look at his
head, look at his head, whoever persists will end up like this too,"
and then I jerked the rope and threw the head in the middle of the
force. . . .) (P. 68)

This act of inhumanity and defiance was triggered by an insult to Getúlio's manhood. "Possa ser—disse o tenete. —Mas na companhia de
um sargento corno e desertor, com um pirobo por chofer, não acredito
muito, não" (p. 73). ("'Maybe,' the lieutenant said. 'But when you are
in the company of a sergeant who is a cuckold and a deserter with a
queer for a driver, I cannot very well believe that'" [p. 65].) Throughout the extended monologue the reader perceives that part of the reason for Getúlio's anger comes from his having been betrayed by his
wife. "A dor de corno, uma dor funda na caixa, uma coisa tirando a
força de dentro. Nem sei. Uma mulher não é como um homem"
(p. 38). ("The pain of being a cuckold, a deep pain in the chest, something draining your strength from inside. I don't even know how to
say it. A woman is not like a man" [p. 34].) He tells of past tender-

nesses, but quickly implies that he killed his wife and his unborn child for a supposed act of infidelity. "Mas não disse nada e, na hora que enfiei o ferro, fechei os olhos. Nem gemeu. Caiu lá, com a mão na barriga" (p. 39). ("But I said nothing and when I plunged the iron, I closed my eyes. She made no sound. She fell there, with her hands on her belly" [p. 35].)

Much of *Sargento Getúlio*'s tone is somber and humorless; the horror of disquisitions on methods of murder and torture seems endless, evoking a strong feeling of reader disgust. Getúlio's being is permeated with "Schadenfreude." This perverse delight is Getúlio's overriding passion. In his choice of a woman he selects his mirror image, Luzinete, a larger than life reflection of himself. "É um diabo duma mulher grande, duas braças de mulher de cima para baixo, cinco arrobas de mulher de legítima . . ." (p. 108). ("She is one devil of a big woman, two armlengths of a woman from top to bottom, seventy-five kilos of genuine woman well measured . . ." (p. 94). She equals his thirst for brutality and impels him to complete his mission. "Disse Luzinete, e por que tu não acaba com aqueles pestes de uma vez logo e vai embora com sua missão?" (p. 135). ("Luzinete said, 'and why don't you finish all those accursed people once and for all and go on with your mission?' " [p. 118].) She is as accepting of violence as a natural state as he is. Her death and that of Amaro leave Getúlio truly alone.

III

Ribeiro's tale is marked with strong psychological concerns. The work is framed only by Getúlio's perceptions of reality. These perceptions are at times lyrically poignant and at others mask the rambling convictions of a madman. Getúlio is now totally obsessed with completing his mission. While his tales of violence may be compelling, the total effect of his extended monologue is that Getúlio is truly a grotesque of Nature, a bestial aberration:

> Mas de vinte nas costas, veja vosmecê, é como mulher, não se consegue lembrar todas. A primeira é mais difícil, mas depois a gente aprende a não olhar a cara para não empatar a obra. De perto demais não é bom. Se agarram-se na gente, puxam a túnica para baixo. (Pp. 14–15)

(Over twenty people to my credit, imagine, it's like women, impossible to remember them all. The first one is the most difficult, but after that you learn not to look at the face so as not to bungle the job. When you're too close it's no good. They grab at you, they pull your jacket down.) (P. 14)

Symbolically, he has now turned on the very same political system that had so frequently used him in the past.

One of the keys to understanding this "tale of virtue" is that the reader is able to see through the constant and twisted philosophizing, perceiving a being, like Dostoyevsky's unnamed narrator, whose imagination impels him to exaggerate the slightest insult or feeling of inferiority. However, unlike his Russian counterpart, Getúlio never considers the consequences of his actions. He is as impulsive as his parallel consciousness is inert. Both men are totally out of step and at variance with the tenor and tenets of their times.

The anti-intellectualism of Getúlio is largely attributable to envy and incomprehension. He is amazed that his companion Amaro is able to remember the words to popular songs and prayers. He loathes the prisoner because he has had a high school education. Getúlio dwells upon that fact throughout the novel:

> Tem ginásio, tem ginásio! nunca vi ginásio fazer caráter, não responda porque é melhor, lhe meto a cabeça num bocapio e deixo o resto com os guarás. . . . (P. 27)

> (You went to high school, you went to high school! a high school never made a man out of a bum, and don't answer because it's better for you, I'll stick your head in a straw bag and leave the rest to the wild dogs. . . .) (P. 24)

It is an anti-intellectualism born of a being unable to fathom the people and places around him:[9]

> Quero ficar olhando muito Aracaju, curtindo minha raiva e pensando em minha vida e querendo saber o que é que faz tanto povo lá, amuntado lá, naquelas ruas grandes. Quando eu falo ninguém entende lá, quando um fala lá eu não entendo. (P. 153)

> (I want to take a very long look at Aracaju, nursing my anger and thinking about life and wondering what so many people are doing there, piled up on those big streets. When I speak nobody there understands, when someone speaks there I don't understand.) (P. 134)

Getúlio is only at home on the "sertão," for he senses his own limitations. "Eu mesmo decoro pouco, que não sou de muito aprendizado, mas se eu fosse eu decorava mais, porque aprecio, todo mundo aprecia . . ." (p. 35). ("I memorize very little, being a man of little learning, but if I had more learning I would memorize more verses, because I enjoy them and everybody enjoys them" [p. 32].) Of Amaro's death he observes: "Se não fosse homem, eu sentia saudade" (p. 36). ("If it weren't for his being a man, I would miss him" [p. 33].) However, his animal nature is continually underscored as he remarks of a simple checker game: "Nunca que eu vou acertar a fazer isso. Não tenho paciência para ficar estudando essas pedras nesse tabuleiro, esquenta a cabeça, não tem propósito" (p. 87). ("I will never figure that out. I have no patience to keep studying these pieces on this board, it heats up one's head, it has no purpose" [p. 77].)

IV

A comparison of the thematic stance underlying the motif of the "stone wall" in *Notes from Underground* may help to clarify the scope and significance of Ribeiro's vision. Dostoyevsky's narrator remarks: "Of course, I won't be able to breach this wall with my head if I'm not strong enough. But I don't have to accept a stone wall just because it's there and I don't have the strength to breach it." [10] However, Dostoyevsky's underground man, in considering all the consequences of his actions, is rendered immobile and withdraws into a solipsistic realm of his own spiteful consciousness. Getúlio, on the other hand, the man of direct action, proceeds into the waiting militia. His sense of self is engendered by his life as a sergeant and the fear that that position instills in others. "Pior é não ser ninguém . . ." (p. 136). ("The worst thing is to be nobody . . ." [p. 119].) This pride leads him to seek his own immortality in the completion of his near impossible mission. Thus, he knowingly advances directly toward certain death.

In the novel's concluding chapter, Ribeiro's narrative tone becomes lyrical and mythic as Getúlio's epic journey is nearing an end. The hero is being made ready for his apotheosis. Witness the psychic transformation of Getúlio's being: "Eu acho, pois então, aquele homem que o senhor mandou não é mais aquele. Eu era ele, agora eu sou eu" (p. 152). ("I think, well then, that man you sent out is no longer that man. I used to be him now I am I" [p. 133].) In completing this mission Getúlio has been transformed from a man at odds with his own world to one whose sense of will and purpose is carried beyond life itself. The mythic qualities of the last chapter are formidable. "Eu era ele e agora eu sou eu. Isso mesmo eu digo com as vistas nas vistas dele e lhe deixo lá, amarrado e sem dente e com minha cara de cinza e com minha mulher de lua . . ." (p. 152). ("I used to be him and now I am I. I will say this with my eyes on his eyes and will leave you there tied and toothless, and with my ash face and with my woman in the moon . . ." [p. 133].) In this anthropomorphic transfiguration, Getúlio becomes one with the earth of the "sertão:"

> Isso eu tenho, essa terra toda eu tenho, porque quem me pariu foi a terra, abrindo um buraco no chão e eu saindo no meio de umas fumaças quentes e como eu outros ela sempre vai parir, porque essa terra é a maior parideira do mundo todo. (P. 153)

> (This I have, this whole land I have, because I was given birth by the land through a hole in the ground and I came out in the middle of hot smoke and she will bear others like me, because this land is the greatest breeder in the whole world.) (P. 134)

> E eu sendo eu, sendo eu, quando eu era menino eu comi barro e entrei por dentro do chão, comendo barro, cagando barro e comendo de novo. . . . (P. 155)

> (And I being I, being I, when I was a boy I ate clay and entered the ground eating clay, shitting clay and eating again.) (P. 136)

> A minha cara de cinza, o meu cabelo de terra, a minha bota de couro, a minha arma de ferro, hem, coisa? não semos tudo o mesmo? agora não muito, porque eu sou eu, Getúlio Santos Bezerra e meu nome é um verso que vai ser sempre versado e se tem lua alumia e se tem sol queima a cara. (P. 155)

> (My ash face my hair of earth, my leather boot, my iron gun, huh creature? aren't we all the same? not much so now because I am I, Getúlio Santos Bezerra and my name is a verse which is always going to be versed and if there is a moon out it glows and if the sun is out it burns the face.) (P. 135)

Within this cosmic at-one-ment with the life force of Nature, Ribeiro disorders prosaic reality as he metamorphosizes Getúlio into a primitive emanation of pure will that endures in the dry lands of the Northeast. "Eu moro no mundo. Moro andando. Ai, aaaaaaaai, aai, aai, ai, ai, aaaaaaaai, aaaai, ai um boi de barro . . ." (p. 29). ("I live everywhere. I live walking. Ay, aaaaaaaay, aay, aay, ay, ay, aaaaaaaay, aaaay, ay, a clay bull, ay a clay bull . . ." [p. 27].) Getúlio's being has been transformed mythically. "Me encontro-me sujo de barro assim e como do barro como de comer, por causo do gosto pardo" (p. 29). ("I am now covered with clay like this and I eat of the clay as though it were food, because of the brown taste" [p. 27].) The violent will of this hellish creature is now transfigured into the clay of the backlands. He is the eternal clay bull.

The novel ends with a montage of verbal exclamations, words run together, but Getúlio's will persists as do his final thoughts. "Boi de barro, aiumboi aiumboide barroaê aê aê aiumgara jauchei de barro e vidaeu sou eu e vou e quem foi ai mi nhalaran jeiramur chaai ei eu vou e cumpro e faço e" (p. 157). ("Claybull claya-ay a-ay a-ay ayapan nierfull of clay and life I am I and will and who was ay mywiltedo rangetree ay hey I will and carry out and do and" [p. 137].) Considered within this mythic perspective, Getúlio's dream (pp. 124–26) (p. 107–09 in English edition) of populating these dry lands of Sergipe with an army of violent sons serves as a prophetic warning. "Eu botava uns nomes de macho e depois a gente tomava essas terras que tem aí e armava umas tropas de mais macho e ficava dono do mundo aqui . . ." (p. 124). ("I would give them real male names and after that we would take these lands around here and we would organize some troops with more men and we would be masters of the world here . . ." [p. 107].) Narratively, his dream becomes a Brazilian tall tale of vengeance. This theme of one man's anger, "Me dá uma raiva por dentro, acho que careço ter raiva" (p. 37) ("I get angry inside, it seems I have a need to be angry" [p. 34]) is subjoined to the motif of the innate anger and violence of an animistic "sertão." An apocalyptic warning is tendered on the final words of chapter six. "Já viu você que filho esse que eu tenho? Arretado" (p. 126). ("You see the kind of son I have? Invincible" [p. 109].) It is at this juncture of the novel that Ribeiro masterfully commingles the art of the modern day mythmaker with, in Jorge Amado's words, "a persistent concern with exposing, both individual and social problems" (p. 139).

João Ubaldo Ribeiro's modern hero, Getúlio, has broken through the barriers of his own deformed soul to find redemption in death.[11] Freed from its purely Christian connotation, the archetype of redemptive suffering is applicable to Getúlio's death in the service of his successfully completed mission. He is transfigured and redeemed through his willingness to accept death ". . . in the process of a transcendent value, a worthy end. . . ."[12] Only by means of this willed death can he be reborn within the soil of backlands, rejuvenating it with his force and vitality. He is finally able to state: "Mas possa ser que chore agora, porque estou com um pouco de vontade de chorar . . ." (p. 156). ("Maybe I will cry now, because I feel like crying . . ." [p. 136].) The act of crying transcends a merely psychological indication that the hero has changed. It acquires the mythic symbolism of an act of consecration and preparation for death and resurrection. Getúlio's spiritual coalescence with the clay of the Brazilian sertão perpetuates his will, a forceful will that is needed for future political and social change. He affirms: "Pode crer que eu estou vivo no inferno . . ." (p. 156). ("I am alive in Hell . . ." [p. 136].) He is now eternal, forming a union with all that is bestial and chthonic. Like Jerome S. Bruner's observation in "Myth and Identity," Ribeiro, through the conscious use of mythological correspondences, "externalize(s) the daemon where it can be enmeshed in the texture of aesthetic experience. . . ." [13] As Amado concludes: "Among the mass of books published in Brazil in the last ten years, *Sargento Getúlio* stands out as one of the few works contributing to the development of a literary art that is genuinely Brazilian" (p. 141). Out of one man's epic quest for redemption, Ribeiro has fashioned one of the most complex and compelling Brazilian novels of the present age.

NOTES

[1] Earl E. Fitz, *Clarice Lispector* (Boston: Twayne, 1985), p. 15.

[2] David W. Foster, "Major Figures in the Brazilian Short Story," *The Latin American Short Story*, ed. Margaret Sayers Peden (Boston: G. K. Hall, 1983), p. 12.

[3] Clarice Lispector, *Laços de família* (Rio de Janeiro: Nova Fronteira, 1983), p. 145. See also Robert DiAntonio. "Myth as a Unifying Force in 'O crime do professor de matemática,' " *Luso-Brazilian Review*, XXII, 2 (1985).

[4] Richard Ellmann, *The Modern Tradition* (New York: Oxford, 1965), p. 617.

[5] Djelal Kadir, "The Survival of Theory and the Surviving Fictions of Latin America," *Modern Fiction Studies* 32 (1986): 396.

[6] The term "Romance Novo" or New Novel will be used in further discussions to represent the works of those novelists who came into prominence after the military coup of April 1, 1964, those writers whose works reflect current anti-mythic and post-modernist tendencies. The term "New Novel" is an appellation that has been applied almost every other decade. It has previously been applied to the novel of the Northeast and to the works of José Américo de Almeida. In 1954 Fred P. Ellison entitled his book *Brazil's New Novel*. E.R. Monegal employs "novo romance" to refer to the generation of writers that included Clarice Lispector, Adonias Filho, and Nelida Piñon. He points out their debt to the French "nouveau roman." In *Literary Disrup-*

tions Jerome Klinkowitz employs the term post-contemporary fiction. It seems that we are consumed with a taxonomy of newness. Assis Brasil calls today's writers "Os Novos." For the purposes of this study the evanescent nature of the term is noted, but for ease and brevity it will be used.

Lispector Study

The epigraph to this study is from Carl Gustav Jung, *Psychological Reflections*, ed. Jolande Jacobi (New York: Harper, 1961), p. 181.

[1] Mircea Eliade, *Ordeal by Labyrinth*, trans. Derek Cotman (Chicago: University of Chicago Press, 1978), pp. 165–66.

[2] Lucas, p. 40. Severino, p. 47.

[3] In excellent studies critics like Assis Brasil, Massaud Moisés, Rita Hermann, Wilson Martins, and Giovanni Pontiero long ago established the link between Lispector and the existentialists. However, the work of Benedito Nunes stands out as the most purely philosophical, linking Lispector's prose to Camusian and Sartrean tenets. *O mundo de Clarice Lispector* (Manaus: Edições do Govêrno do Estado, 1966).

[4] Within this wide spectrum of approaches is found Maria Luisa Nunes's study of character awareness, "Narrative Modes in Clarice Lispector's *Laços de família*: the Rendering of Consciousness," *Luso-Brazilian Review* 14, 12 (1977), 174–84; also Terry L. Palls's study of the similarities between Virginia Woolf's use of epiphanies in "The Miracle of the Ordinary: Literary Epiphany in Virginia Woolf and Clarice Lispector," *Luso-Brazilian Review* XXI, 1, (1984), 63–78. To briefly mention other aspects of critical studies too numerous to cite fully: Bella Jozef's studies of dialogue as "polyphonic structure;" Naomi Lindstrom's analysis of the woman's experience and feminine discourse; Silvio Castro's studies of the innovative use of language; Earl Fitz's studies of leitmotif; Teresinha Alvez Pereira's comparative study linking Lispector's work to Julio Cortázar's prose. Olga da Sá, Earl E. Fitz, and Olga Borelli also have written insightful books dealing with various aspects of Lispector's art. For the most comprehensive listing to date see Earl E. Fitz's "Bibliografia de y sobre Clarice Lispector," *Revista Iberoamericana* 50, 126, (1984), 293–304.

[5] Lucas, p. 111.

[6] Clarice Lispector, *Laços de família* (Rio de Janeiro: Nova Fronteira, 1983), p. 129. The translation is taken from *Family Ties*, trans. Giovanni Pontiero (Austin: The University of Texas Press, 1972), p. 133. Further citations will be made by page numbers directly entered in the text.

[7] Gertrude Jobes, *Dictionary of Mythology, Folklore and Symbols* (New York: The Scarecrow Press, 1962), p. 809.

[8] John J. White, *Mythology in the Modern Novel* (Princeton: The Princeton University Press, 1971), pp. 11–12. Although now in frequent use by

literary critics, the word "prefiguration" is of religious origin, a translation of the Latin term "figura." Of particular interest is Chapter IV, "The Unilinear Pattern of Development."

⁹Mircea Eliade, "The Yearning for Paradise in Primitive Tradition," *Myth and Mythmaking*, ed. Henry A. Murray (Boston: Beacon Press, 1960), pp. 61–62. See also Maria Leach, *The Standard Dictionary of Folklore, Mythology and Legend* (New York: Funk & Wagnalls, 1972), p. 844. Of particular note is her definition of Paradise: "An otherworld where perfect life is lived: the word is derived from Persian words meaning an encircling wall, probably the king's garden."

¹⁰Joseph Campbell, "The Historical Development of Mythology," *Myth and Mythmaking*, ed. Henry A. Murray (Boston: Beacon Press, 1968), p. 33.

¹¹Assis Brasil, *Clarice Lispector, ensaio* (Rio de Janeiro: Simões, 1969), pp. 72–73. The translation is from *Modern Latin American Literature*, eds. David William Foster and Virginia Ramos Foster (New York: Unger, 1975) vol. 1, p. 488.

¹²Bella Jozef, "La recuperación de la palabra poética," *Revista Iberoamericana*, vol. 50, no. 126 (1984), 256.

¹³Herbert Thurston, SJ, ed., *Butler's Lives of the Saints* (New York: P. J. Kennedy and Sons, 1956), pp. 184–87. Also see Maria Leach, *The Standard Dictionary of Folklore, Mythology and Legend* (New York: Funk and Wagnalls, 1975), pp. 1061–73. Of particular note are the references to the "Fiesta del Gallo" and the ceremony of the "Toro de San Marcos," both remnants of paganism that have been condemned by the ecclesiastical authorities.

¹⁴Robert Alter, "The New American Novel," *Commentary*, vol. 60, no. 5 (Nov. 1975), 46.

¹⁵Lispector's style is not rooted in a profound analysis of psychological or sociological events or characters, but more frequently there exists a strong penchant for dramatizing seemingly inconsequential and mysterious occurrences: the ritual burying of a dog, the stealing of a flower, the viewing of a buffalo, the contemplation of a vase of roses, etc. These occurences produce evanescent moments of existential illumination. (See Palls, cited in note 4) This narrative tendency evolves as a source of richness, since the resultant ambiguities—was the girl's confrontation with the masqueraders merely symbolic? —aid in sharpening the reader's attention, allowing for a more intimate participation in Lispector's narrative world.

¹⁶T. S. Eliot, *The Waste Land and Other Poems* (New York: Harvest, 1962), p. 29.

¹⁷Jobes, p. 809.

¹⁸Ibid., p. 809.

¹⁹Edith Hamilton, *Mythology* (New York: Mentor Book, 1953), pp. 89–90.

²⁰Jung, p. 41.

[21] It is the contention of this present study that Clarice Lispector's use of mythological correspondences and prefigurative techniques, throughout the corpus of her writings, is an integral and valued component of her stylistic identity.

[22] Charles I. Glicksberg, *The Self in Modern Literature* (University Park, PA: Pennsylvania State University Press, 1969), p. 185.

Ribeiro Study

The first epigraph is Lourenço Moreira Lima from Ângelo's *A festa* p. 19, trans. Thomas Colchie, p. 16.

The second epigraph is from Carl Gustav Jung, *Psychological Reflections*, ed. Jolande Jacobi (New York: Harper, 1961), p. 296.

The third epigraph to the study is General Garrastazu Médici in a speech delivered on June 6, 1970. Also quoted from Ângelo's *A festa*, p. 26, trans. Colchie, p. 25.

[1] Subsequent chapters will stress and document this pervasive concern of Brazilian fiction.

[2] George A. Panichas, "Introduction," *The Politics of Twentieth-Century Novelists*, ed. George A. Panichas (New York: Hawthorn, 1971), p. xxvi.

[3] Peter S. Prescott, "A Good Barbarian," *Newsweek* 30 Jan. 1978, p. 68.

[4] João Ubaldo Ribeiro, *Sargento Getúlio* (Rio de Janeiro: Nova Fronteira, 1982), p. 161. Érico Veríssimo's back cover quote is undocumented.

[5] João Ubaldo Ribeiro, *Sergeant Getúlio* (New York: Avon, 1984), p. 139. Amado's afterword and the novel itself were translated by the author, Ribeiro. All subsequent quotes will be taken from these editions and page numbers will be directly entered into the text.

[6] Charles I. Glicksberg, *The Self in Modern Literature* (University Park, PA: Pennsylvania State University Press, 1963), pp. 39–40.

[7] Jon Vincent, *João Guimarães Rosa* (Boston: Twayne, 1978), p. 65.

[8] See Robert Arlett, "Daniel Martin and the Contemporary Epic Novel," *Modern Fiction Studies* 31 (1985), 173–86. In this analysis, Arlett offers a component definiton of the contemporary epic novel stating, "Since Plato, as they have found 'Epic' a useful term in their engagement with the major works of an age or civilization, writers have tended to define epicism in ways that fit their particular critical uses" (p. 173). He goes on to observe that many modern novels such as Barth's *Chimera*, Bellow's *Herzog*, Vonnegut's *Slaughterhouse-Five*, and Pynchon's *Gravity's Rainbow* "frequently invite—by scope, structure, or allusion to their own literary status—epic consideration" (p. 174).

[9] From a sociopolitical perspective, one could argue that Getúlio's besti-

ality is born of a political failing, extreme poverty, and a lack of education. Jorge Amado in his afterword observes that Ribeiro's novel, due to its "deep knowledge of the language spoken by the people, . . . [has] the capacity to reach the class of readers who are really interested in deep social changes" (p. 140). It is the contention of this study that this novel transcends a purely sociological and political reality, acquiring also a mythical and ontological significance.

[10] Fyodor Dostoyevsky, *Notes from Underground*, trans. Andrew R. MacAndrew (New York: Signet, 1961), p. 99.

[11] See Theodore Ziolkowski, *Fictional Transfigurations of Jesus* (Princeton, NJ: Princeton University Press, 1972), pp. 3–54. One of Ziolkowski's key points regarding the archetype of redemptive suffering is that the suffering must be willed. The character must accept suffering and even death in the service of achieving a value or goal.

[12] F. W. Dillistone, *The Novelist and the Passion Story* (New York: Sheed & Ward, 1960), p. 22.

[13] Jerome S. Bruner, "Myth and Identity," *Myth and Mythmaking*, ed. Henry A. Murray (Boston: Beacon Press, 1960), p. 279.

THE PASSAGE
FROM MYTH
TO ANTI-MYTH
IN CONTEMPORARY
BRAZILIAN FICTION

 The passage from the poetics of myth to the po-
etics of anti-myth constitutes a significant force
in the aesthetic of contemporary Brazilian literature. A purely mythic vision of reality was no
longer suited to the sociopolitical ambience of
the 1960s and 1970s. The anti-mythic world
view held sway as a more valid expression of this
age. Richard Kostelanetz, cultural historian and
literary critic, in discussing the "urgent contem-
poraneousness" that he perceives as the prime
characteristic of "significant writing," states:

The major authors of our time have looked unflinchingly at our condition; and out of its anti-poetic ugliness, they have fashioned works
of an original, compelling and relevant form, a literature illuminating
and more profound than "beautiful," which at its best perceives some
of the contemporary reality that evades our limited perspective.[1]

Anti-myth is an accommodation or inversion of the myth-making process. The anti-mythic novelist is today's "shaman" who can no longer view the cosmic and human experience as a plausible and coherent whole. This sense of fragmentation of reality translates itself into a narrative focus which envisions human experience as basically purposeless. Glicksberg, in discussing what he calls the central clue to the mystery of existence, states, "Lost in a world of energy that threatens to run down, the absurdist hero is a victim whose only weapon against fate is that of irony."[2]

The anti-mythic experience is one of continual remythologizing of man's thinking. Anti-literature reverses the conventions and traditions of the well established myths. Anti-myth then becomes a fusion of various aspects of the traditional myth-making process applied to the modern philosophical situation. The passage from myth to anti-myth is in essence an aesthetic shift in focus, a desire to reorder and restructure man's priorities. The modern Brazilian novel cynically debunks and defies established myths and past truths. This perception of purposelessness is squarely confronted by writers like Márcio Souza, Ignácio de Loyola Brandão, Roberto Drummond, Ivan Ângelo, Flávio Moreira da Costa, and Rubem Fonseca. From their persistent vision of selfless heroes confronting unfathomable social, political, and existential situations emerged a strong anti-mythic quality that characterized the times.

※ ※ ※

In Brazil the short narrative has always been a popular genre. Some Brazilian authors seem to prefer this form to the novel. Luiz Vilela, Osman Lins, Dalton Trevisan, Roberto Drummond, and Lygia Fagundes Telles have created impressive collections of short fiction. Their writings form part of a Brazilian tradition of excellence that has included writers like Machado de Assis, Mário de Andrade, Antônio de Alcântara Machado,[3] Darcy Azambuja, Clarice Lispector, and João Guimarães Rosa. Short fiction has been an important component of Brazilian literature in the past, much like the novel in North American literature and poetry in Chilean literature. The development of the Brazilian short story has been a subject of several excellent studies. Some of the most notable are by Alexandrino Severino, Malcolm Silverman, Alfredo Bosi, Assis Brasil, David William Foster, Massaud Moisés, and Antônio Hohlfeldt.

One of the most interesting collections of short stories to appear in many years is Edilberto Coutinho's *Maracanã, adeus* (1980; *Good-*

bye, Maracanã Stadium). This collection of "onze histórias de futebol" (eleven stories about soccer) won the prestigious Casa de las Americas prize. It also won the Prêmio Nacional de Conto e Novela awarded by the Brazilian Academy of Letters. These stories perceive the passions, ironies, and desperate sense of sublimation in the dreams of an entire nation. As critic Jorge de Sá states, "Quando onze jogadores entram em campo vestindo a camisa do NOSSO time, é a NOSSA vitória que estará em jogo. Somos nós mesmos lutando contra onze adversários. O empate não interessa, só a vitória compensa o fracasso diário."[4] ("When eleven players come on the field dressed in OUR team's shirts, it is OUR victory that is being played out. We are the ones fighting against the eleven adversaries. A tie doesn't interest us, only a victory will compensate for our daily failures.") Coutinho's stories, like Robert Coover's *The Universal Baseball Association, Inc.* (1968) and W. P. Kinsella's *The Iowa Baseball Confederacy* (1986), use a country's national pastime to explore larger issues—both national myths and societal and personal failings.

In *Sangue de Coca-Cola* (1985; *Coca-Cola Blood*) Roberto Drummond, while parodying the carnivalesque diversions created by the Médici government, details the grotesque and chaotic reality that lies just below the surface of a national myth. "Então tu pegas esse telefone vermelho no teu quarto e, com a voz de galã de radionovela, essa tua voz com que lias os teus discursos que eram líricas declarações de amor à Pátria, a Pátria que entregaste às multinacionais ao som de sambas patrióticos, com a voz de galã de radionovela."[5] ("Then you grab the red telephone in your room and, with a radio soap opera star's voice, that voice of yours with which you read your speeches, speeches that were lyric declarations of love to the Country, the Country that you handed over to multi-national business interests, to the sound of patriotic sambas. . . .")

The ideology of anti-myth, the philosophical and ideological matrix of the "Romance Novo," possesses a strong sociopolitical component. *Galvez, Imperador do Acre* (1975; *The Emperor of the Amazon*) by Márcio Souza, is a work that articulates an all-consuming cynicism concerning politics, religion, and the human comedy. This novel contains a proliferation of pseudo-historical details and absurd happenings. Souza superimposes his vision of a failed Utopia upon quasi-historical accounts of reality.

The writings of this period express a strong reaction to, and at times, even a parodying of the traditional existential conception that contemporary man is able to "create himself." Man is often presented symbolically as a crippled anti-hero limping through the wastelands of Latin America, be they conceived as dystopian futures or the Brazilian sociopolitical present. This fiction also contends that the modern absurdist vision can indeed be written from a moral perspective. Underlying what is seemingly a negative world view is a desire to redirect the consciousness of our times, to construct a psychic defense mechanism and to create a realistic condemnation of the metaphysical and political status quo.[6]

※ ※ ※

One of the most structurally and technically innovative uses of anti-myth of the past twenty years is Darcy Ribeiro's *Maíra* (1978). This is a work that is of the experimental school, utilizing varying narrative voices and focuses. However, unlike many works whose formal ingenuity supersedes content, Ribeiro's *Maíra* is an artful blending of form with content. The myth anti-myth polarity in this work is dynamically and uniquely presented. Old myths clash with a sociopolitical and religious present. Ribeiro's message is charged with social commentary, but it is a muted commentary that is born of an aesthetically conceived novel. This one work dramatically encapsulates the passage from myth to anti-myth in contemporary Brazilian fiction.

Darcy Ribeiro's *Maíra*: Fictional Transfiguration and the Failure of Cultural Pluralism

The world is God's suffering, and every individual human being who wishes even to approach his own wholeness knows very well that this means bearing his own cross. But the eternal promise for him who bears his own cross is the Paraclete.

Carl Gustav Jung

Vocês pensam que o Esperado, o Novo Messias, possa nascer entre os mairuns, por exemplo? (You think that the Awaited One, the New Messiah might come, for example, from the Mairuns?)

Darcy Ribeiro

To achieve an understanding of any work of fiction, one begins by analyzing the contours, techniques, and shaping forces that brought that specific work to fruition. At the same time, the danger exists of

65

merely isolating narrative conventions and not integrating them into a coherent and comprehensive vision. For Darcy Ribeiro, stylistic identity and narrative originality are rooted in his use of prefigurative techniques, in particular, his use of fictional transfiguration. His handling of this narrative technique attains major significance within the novel *Maíra* (1978), becoming relevant to its total conception and comprehension.

In discussing fictional transfiguration, Theodore Ziolkowski states, "It is a fictional narrative in which the characters and actions, irrespective of meaning and theme, are prefigured to a noticeable extent by figures and events popularly associated with the life of Jesus."[1] The use of prefigurative techniques and mythological correspondences as an ennobling or structuring device is also studied by John J. White. White observes, "Rather than being viewed in isolation, mythological motifs will be related to the more general technique of prefiguration, a literary device which embraces both this and other kinds of patterning in the presentation of character and plot"[2] The use of these mythological motifs is an integral part of an author's style since they suggest indirect authorial statement. They anticipate plot and "offer the novelist a shorthand system of symbolic comment."[3]

A critical consideration of Darcy Ribeiro's conscious use of fictional transfiguration and prefigurative techniques to underscore his anti-mythic vision of a culturally pluralistic Brazil is the central theme of the following study.

I

Darcy Ribeiro's career as a writer parallels, to a great extent, that of Mário de Andrade before him. Both men had long been immersed in the research and teaching of ethnology, folklore, and popular culture prior to taking up the novel and winning worldwide acclaim. "A surpresa que Darcy Ribeiro deu aos seus inúmeros amigos . . . foi a revelação de uma qualidade oculta desse cientista social, homem de cultura e político que enobrece sua geração."[4] ("The surprise that Darcy Ribeiro gave his innumerable friends . . . was the revelation of an occult quality in this social scientist, man of letters and politician who has so ennobled his generation.") *Maíra* is the first novel of a trilogy that includes *O mulo* (*The Mule*) and *Utopia selvagem* (*Savage Utopia*).

As a renowned anthropologist, politician, and teacher, Darcy Ribeiro has long been an outspoken critic of the scandalous and systematic extermination of Brazil's Indian population. While one can appreciate the novel's responsiveness to the conditions of life that have been patently destructive to the indigenous people of the Amazon, one can at the same time perceive in its management of textual complexities and rhetorical figures a remarkable structural congruence. In this sense, *Maíra* transcends the stereotypical novel of social protest, acquiring the proportions of a truly protean work of art. It is one of the benchmarks of contemporary Brazilian fiction.

There exist some interesting thematic parallels between Ribeiro's *Maíra* and N. Scott Momaday's Pulitzer Prize winning novel *House Made of Dawn*. Momaday's novel portrays a mythless Los Angeles where the Native American's alienation and need for spiritual redemption is played out.[5] Joseph F. Trinner's thesis statement regarding Momaday's novel is that the work "warns Native Americans that they may lose more than they gain if they assimilate into the American mix."[6] Ribeiro's novel philosophically mirrors Trinner's observation; however, *Maíra* carries more than a warning. It is an apocalyptic projection of a sociopolitical system gone haywire, a novel that "offers not only a compelling picture of an Indian tribe's life, but also a fascinating allegory of Christianity, capitalism and the contradictions of cultural pluralism."[7]

The work begins forcefully with a police investigation of the mysterious death of a young white woman. She is found deep in the Amazon jungle on the tribal land of the Mairuns, having just given birth to stillborn twin sons:

> *Sobre a praia, distante vinte metros aproximadamente da linha-d'água, jazia, em decúbito dorsal, uma jovem mulher branca, meio despida, com o corpo pintado de traços negros e vermelhos, formando linhas e círculos.* (P. 15)

> (On the beach, approximately twenty meters from the waterline, lay a young white woman in a supine position half naked, her body painted with streaks of black and red forming lines and circles.) (P. 5)

The novel's opening is reminiscent of Hemingway's "The Snows of Kilimanjaro," in which a leopard is discovered far from its natural habitat in the rarified air of the snow covered mountain. Symbolically, both Alma, the dead woman, and the leopard died while seeking something seemingly unattainable. Their search brought them both to places well beyond the limits of their established worlds. Both works open by introducing similar enigmas. The jarring image of Alma's mysterious death posits the novel's theme of spiritual quest and simultaneously thrusts the story from the level of a factual occurrence to one of metaphysical and mythical import.

Ribeiro proceeds to describe in strongly poetic terms the mythic atmosphere surrounding the Mairun tribe's traditions, their reverence of the life force of the land, and their sense of consanguinity with all things. The daily life of this small group of indigenous people dramatizes the irony of the tension between myth and history. They live spontaneously, sensually in a mega-spiritual world, a world in which the sensory objects of the natural landscape enter into a celebration of existence. The ritualistic burial of an old chieftain is detailed in a scene showing a depth of feeling for the life-death continuum. "Anacã está sepultado. Logo morrerá. A vida deve, agora, renascer" (p. 22). ("Anaca is buried. Soon he will die. Life must now be reborn" [p. 12].)

The conscious use of mythic elements and nominal symbology begins with the presentation of Isaías, the novel's main character. Isaiah, in the Old Testament, was the Prophet of Faith who conceived of God as transcendent and holy. His doctrine of Messianism predicted a savior-king who would bring about a reign of peace and prosperity. The irony of this prefiguration begins immediately as Isaías, or Avá, his Mairun name, is portrayed as a tormented soul who as a young boy was taken from the tribe and converted to Christianity. He had studied in Rome for many years, but could never bring himself to be ordained a priest. Unlike his biblical namesake, he is ravaged with self-doubt. "Eu que sou o Isaías da Ordem Missionária e ao mesmo tempo o Avá do Clã Jaguar, do povo Mairum? Não, jamais. Longe de mim esta ambiguidade" (p. 27). ("I who am Isaías of the Missionary Order and, at the same time, Avá of the Jaguar clan of the Mairun people? No, never. This ambiguity is far away from me" [p. 17].)

His faith has diminished as he is trapped between two cultures, two religions. "Cada um que saia da aldeia vai ser como eu, ou seja, coisa nenhuma. Os que ficarem lá, só herdarão a amargura de serem índios" (p. 25). ("Everyone who leaves the village will become someone like me; that is, nothing. Those who remain there will only inherit the bitterness of being Indian" [p. 14].) He now longs to live the everyday life of the Mairuns, to cleanse himself of civilization and Christianity. The Mairuns await his arrival, their new chieftain, their Messiah. Ribeiro's fictional transfiguration presents Isaías/Avá as the mythic amalgam of traits borrowed from both Isaiah and Jesus. He is the savior who is to rebuild his dwindling tribe, to redeem it from destruction, and in the process find self-redemption. He is imbued with ideas for change, but lacks the psychic will to carry them out. The tribal life of the Mairuns that Ribeiro configures is a stylized earthly Paradise. This is now the only Paradise to which Isaías aspires. "Uma coisa só: viver a vidinha de todo dia dos mairuns. Comer peixe assado ou cozido que hei de pescar e uma carninha de-vez-em-quando, se estiver com sorte. Minha ambição é voltar ao convívio da minha gente e com a ajuda deles me lavar deste óleo de civilização e cristandade que me impregnou até o fundo" (p. 162). ("One thing only: to live the everyday life of the Mairuns. To eat grilled or boiled fish that I've caught myself, with now and then if I'm lucky a little meat. My desire is to live among my people once again, and with their help to cleanse myself of this oil of civilization and Christianity that has permeated me" [p. 142].)

This nostalgia for the Indian world of his youth impels Isaías to attempt to rediscover himself through his ancestry. Seeking one's identity is a consistent theme throughout the contemporary Native American literature of North America. Writers like Momaday, D'Arcy McNickle, and James Welch fictionalize the theme of two cultures in conflict. *Maíra*'s conflict is embodied in the single personage of Isaías/ Avá. "Eu pelo menos sei que nada posso, se consola: poderia eu, ex-Isaías, atual Avá, que nem Avá sou ainda . . ." (p. 162). ("At least I know what I can't do, he consoles himself. How could I, ex-Isaías, now Avá but not yet actually Avá. . . ." [p. 142].)

Ribeiro's conscious use of prefigurative techniques is central to an understanding of his art. The aforementioned character Alma is skillfully drawn. She is a Mary Magdalene figure who finds redemption not in the ways of the church or contemporary institutions, but in the primitive rituals of the Mairuns. Alma is a refugee from twentieth-century life. Faithless, she evolves as the author's paradigm for the modern urban Everyman/Everywoman who has been unable to find solace in education, drugs, sex, or psychoanalysis. "Cansei, cansei de mim e também de salvar o mundo, conspirando sem possibilidade de êxito. Cansei do medo medonho de enfrentar, com as minhas pobres carnes doídas, as dentadas dos cães ferozes. Desbundei!" (p. 164). ("I was tired, tired of myself and of trying to save the world, conspiring but with no possibility of success. I was tired of the awful fear of confronting, with my mangled flesh, the fangs of ferocious dogs. I was out of control" [p. 145].) She is accepted and even admired for her spontaneity. "Pensa: estou cansada de planejar; agora vou é na intuição, sem necessidade de razões. Nem de fé, se fé me faltar" (p. 164). ("She thinks: I am tired of planning things. Now I am going to rely on intuition without the necessity for reasons or for faith lest it ever fail me" [p. 144].) In her transformation to mirixorã Canindejub, she has found fulfillment.[8] "Cada dia cuido de gente que me quer e precisa dos meus cuidados. Cada noite dou e como homens que eu quero e que me desejam. Quem não gosta da mirixorã Canindejub? . . . me sinto uma sacerdotisa, uma sacerdotisa do amor, do amor gratuito, do amor gozoso" (p. 324). ("Every day I take care of people who want and need me. Every night I give myself to men, fucking whom I like and whoever desire me. And who does not like the paramour Canindejub? . . . I feel like a priestess, a priestess of love, of free love, of joyous love" [p. 289].) Far from contemporary institutions she has reordered her life, and it now takes on an inverted religious quality. "Só pensava no verdadeiro gozo de viver que, afinal, encontrei aqui" (p. 326). ("I was only thinking of the true joy of living, which, at last, I have found here" [p. 291].) "Não sei por que, mas me ofendeu muito a idéia de ser puta de índio. Agora não me importo. É uma função, nao é um ofício como o de guarda-livros, de assistente social ou de dentista. Não, é uma função, um sacerdócio" (p. 324). ("I don't know why, but I was very offended by the idea of being a whore for Indians. That doesn't matter to me now. It is a function, not a profession like those of librarian, social worker, or dentist's receptionist. No, it is a function, a religious vocation" [p. 289].)

While Darcy Ribeiro has employed existing mythological correspondences and prefigurations in the characterization of Alma and Isaías, he also has created his own cosmology. Within this cosmology Maíra, the sun, and Micura, the moon, preside over this dying race. They are made to enter directly into the narration. Stylistically, this innovative technique transcends mere experimentalism by directly incorporating into Ribeiro's fictional world elements of a magical and fantastic nature. "Aí está este Avá que muito quis ser Isaías. Nele mergulho: -Éta merda de corpo este, desgastado de tão mal gastado. . . . Fale, desgraçado. Fale, Avá" (p. 309). ("There is that Avá who so much wanted to be Isaías. I am diving into him: this shit of a body, worn out from such abuse. . . . Speak, wretch. Speak, Avá" [p. 275].)

The creation myth of the Mairuns presents a very human god, a god born of "the belch of the Father-God." "Sou Maíra—lembrou—sou o arroto de Deus-Pai" (p. 157). ("'I am Maíra,' he remembered, 'I am the belch of the Father-God'" [p. 137].) In this fictional mode Ribeiro can wryly debunk the myths and mores of our age. Maíra is a chimerical god, almost childlike—a reflection of his people. "A uns que queriam ser bonitos Maíra fez clarinhos mas muito fedorentos, são os caraíbas. A outros que quiseram tostar a pele num moreno dourado, Maíra fez negros como tições" (p. 144). ("To some who wanted to be beautiful, Maíra gave white skins but made them very smelly: they are the Europeans. Others who wanted to tan their skin to a nice golden brown, Maíra turned black as a brand" [p. 125].) "Sem querer, por inocência, Maíra havia fundado a morte" (p. 143). ("Without meaning to, out of innocence, Maíra had created death" [p. 125].)

In this Mairun cosmogony Maíra and Micura at times descend to earth "para brincar de gente. Mas principalmente para sentir o mundo no corpo e no espírito Mairun" (p. 207). ("to play like people, but principally to experience the world through the Mairun body and spirit" [p. 180].) A panoply of experiences, attitudes, and primitive wisdom is communicated within this cosmogony. It is a mythic vision providing an almost puerile explanation of reality. In its simplicity, baseness, and sensual nature is found the key to the Mairun's world-view that is perceived by the novelist as no longer operable as civilization encroaches upon the harmony of the Mairuns' way of life.

> É bom viver como ensinou Maíra. . . . Como nós só queremos rede e bubuia, ele deu a outros a obrigação de trabalhar duro, sem sossego, fazendo coisas. . . . Somos bons é para namorar carinhoso e sururucar demorado. . . . E não nos afobamos. Mulher está aí mesmo para a gente namorar quando quiser. . . . O melhor das criações de Maíra é que sempre nascem crianças para a gente com elas brincar, rir e criar com amor e paciência. . . . É assim que gostamos de viver. . . . Até trabalhar moles devagarinho, não é ruim, sobretudo se não for na hora do sol quente.
>
> Melhor ainda é descansar, deitar com mulher na rede de barriga cheia, dormir e sururucar demorado. Assim fazem Maíra e Micura quando andam por aqui. É a alegria de viver do povo Mairum. Isto quem nos deu foi Maíra. (P. 209)
>
> (It is good to live the way Maíra taught. . . . As we prefer to lounge in a hammock or drift with the current, he obligated the others to work hard, without repose, and make things. . . . We are best at gentle loving and slow fucking. . . . And we don't overtax ourselves. . . . Women are there for a man to make love to if he wants to. . . .
>
> The best of Maíra's inventions is that children are always being born for people to play with, laugh with, and bring up with love and patience. . . . This is how we like to live. . . . As for work, it's not too bad provided it is slow and easy and the sun is not too hot.

> Better still is to rest, to have a full belly, and to lie in one's ham-
> mock with a woman and fuck slowly. . . . That's what Maíra and
> Micura do when they come around here. It's the joy of living of the
> Mairun people; Maíra gave us this.) (Pp. 182–83.)

II

In a very real sense, Ribeiro's characterization of Isaías/Avá's life is an
accommodation of the "Jesus redivivus," reaching its thematic apogee
in the elegantly wrought section "A Semente de Aroe" ("The Seed of
the Guide of Souls"). Avá's life among the Mairuns has become that
of an outsider, an invisible person. Only the oxim, the sorcerer, now
feels any kinship to Avá. Avá is growing ill and the oxim wishes to
prepare him for the ritualistic transfiguration of his tribe. Through the
use of bloodletting, rattles, cigar smoke, and dried fish, Avá "Será re-
conhecido, então, como primeiro anhereté no lado de cima, desa-
fiando Maíra ali debaixo de sua luz, com poder talvez para fazer tudo
que queira. Não só no mundinho dos mairuns, mas no mundo todo
do Sol Vermelho" (p. 357). ("He will then be recognized as the first
master sorcerer, of the side above, challenging Maíra there under his
light, with power perhaps to do anything he wishes. Not merely in the
little world of the Mairuns, but in the whole world of the Red Sun"
[p. 320].) This mystical experience, this quest for Christian and primitive transcendence is described by Joseph Campbell in *The Hero with
a Thousand Faces* as ". . . a passage, back and forth, across the world
threshold."[9] Campbell also reveals the tenor of the image of transfiguration as "amounting to a glimpse of the essential nature of
the cosmos"[10] so as to become "ripe, at last for the great at-one-
ment."[11] However, Avá is unable to give himself over; he resists "self-
annihilation." He cannot free himself or fully believe in the oxim's
vision. "Isaías anda sobre as dunas, metido no couro de Avá" (p. 365).
("Stuck in the skin of Avá, Isaías walks along the dunes" [p. 327].) "O
mal de Isaías é ser ambíguo. Ser e não-ser. Não é índio, nem cristão"
(p. 360). ("The trouble with Isaías is that he is ambiguous. To be and
not to be. He is neither Indian nor Christian" [p. 322].) "O Avá escuta
e reescuta as intermináveis recomendações e prescrições do oxim. É o
mais dócil, mas também o mais resvaladiço dos clientes" (p. 357).
("Avá listens again and again to the interminable recommendations

and prescriptions of the oxim. He is the most docile but also the most slippery of his clients" [p. 320].)

In direct contrast, the young Mairun warrior Jaguar is depicted as the antithesis of Avá. He is at peace with himself and the ancient mythologies of his people. He is fearless and assertive. "Minha, mais ainda, aquela onça foi . . . minha, como minha irmã Mbiá, antes de menstruar, minha, mais minha, toda minha . . ." (p. 293). ("That jaguar was mine . . . even as my sister Mbiá was mine before she began to menstruate" [p. 260].) The atavistic quality of the Mairun's life is best exemplified in the following passage, one in which Jaguar's metamorphosis is accomplished: ". . . aquela onça foi, quando eu por dois dias a duas noites andei debaixo do peso do seu couro, do peso das suas garras, do peso da sua cabeça. E quase fui dela. Principalmente quando entraram em mim os sentimentos de força e de glória com que ele desnucou um-por-um e depois dilacerou tantos bichos grandes, inclusive um caçador caraíba" (p. 293). ("That jaguar was all mine when, for two days and two nights, I walked under the weight of its pelt, the weight of its claws, the weight of its head. And I was almost his, chiefly when thoughts of its strength and glory entered my head, of how it had killed other animals by breaking their necks, one by one, including that of a white hunter" [pp. 260–61].) He, unlike Avá, succeeds in reaching a spiritual "at-one-ment" with the life force of nature. His transformation suggests the Bororo Indian legends of the mythic jaguar-man:[12] "Agora que sou o onção vivente" (p. 293). ("Now that I am the living puma" [p. 261].)

Isaías/Avá, like other contemporary literary heroes whose lives are prefigured by the life of Jesus, is not the total embodiment of Christ, not the "imitatio Cristi," but a negative accommodation of Jesus in his capacity as a mythic figure. Avá has returned to his people, and his lack of faith has rendered him a shadow image to the Mairuns. The Messiah has returned and he is impotent. "Todos são cordiais, demasiado cordiais. É tratado como uma espécie de visita que um dia irá embora. Uma visita querida, ainda que demorada, muito demorada. . . . Cada vez mais fechado em si, ele não facilita nenhuma aproximação" (p. 354). ("Everyone is cordial, excessively so. He is treated as if he were merely a visitor who would one day go away. A welcomed visitor even if he should have long ago departed. . . . Each time, he becomes more closed, refusing to facilitate contact" [p. 316].)

This negative accommodation, this inverted mythic pattern, becomes an anti-mythic assault on itself, for as Father Vincent Ferrer

Blehl observes, "The Christ figure of modern literature in his moral actions often does not reflect Christ at all. The writer is free, of course, to make whatever he wishes of the Christ figure, but the writer's beliefs will determine the significance of his imagery and symbolism." [13]

III

A comparison of the thematic stance underlying *Maíra* and *House Made of Dawn* may help clarify the significance of Ribeiro's vision. Momaday's novel implies that a feeling of personal affirmation can be born of a realization that one's cultural identity and sense of place are able to be maintained within a larger, more monolithic cultural identity. Michael Raymond states that "*House Made of Dawn* continually and artistically suggests that myths or the people that make up a pluralistic society are rarely independent, insular units. By advocating compatibility in cultural pluralism and the authenticity of individual identity within that pluralism, Momaday emphasizes the potential for the individual to find a sense of place in contemporary life." [14]

For Ribeiro the Christianized Brazilian world can offer nothing of value to the Mairuns. His assertions mirror those of Jung, who maintains that to replace or destroy the practices and myths of a people is a form of spiritual genocide: "Myths . . . have a vital meaning. Not only do they represent, they *are* the mental life of the primitive tribe, which immediately falls to pieces and decays when it loses its mythological heritage, like a man who has lost his soul." [15] Despite the combining of cultures—the Brazilian and the indigenous—the cultural mix so long proclaimed as a positive sociological force is symbolically damned, like the symbolism in Alma's twin sons being delivered stillborn on a jungle river bank. The characterization of the renegade Juca, a Judas figure who has adopted Brazilian ways, is presented as a portrait of lost cultural identity. Juca has betrayed his people and has become a pawn of the land-grabbing politicians.

Certainly the character of Isaías/Avá is the narrative matrix of the novel, but swirling around his inner struggle, Ribeiro has depicted the corruption of the FUNAI (Fundação Nacional do Indio) workers and the lassitude of the Catholic missionaries. There is also present the self-righteous zeal of "seu Bob," a born-again missionary, and his wife Gertrudes, a linguist who "está fazendo o *master*" (p. 389) ("is getting her doctorate" [p. 349]) at "Bright University" (p. 389). They live in an impregnable fortress-home in the heart of hostile Indian territory. Both are representations of well-intentioned American interventionism. Finally there is the ubiquitous Brazilian political system that ebbs and flows with the whims and greed of the governmental elite.

On the first level of meaning *Maíra* is certainly a novel of social criticism, a fine example of *littérature engagée*, but, more importantly, it is a modern day parable of man's search for spirituality in a despiritualized world. This parable is highlighted by another of *Maíra*'s innovative structuring principles, that of the liturgy of the mass, a requiem mass that Ribeiro is offering in the form of a novel.

The self-centered concern of both the missionaries and the FUNAI workers is symptomatic of a society without vitality. *Maíra* is a unique social document in that it captures the metaphysical suffering of an individual which, in a broad sense, is the correlative of the wider suffering of an entire people. *Maíra* communicates no message of individual or collective triumph, no faith in the indomitableness of the human spirit, only a brilliantly articulated "cri de coeur."

At the work's end an avaricious senator has gained control of the Indian lands; the missionaries will continue to function, but now will do the bidding of politicians. Avá is left to perform the absurd task of making a literal translation of the Bible into the Mairun tongue. "De que vale uma tradução perfeita se eles não entenderem?" (p. 389). ("What is the use of a perfect translation if none of them understands it?" [p. 349].) He will go on day after day turning the Book of St. Matthew into gibberish. The futility and absurdity of this activity constitutes one of the book's final and enduring images. In this aspect of the novel can be seen an extended metaphor with Avá again representing an ineffectual and impotent Messiah. This theme of the failed Messiah is underscored in the work's concluding chapter, "Indez" ("Coda"), in which various scenes are rapidly juxtaposed, creating a panoramic sense of immediacy. The reader is at once able to experience and react to a multiplicity of events, both past and present. The sensual nature of Alma's death and the futility of Avá's present state are telescoped within this montage of images, propelling the novel to its conclusion.

Maíra has moved to this conclusion in a garble of confused voices advocating not a cultural pluralism within the integrity of individual mythologies, but a chaotic vision of a doomed nation. Thus, Ribeiro's *Maíra* is a poetic evocation of these vanishing people, a Requiem for a fading way of life. Ribeiro has brilliantly apotheosized the personages from this decimated and dwindling nation. Their loss is lamented by Ribeiro, and its tragedy is eloquently brought to the reader's attention and given meaning.

NOTES

[1] Richard Kostelanetz, "Contemporary Literature," *On Contemporary Literature*, ed. Richard Kostelanetz (New York: Avon Books, 1969), p. xxvi.
[2] Charles I. Glicksberg, *The Ironic Vision in Modern Literature* (The Hague: Martinue Nijhoff, 1969), pp. 259–60.
[3] See Robert DiAntonio, "The Passage from Myth to Anti-Myth in Antônio de Alcântara Machado's 'Gaetaninho'," *Annali-Sezione Romanza* 28, 2 (1986) pp. 151–56.
[4] Jorge de Sá, "Sugestões de aproveitamento didático de *Maracanã, Adeus*" ("Teaching Suggestions for *Maracanã, Adeus*") Edilberto Coutinho, *Maracanã, Adeus* (Rio de Janeiro: José Olympio, 1980), p. 121.
[5] Roberto Drummond, *Sangue de Coca-Cola* (Rio de Janeiro: Nova Fronteira, 1985), p. 23.
[6] See Josephine Hendin, "Experimental Fiction," *Harvard Guide to Contemporary Writing*, ed. Daniel Hoffman (Cambridge, MA: Harvard University Press, 1979) pp. 240–86.

Ribeiro Study

The first epigraph is from Carl Gustav Jung, *Psychological Reflections*, ed. Jolande Jacobi (New York: Harper, 1961), p. 325.
The second epigraph is from Darcy Ribeiro, *Maíra* (Lisbon: Publicações Dom Quixote, 1983), p. 242. The English edition is *Maíra*, trans. Thomas Colchie (New York: Aventura, 1984), p. 212. Further citations will be taken from these editions, and page numbers will be entered into the text.
[1] Theodore Ziolkowski, *Fictional Transfigurations of Jesus* (Princeton: Princeton University Press, 1972), p. 6. Ziolkowski's working definition of fictional transfiguration allows for a broad interpretation of a Jesus-figure. One scene could suffice, one instantly recognizable scene "where the action, the imagery, and organization of the scene" point to a "transfigured Jesus" (p. 6). Isaías/Avá is the image of a Man of Sorrow, a "Schmerzensmann." Within *Maíra* is found a veritable panoply of Biblical accommodations. There is present the persona of the Messiah returning, the agony in the gar-

den, the betrayal, the Magdalene, Juca-Judas, the transfiguration scene, and the final image of Paradise lost.

[2] John J. White, *Mythology in the Modern Novel* (Princeton: Princeton University Press, 1971), p. 11.

[3] White, p. 12.

[4] Irineu Garcia, "*Maíra*, ofício litúrgico de Darcy Ribeiro," *JL-Jornal de Letras, Artes e Idéias*, no 2 (1981):17. This article is quoted from its reprinted version of page 4 of the Portuguese edition of *Maíra*, cited in note 2.

[5] N. Scott Momaday, *House Made of Dawn* (New York: Signet, 1969).

[6] Joseph F. Trinner, "Native Americans and the American Mix in N. Scott Momaday's *House Made of Dawn*," *Indiana Social Studies Quarterly* 28 (1975), 88–89.

[7] Jim Miller, "Listening to Foreign Voices," *Newsweek* 26 Sept. 1983, p. 88.

[8] Alma, unlike Momaday's character in *House Made of Dawn*, Angela St. John, was indeed able to find spiritual redemption through her contact with Indian life. The two characters, away from the confines of the white world, express themselves openly and sexually, but only Alma is totally drawn into an acceptance of the indigenous life-style. There also exist marked parallels between the characterization of Alma and that of Sônia Dimitrovna in Antônio Callado's *Quarup* (Rio de Janeiro: Editora Civilização Brasileira, 1982), trans. Shelby (New York: Alfred Knopf, 1970): "Sônia que não escutou nada só tinha que seguir a musculosa traseira castanha com miçanga azul e cada vez entraram mais na mata . . ." (p. 210). "Sonia didn't hear a thing all she had to do was keep following that muscular brown backside with its swinging blue beads and they were going deeper and deeper into the jungle . . ." [p. 236–37].)

[9] Joseph Campbell, *The Hero with a Thousand Faces* (Princeton: Princeton University Press, 1968), p. 230.

[10] Campbell, p. 234.

[11] Ibid., p. 237.

[12] Maria Leach, *The Standard Dictionary of Folklore, Mythology and Legend* (New York: Funk & Wagnalls, 1972), p. 1122. Alfred Métraux, longtime director of the Institute of Ethnology in Tucuman, Argentina, relates that the myths of the Brazilian tribes of the Amazon are replete with figures of a jaguar-man who at times appears as a werewolf-like creature. Transformation or metamorphosis "constitutes one of the favorite themes of South American mythology and folklore. A large number of these transformations are ascribed to the culture hero or the divine Twins. . . ." (Maíra-Micura?) This "transformer aspect of creators-culture-heroes" is present also in the myths of North American Indian tribes. The ceremony of the Bororo jaguar dance might have been the seminal inspiration for this scene.

[13] Vincent Ferrer Blehl, SJ, "Literature and Religious Belief," *Mansions*

of the Spirit, ed. George A. Panichas (New York: Hawthorn Books, 1967), p. 111.

[14] Michael W. Raymond, "Tai-Me, Christ, and the Machine: Affirmation through Mythic Pluralism in *House Made of Dawn*," *Studies in American Fiction*, XI, 1 (spring, 1983), 71.

[15] Jung, p. 314.

THE
ABSURDIST
VISION

A perception of the Absurd has always been a dynamic component of the Brazilian literary temperament. In broad terms the writings of Ronald de Cavalho, Mário de Andrade, and Oswald de Andrade can be considered precursory to the present day absurdist novel. A sense of irreverent questioning can be traced back as far as the colonial works of Grégorio de Matos. In Oswald de Andrade's *Seraphim Ponte Grande* (1933; *Seraphim Grosse Pointe*) the protagonist-narrator states, "Do meu fundamental anarquismo jorrava sempre uma fonte sadia, o sarcasmo." ("Out of my basic anarchy a healthy talent always flowed—sarcasm.")[1] Andrade's work displays a powerful sense of the ludic, an authorial playfulness that disavows itself from existing literary language and forms. Haroldo de Campos, in his essay "Serafim: um grande não-livro" ("Seraphim, a Great Nonbook"), relates this precursory anti-novel to the theories of Philippe Sollers. "É uma dessas obras que põem em xeque a idéia tradicional de genêro e obra literária, para nos propor um nôvo conceito de livro e de leitura." ("It is one of those works that puts the traditional idea of genre and literary production in check in order to put forth a new concept of book and of reading.")[2]

Andrade assails the establishment myths of his time. The fragmented energy in *Seraphim Ponte Grande* foreshadows the style and techniques of the absurdist writings of the 1960s and 1970s. Irving Howe has stated that "a major impulse in modernist literature is a choking nausea before the idea of culture."[3] This narrative attitude of off-handed flippancy is well suited to explore and lampoon Brazilian society and morals. "Com pouco dinheiro, mas fora do eixo revolucionário do mundo, ignorando o Manifesto Comunista e não querendo ser burguês, passei naturalmente a ser boêmio." ("Short of cash but outside the revolutionary axis of the world, ignorant of the Communist Manifest yet not wanting to be bourgeois, I naturally became a bohemian.")[4]

Oswald de Andrade's sardonic narrative posture mirrors and portends the tone expressed by Ignácio de Loyola Brandão's 1985 novel, *O beijo não vem da boca* (*The Kiss Doesn't Come from the Mouth*). Loyola's work is punctuated with a tongue-in-cheek rethinking, reevaluation, and redefinition of Brazilianism. In particular, he attempts to answer the question, "O que é ser brasileiro?"[5] ("What's it like to be a Brazilian?") By means of the artifice of listing a drawn out series of answers, he evolves an anti-novelistic, component definition. A few examples will suffice: "aceitar passivamente a inflação . . . jogar na loto . . . fritar lingüiça de porco . . . ter todos os cartões de crédito . . . ter um contrabandista amigo para as bebidas . . . mentir como o governo . . . acreditar na macumba . . . adorar bundonas . . . acreditar que ninguém pode com o brasileiro?"[6] ("passively accepting inflation . . . playing the lottery . . . frying pork linguiça sausage . . . having every credit card . . . having a smuggler friend who gets your liquor . . . lying like the government does . . . believing in voodoo . . . adoring big-assed women . . . believing that no one can cope with Brazilians and their ways.")

Flávio Moreira da Costa's *O desastronauta: OK Jack Kerouac nós estamos te esperando em Copacabana* (1971; *The Anti-Astronaut: OK Jack Kerouac We're Waiting for You in Copacabana*) is also an important anti-literary work. This experimental book was conceived in the novel as collage tradition, utilizing various forms of discourse.

The work, in a vivid example of authorial self-referentiality even includes a photograph of da Costa as a young man. The book's colloquiality, its off-handed irreverent attitude toward its subject matter is, in essence, a challenge to the traditional role of status quo literature. From within the work itself the narrator comments on the book's lack of continuity. "Se você é do tipo que quer as coisas explicadinhas e tá-tá-tá-e-coisa, o problema é seu, porque eu sou o caos."[7] ("If you're one of those guys that wants every little thing explained, bingity-bong and there it is, it's your problem, because I'm chaos itself.") This anti-novelist challenge to literary assumptions predates and philosophically mirrors a similar passage by American author Kurt Vonnegut.

> Let others bring order to chaos. I would bring chaos to order, instead, which I think I have done. If all writers would do that, then perhaps citizens not in the literary trades will understand that there is no order in the world around us, that we must adapt ourselves to the requirements of chaos instead.[8]

O desastronauta's importance in modern Brazilian fiction is that it recreates a genre freeing it from past constraints and assumptions. Thus, this work opens the way for a new generation of Brazilian anti-heroes and heroines. Through the presentation of the tragic-comic lives of a series of failed misfits, the New Novel attempts to define contemporary society, defining it by the very limitations it placed on these exaggerated narrative personages.

Chronicling in absurd fashion the inept quests of these anti-heroes and heroines, the New Novel is, in reality, questioning long held myths regarding the entire fabric of the country's social organization. While the narrative focus may appear to be on the "João-Ninguém," the inept and inconsequential Everyman/Everywoman, this focus is actually a technique designed to explore the prevailing traditions and underlying constraints of Brazilian society.

Bruce Jay Friedman in his anthology *Black Humor* (1965) never sets forth a complete definition of a fictional style that has been simultaneously classified as grotesque, sick, macabre, scatological, satirical, cosmic, entropic, and absurd, plus the translated terms "humour noir" and "schwater Humor." He states "I would have had more luck defining an elbow or a corned-beef sandwich"[9] Friedman does imply that all the writers in his collection (Albee, Heller, Pynchon, Barth, Nabokov, Southern, Celine, and Donleavy) have moved well beyond traditional satire. The actual political events of the times had usurped the novelists' material, and these writers were forced to create in the "darker waters out beyond satire."[10]

Márcio Souza, Moreira da Costa, Sant'Anna, and Loyola Brandão are Brazilian writers who have frequently used absurdist elements in their prose. Other writers like Darcy Ribeiro in *Maíra* occasionally utilize aggressively absurd parody. Ribeiro introduces a comically implausible presentation of "seu Bob" and "his wife" to satirize the ubiquitous American missionaries who cover the Latin American landscape. They are, by extension, paradigms for ideologists—whether well-intentioned or not—whose sole purpose is to present truth in their terms. This parody of American intrusionism is made more intense by the fact that the missionaries have to live in a fortress-like home. Surprisingly, even Clarice Lispector avails herself of this narrative technique, creating an unforgettable grotesque character-symbol in *A hora da estrela*, Madame Carlota.

Yet another example of the Brazilian counterliterary narrative is *Confissões de Ralfo* (1975: *Ralph's Confessions*) by Sérgio Sant'-Anna. Ralfo describes himself as a knight errant with both good and bad intentions. He is a man without a past, a decadent Ulysses. Sant'Anna's writing also suggests that the fictional narrative need not be considered sacred ground. His chapter "Dias tranqüilos ou (Sofia e Rosângela)" ("Tranquil Days or [Sophia and Rosângela]") is a hilariously grotesque adventure, a portrait of a strange "menage à trois." Ralfo is involved with two obese twins, two artists with insatiable sexual appetites. An absurdist satiric nonchalance pervades the novel. "Leio de tudo: os crimes, política (o mundo vai mal como sempre, e o país não vai nada). . . ."[11] ("I read everything: police reports, politics [the world is going badly, as always, and the country isn't going at all]. . . .")

In the last century Brazilian novelists like José de Alencar (1829–1877) created a literature in which native Indians were presented as noble warriors amid the splendor of a romanticized paradisal forest. *Iracema* (1865) became the literary and historical interpretation against which Márcio Souza develops his contemporary anti-myth.

In *Galvez, Imperador do Acre* (1976; *The Emperor of the Amazon*), Souza parodies the romantic adventure narrative. This work was an international best seller, enjoying critical acclaim and a vast popular following. His absurdist treatment of this work is an explicit example of the literature of exhaustion. That is to say, Souza employs an "exhausted" literary form from the past to make an ironic and negative commentary concerning the present. Souza lampoons the idea of the Amazon as an innocent and paradisal state. Again, it was Joseph Campbell who stated that the artists of our era continue to search for mythologies when past myths have been replaced by an objective world view. "Heaven has become an empty place for us, a fair memory of things that were."[12] In his now famous *Time* magazine essay, he goes on to state that "old myths are no longer operative, and effective new myths have not arisen to replace them."[13]

In *Galvez, Imperador do Acre*, absurdity is a dual reflection. It is a stylized vision of the disorder inherent in Brazilian history and politics and a cynically comic overview of all human endeavor. However, Souza's absurdist "weltanschauung" does not lament, nor decry, man's fate. One of the work's central metaphors is that life is theater and, most importantly, shoddy and poorly performed theater. The themes of form superseding substance and the primacy of artifice and illusion are constant ones. Souza's novel is a multitextured narrative that converges upon myth, history and social satire.

Souza, this Brazilian absurdist, highlights the comedy, not the tragedy, in the human experience. The Brazilianization of the code of the Absurd is more intuitive than philosophical. It seems almost a reflex action, an ironic defense mechanism. Through the use of irony, burlesque, and self-deprecating black humor, Márcio Souza creates a uniquely Brazilian novel. In Souza's absurdist fantasy *O ordem do dia* (1983; *The Order of the Day*), Mãe Tereza (Mother Teresa), a voodoo priestess, is portrayed in a trance-like state sacrificing live chickens to aid the economics minister of the Médici government in deciding upon policy. Mãe Tereza is then shown to be one of the most politically powerful and indispensible members of that military government. The situation is Brazilian in its mockingly political burlesque, but it is also as universal as Franz Kafka's empty castle motif, or Joseph Heller and Kurt Vonnegut's aesthetic acceptance of bureaucratic ineptitude as both literal fact and ontological metaphor.

Márcio Souza's 1982 novel *Mad Maria* is also a satiric political allegory presented in an inventively playful style. Again, Souza develops a fictive universe that disrupts the reader's expectations. In the style of the absurdist anti-novel, the work utilizes a variety of narrative strategies to reveal the underlying incongruities of the human comedy. Souza's *Mad Maria* conjures up a lurid tableau in which foreign laborers attempt to build a railroad across an inhospitable stretch of the Amazon.

Throughout these two novels Souza's poetics strive to re-establish man's vital sense of existence. Although it may appear contradictory, the metaphysical foundation of his absurdist novels is based upon the idea that man's experience must affirm life and, more importantly, celebrate his courage and individuality.

The Absurdist Code in Márcio Souza's *Mad Maria*: Ideologic and Ontological Catharsis

> Our banal everyday life makes banal demands
> on (us) . . . which actually need a heroism that is
> not seen from without.
>
> Carl Gustav Jung

> —*Eu sei que é absurdo. Mas o que é que não é*
> *absurdo, meu rapaz?* ("*I know it's absurd. But*
> *what do you know that isn't absurd?*")
>
> Márcio Souza

Márcio Gonçalves Bentes de Souza, Márcio Souza, who was born in Manaus in the Brazilian state of Amazonas in 1946, is one of the most prolific and influential novelists writing in Portuguese today. He has worked as a movie critic, studied social sciences in São Paulo, made films, and has written and directed experimental theater in his native Manaus. This combination of interests may well have forged one of the central symbols in his works, that of life as theater, illusion, and farce. His works denaturalize basic cultural assumptions and national myths, revealing the underlying incongruities of the human comedy.

In *Catharsis in Literature*, Adnan Abdulla concludes, "Catharsis in modern critical theory tends to be regarded in terms of communication. (Hans Robert) Jauss's major interest in catharsis lies in his investigation of it as a communicative framework within which social change is introduced. In this way catharsis becomes a tool of social change in the sphere of literary artifacts, in the sense that the audience either tries to emulate the model (the hero), or refuses to do so."[1] Souza's *Mad Maria* expresses a highly comic vision of the collective spirit of the Brazilian national character. It is a visionary work that actively reflects upon Brazilian reality by means of a cathartic confrontation of reader, text, and author.

Souza's novel accommodates and parodies the adventure narrative. His work explores life's contradictions and absurdities on varying levels of consciousness. On the surface non-symbolic level, it is a fascinating tale of the civilizing of the Brazilian wilderness. However, the book's value as pure entertainment is belied by the author's forward.[2] Souza, the master illusionist, blurs the line between straight narrative, serious intention, and humor:

> Ha muito de verdadeiro. Quanto à política das altas esferas, também. E aquilo que o leitor julgar familiar, não estará enganado, o capitalismo não tem vergonha de se repetir. . . . Mas este livro não passa de um romance. Preste atenção: (P. 11)

> (I have tried to be meticulous—likewise with the politics of the powers that be. And wherever the reader judges something to be familiar, he is probably not mistaken. Capitalism has seldom been ashamed to repeat itself. . . . Don't worry, though, it's only a novel. All that's required is that you pay some attention. . . .) (P. vii)

The present analysis will concentrate upon Márcio Souza's use of catharsis as a narrative code to highlight his absurdist vision of the human condition.

At the onset of the work an international crew has been recruited to construct a railroad across an inhospitable stretch of the Amazon. The crew is composed of a cynical English construction engineer; German, Barbadian, and Hindu laborers; and a young idealistic doctor from St. Louis, Missouri. Ethnic misunderstandings and racial violence abound as the reader is explicitly made aware of the continual overlay of social criticism.

Souza's novel presents this lurid tableau with strong overtones of sociopolitical allegory. The absurdist writer's approach to his or her subject is seemingly playful. The characters are stereotypical cardboard creations, more symbolic than substantive. However, *Mad Maria*'s grim allegory of the contradictions of cultural pluralism is also a forceful and combative work.

The symbolic representation of the Brazilian national will and character is embodied in the charismatic and resilient personage of a Caripuna Indian.

> Não era um ambiente especialmente confortador para o seu amigo caripuna, mas ele nem parecia notar, continuava sorridente e carinhoso, acendendo cigarros com fósforos que ele riscava com os pés, para divertimento dos enfermeiros e alguns doentes em estado menos deplorável. (Pp. 230–31)

> (Thus, it was not an especially comforting atmosphere for her Caripuna friend, but he never seemed to really notice: he kept on smiling with affection, lighting cigarettes with matches he would strike with his feet to the considerable delight of the nurses and those of the patients in less deplorable states.) (P. 260)

As the Indian observes the foreign workers cutting across his tribal land, he is simultaneously frightened, amused, and even drawn to the lives of these strange men.

> Os civilizados eram uma tribo difícil de entender . . . ele observou tudo e sentiu medo. Não pelos tiros, mas pelas descargas de ódio que os brancos faziam chegar até ali. . . . Era como se a cerimônia dos brancos em relação à morte fosse o próprio ato de trazer a morte, e isto era difícil de aceitar. Os civilizados eram poderosos, fabricavam coisas boas, tinham sempre comida embora não plantassem ou caçassem. (Pp. 32)

> (The *civilized* were a difficult tribe to understand . . . he had seen everything and was frightened—not by the rifle shots but by the furious outbursts of hatred that the *whites* spewed forth echoing through the jungle. . . . It was as if only the very act of bringing death to themselves constituted a ceremony, and this he found difficult to accept. The *civilized* were powerful, nonetheless: they could build great constructions and they always had food, though they did no planting or hunting.) (Pp. 28–29)

Souza's novel is filled with the arrogance of cultural condescension; however, this arrogance is presented in an absurdist manner that allows the reader to first enjoy the work's comic apsects and then react emotionally. This is the essence of Abdulla's and Jauss's observations regarding the role that catharsis plays in the aesthetic process.

—Que dizer que o progresso às vezes depende de situações como esta?
—E o fardo do homem branco. (P. 145)

("Ye mane to convince me that progress depends upon me crawlin' on me belly through the likes o' this slime?"
"It's the white man's burden.") (P. 163)

—Ele nunca abandonou a cidadania inglesa. Sempre disse que vivia na América como se estivesse na Índia ou coisa parecida. (P. 147)

("He never gave up his English citizenship. Always claimed to be livin' in America just like it were India or anywhere else.") (P. 165)

—Exatamente, John, brasileiros.
—É a mesma merda (P. 304)

("That's right, John, *Brazilians*."
"They're all the same malingering *babus!*") (P. 343)

Joe Caripuna is caught stealing trinkets from the "civilizados," and for the theft of some combs, pens, and mirrors he is brutally beaten, having both his hands slashed off. The violence of the act is described graphically by Souza. "Os civilizados seguraram ele esticado no chão e colocaram os dois braços dele sobre um dormente. Um civilizado pegou um machado e decepou na altura do antebraço as suas mãos" (p. 85). ("The *civilized* held him securely on the ground and stretched his two arms across a railroad tie. One of the *civilized* then took out his machete and struck off his hands at the level of the forearms" [p. 92].) Here Souza departs from the typical myth of the absurd by implying that man himself is instrumental in contributing to the hellish ambience in which he lives.

The building of the Madeira-Mamoré Railroad (with home offices in Portland, Oregon) is designed to connect two inconsequential Amazonian towns. The construction of this railroad evolves ontologically as Souza's paradigm for the life journey:

—Fui eu que inventei esta ferrovia que deverá levar um trem do nada a parte alguma, no meio do deserto? Ora, meu rapaz, no máximo eu posso ser um dos loucos, talvez o caso mais grave, mas assim mesmo um simples louco. (P. 143)

("Was it I who invented the idea of this confounded railroad that is meant to lead a train from no place to nowhere, out here in the middle of the jungle? Come now, my lad, the most I can be accused of is playing idiot—perhaps one of the worst cases, but, still, a simple idiot, like everyone else.") (P. 161)

The workers, all races and creeds, are aware of the Sisyphusian absurdity of their task. Like the characters in Joseph Heller's *Catch-22*, they are in a no-win situation. They are under contract, the jungle surrounds them, and their work is backbreaking and thankless. "—Acho que alguém que perdeu o miolo inventou esta ferrovia" (p. 33). ("'Whoever yer feller was invented the idea o' puttin a railroad through here musta been daft'" [p. 29].)

Souza's *Mad Maria* conjures up a strange world where men die of malaria and loneliness while imported German grand pianos are transported up the Amazon only to be capsized and washed away down river. Joe Caripuna is nursed back to health by the company doctor and a beautiful Bolivian widow. After his maiming, his being acquires magical and mystical proportions. "O índio tinha alguma coisa de sagrado, pequenos deuses que lhe completavam as mãos ausentes" (p. 163). ("Indeed, that Indian has something sacred about him—smallish gods who completed his absent hands" [p. 185].)

The city of Porto Velho, a city reflecting all that is non-Brazilian, serves as the international offices of the railroad company. It is there that minor dignitaries are treated to a performance by Joe Caripuna who had learned to play the piano with his feet. "Joe conseguia tocar, com segurança e sem desafinar, não apenas o *Parabéns para você* mas duas outras canções populares norte-americanas" (p. 309). ("Joe Caripuna had mastered, with perfect ease and no mistakes, not only 'Happy Birthday' but two other popular North American tunes" [p. 348].) Joe had become a dancing bear to show off his social rehabilitation. The satire and black humor, while acerbic, are secondary to the work's historical and ontological overtones.

The railroad is completed, and the locomotive, Mad Maria, will be able to journey "do nada a parte alguma," (p. 143). ("from no place to nowhere" [p. 161]). In its completion many lives were lived out on many levels. The inhuman zooidal existence of the Hindu workers was juxtaposed to a sexually deviate American living in decadent splendor in Rio. Richard Finnegan, the St. Louis doctor, in his attempt to keep the workers alive forcefully dispenses anti-malaria tablets to men who attempt to sell them for cash. The absurdity of their action, combined with the daily violence, tarnishes his idealism. He came to the jungle a symbol of rational twentieth-century man, a man of science. He is now appalled by his observations of the human drama, by his total impotence. "O médico fascinado pela ciência não existia mais, era um inútil" (p. 136). ("The physician fascinated by the wonders of science had already ceased to exist in him, for he was

redundant—no, worthless! —" [p. 154].) In his symbolic presentation
of Finnegan as a failed Messiah, Souza employs language that is sub-
jected to varying forms of parody, experimentation, and wry cynicism.
"Quando o último homem recebeu o seu comprimido naquela eucar-
istia bizarra . . ." (p. 142). ("When the last man had finally swallowed
the emblematic host of that bizarre eucharist . . ." [p. 160].)

Finnegan is yet another emblematic savior who has lost his faith,
continuing to minister to his parishioners but appalled by their actions. He once possessed the Christ-like courage and convictions of
McMurphy in Ken Kesey's *One Flew over the Cuckoo's Nest*; however, the jungle, human greed, and hostility have taken their toll.

> —Que saúde coisa nenhuma. Eu estou protegendo é a eficiência
> do trabalho. . . .
> —Está certo, doutor, isto aqui parece com um hospício, mas
> não há outra maneira de agir. Ou há? (P. 143)

> ("*Health* you say," Collier snarled. "To blazes with you and
> your fatuous health! What concerns me is the efficiency of my labor
> force. . . ."
> "Perfectly correct, doctor, what we have here is akin to bedlam,
> for which there is no other way to act than I do—or do you see
> otherwise?") (P. 160)

On this voyage to absurdity, Finnegan is loved by the sensuous
Bolivian widow. The widow Consuelo (Consolation) eases his passage,
but at the work's end he is no better off than the rest of the men.

> Consuelo representava um provocante antagonismo em relação ao
> seu desabamento como criatura. Uma tristeza foi surgindo nas pare-
> des daquele quarto impessoal e Finnegan, que pretendia agora ver
> no mundo uma comédia absurda, tinha contra o seu corpo, enlaçada
> nas suas pernas, uma mulher. E isto era realmente o diabo. (P. 296)

> (Consuelo Campero represented a tantalizing antithesis to his own
> collapse as a human being. Yet a sadness was welling up from the
> walls of that impersonal boudoir; and Richard Finnegan, who now
> affected to see the world as an absurd comedy, had crushed to his
> chest and coiled around his thighs the body of a woman. And that
> was a hell of a situation.) (P. 334)

I

Márcio Souza punctuates his text with supercilious aphorisms that
serve as chapter headings: "Um dia ainda vamos rir disso tudo"

(p. 171) ("Someday We'll Probably Laugh at All This" [p. 193]); "Quando não puder resistir, relaxe e goze" (p. 250) ("If You Can't Escape, Relax and Enjoy It" [p. 283]); "As delícias da acumulação primitiva" (p. 297) ("The Delights of Primitive Accumulation" [p. 335]). Souza, the author, functions as the pivotal angle in the aesthetic triad, acting as intermediary between the work of art and the reader. From this perspective he renders a metaphysical stance that is both buoyant with persiflage and reflective of his absurdist life view.

Souza adroitly manipulates this absurdist fantasy, feigning the neutrality of the adventure novelist while all the time burlesquing both the American attitudes and Brazilian foibles. From the safety of this narrative distance, his writings are gravid with satire, parody, and humor.

> Percival Farquhar já era um dos homens mais poderosos do Brasil . . . era uma reprodução da energia dos negócios norte-americanos . . . era igualmente respeitado e odiado, o que ele compreendia perfeitamente, pois sabia que num país como o Brasil, repleto de vícios e não inteiramente democrático, a objetividade, ou seja lá que outro nome usassem, era uma virtude menor frente a dissimulação. (Pp. 20–21)

> (Percival Farquhar was also one of the most powerful men in Brazil . . . he seemed to epitomize the energetic North American businessman . . . he was equally hated and respected—something he understood perfectly well, appreciating as he did how in a country like Brazil [steeped in vice and not entirely democratic], objectivity, or what have you, was small virtue in the face of dissimulation.) (P. 14)

Consuelo goes off with Joe Caripuna to New York where he is engaged as a performer on the vaudeville circuit, dying sixteen years later of syphilis. The railroad was inaugurated in 1912, ironically at the very same time the English found a way to effectively harvest rubber in Asia (from stolen Brazilian seedlings). The engineering marvels, the senseless deaths, the heroism were all for naught.

The serious intention that underlies the farcical demythification of Brazilian and American attitudes can be observed in Dr. Finnegan's reaction to the chaos that envelopes him. Finnegan tires of the chain of hatred (the Germans killing the Barbadians and, after the Germans flee, the Barbadians killing the Hindus) and on the verge of madness fires on a group of men fighting. "—Exatamente, idiota. Fogo! Mandem chumbo nesses filhos da puta—gritou o médico" (p. 343). ("'Exactly, you idiot! Fire! Shoot! Pour some lead into these sons of bitches!' Richard Finnegan continued to scream" [p. 390].) Finally a combination of the oral tradition in Brazilian popular literature and the post-modernist flair for direct authorial commentary—part of what Thomas Pynchon refers to as the Luddite spirit—is brought to the fore as the author-narrator decries the use of poetic euphemisms to describe the futility of the deaths of so many men. "Amanhecer no nunca mais é um diabo de expressão, poeta! Quanta sandice. Coisas da vida" (p. 341). ("'Awakened the next morning in the nevermore' is one hell of an expression, O My Poet! So much foolishness. Life's way, perhaps" [p. 387].)

II

Modern Brazilian fiction expresses all the formal exploration, experimental strategies, and aesthetic creativity that reflect current international trends. However, the thematic perspective of much of this fiction is nationally oriented. The political foment of the past twenty years has produced a strong literary response. A comparison of the narrative stance underlying *Mad Maria* and *Sangue de Coca-Cola* (1982; *Coca-Cola Blood*) by Roberto Drummond will aid in clarifying Souza's absurdist aesthetic. There exists a wide spectrum of novelistic approaches that address Brazilian social and political issues from 1964 to the "abertura." The sociopolitical failings of the 1970s were documented in two very different manners by Souza and Drummond.

Sangue de Coca-Cola encapsulates the very contemporary nature of Brazilian postmodern fiction. Drummond's novel is highly experimental, almost schizophrenic in form, yet through its pop magicality, it analyzes the years of the dictatorship, naming names, documenting the repression, and suggesting future guidelines. This aggressive text is the quintessence of the responsive and committed novel that Drummond expounds.[3] "O Brasil anda para trás, recua no tempo, escutas a narração de gols de Pelé e musiquinhas patrióticas e o latir das sirenes, que abafam os gritos dos torturados"[4] ("Brazil is going backward, it draws back in time, you listen to broadcasts of Pele's goals and patriotic little songs and the sirens' shrill chokes off the shouts of the tortured.")

Souza's novel, conceived in a very different manner, utilizes the tenets of the novel of the Absurd, the anti-novel, to respond to the very same issues that Drummond addresses. Both authors aim at a redirecting of national consciousness, one by describing it, portraying its excesses, the other by recasting it in a historical past and viewing it cynically. Both novelists create a fiction that is highly Brazilian in scope. Drummond's has direct significance within Brazil; Souza's also attains universal import.

III

Márcio Souza, a master storyteller, moves plot along with beguiling dexterity. His writing is effortless in its direct use of language. This use of language attempts to artfully produce the impression of the dated artlessness of the adventure writer. However, *Mad Maria* transcends its narrative format as an exhausted literary form. It utilizes the style and format of earlier novels, adapting this present work to draw serious conclusions regarding the modern world. In the way that Thomas Berger accommodates historical accounts in *Little Big Man* and Donald Barthelme employed the fairy tale as a prefigurement to write *Snow White*, *Mad Maria* transcends its tongue-in-cheek format. It is first and foremost an artfully conceived allegory of the excesses of capitalistic colonialism and its effects upon the Brazilian character. It is also an allegory of ontological import.

In this regard Adnan Abdulla observes that "The audience identifies or refuses to identify with the model and this identification or detachment performs a social function. In the case of identification, the audience will have an example to follow; in the case of detachment, the audience will have a bad character that it will avoid or reject emulating." [5]

In *Mad Maria* the grotesque characterization of the naive, accepting personage of the Caripuna Indian becomes the central figure in this one dimensional allegory. Joe Caripuna is, at first, lured to the foreign world by its illusion of wealth (trinkets and mirrors), brutalized by it, and then somehow manages to assimilate it and even to achieve a crass form of transcendence and triumph. His love affair with Consuelo and his decadent, syphilitic, and tawdry show business career are contrasted to the failed multinationals who have been drained of their vitality by the Brazilian jungle. This savagely funny indictment of the failure of cultural colonialism is simultaneously interpretable as the triumph and profanation of the Brazilian national will.

It is generally accepted that there exists a strong interrelationship between the mythological and psychological approaches to literary study. To penetrate a deeper level of meaning in the work, the aesthetic theories of Kenneth Burke can be utilized as a point of departure.[6] It is Burke's conclusion that catharsis is not merely a literary term, but that it also takes into account the text, the reader, and society in general. He insists that these key concepts are inseparable from catharsis: "victimage," "mortification," "transcendence," and "communication." These parallel Joe Caripuna's rise as an anti-hero. Souza's novel mirrors Burke's belief that "the work of art moves *toward the transcendencing* (sic) *of both self-expression and communication.*"[7] In his role as the consummate anti-novelist, Márcio Souza's depiction of Joe Caripuna chronicles in true comic fashion all the stages of Burke's taxonomy. Souza's burlesquing of the Brazilian historical past contains implicit referential analogies to the present situation. Reader identification and aversion are strong components of *Mad Maria*'s anti-aesthetics. The ironic juxtaposition in the work is that Souza uses an Anglo-Saxon perspective, thus creating deeper reader reaction. The final example of authorial intrusion is steeped in cynicism and burlesques the concept of cultural domination that has been portrayed throughout the work. "Ah, que belo país é o nosso Brasil, onde um escritor de língua neo-latina pode fazer um romance inteirinho cheio de personagens com nomes anglo-saxões" (p. 341). ("Ah, what a beautiful land is our Brazil, where an author who writes in a neo-Latin tongue can compose an entire novel filled with Anglo-Saxon names" [p. 387].)

IV

The narrative rendering of any fictional work is designed to create a response, a cathartic reaction in the reader. Márcio Souza's *Mad Maria*, in its absurdist treatment of ontological and ideologic themes, is conceived in such a manner as to engender in the reader's consciousness a strong emotional arousal that leads to intellectual understanding.[8] In essence, Souza's book is "demythificational (serving to deny the validity of cultural referents . . .)."[9]

In Souza's novel life ceremonies define existence: railroad building, love affairs, kitsch entertainment, political intrigues, and international business deals. Life in Souza's work evolves as an ontological journey, like that of the locomotive Mad Maria. The author universalizes this journey, expressing the commonality of experience by the simultaneous use of several languages as a defining technique. He presents a component definition of this failed reality through the artifice of repetition. "E havia também uma locomotiva chamada Mad Mary, Marie Folle, María Loca, Maria Louca, Mad Maria" (p. 341). ("And where there once was a locomotive called Mad Mary, Marie Folle, María Loca, Maria Louca, Mad Maria, Mad Maria, MAD MARIA!" [p. 387].)

Life rituals are the ordering factor that define character. The world outside of these rituals is in desperate need of reorganization. Souza's characters daily confront an inhospitable climate, racial hatred, and a society at the mercy of politically expedient decisions and indecisions. At the work's end Dr. Finnegan loses control and kills six of his own men. His idealism has turned primitive. He now is resigned to his fate, hoping only to survive. "O máximo que ele podia sentir agora era cansaço, muito cansaço, pois só os bobos podiam se importar com alguma coisa além da arte de ficar vivo" (p. 344). ("The most he was capable of feeling now was tired, profoundly tired, since only fools could bother with anything beyond the art of staying alive" [p. 390].)

Charles B. Harris affirms that "All human activity is blighted by this perverse absurdity. Since the blight is irremediable, acceptance of absurdity may constitute the only logical extention of the absurdist vision." [10] In a novelistic world without declared hope, fundamental resignation to the absurd comedy of life becomes a conscious and cathartic act that Souza proffers as contemporary man's fate. His novel underscores man's struggle to find meaning in life. Mad Maria's cathartic code is based upon an ability to conceive as noble the seemingly simple act of living. In discussing the modern writer, Charles I. Glicksberg concludes, "He retreats neither into self-pity and aggrieved silence nor into a realm of beautiful lies. He chooses rather to render the absurdity which he perceives, to know it and make it known." [11] Mad Maria, in the final analysis, is a novelistic quest; it is an attempt to comprehend human relationships, national values, and ontological truths.

The Aesthetics
of the Absurd
in Márcio Souza's
Galvez, Imperador do Acre:
The Novel as Comic Opera

> *Nihilism lies at the center of all that we mean by*
> *modernist literature, both as subject and*
> *symptom, a demon overcome and a demon*
> *victorious.*
>
> Irving Howe
>
> *O meu império era um pedaço de mundo*
> *absurdo. . . . (My Empire was an absurd bit of*
> *world. . . .)*
>
> Márcio Souza

Irony constitutes a vital force in the aesthetics of Márcio Souza's fiction. In his best known work, *Galvez, Imperador do Acre*, he parodies the romantic adventure narrative of the last century, satirizing historical, political, and social institutions in a book that serves as an excellent example of the contemporary Brazilian anti-novel.[1]

Carlos Felipe Moisés considers that Souza ". . . é das mais fortes vocações de contador de histórias dos últimos tempos, em literatura brasileira."[2] ("has one of the strongest vocations for story telling in all of modern Brazilian literature.") Moisés also draws an interesting anti-novelistic parallel. "Galvez guarda ainda muita afinidade com nosso 'herói sem nenhum caráter,' o Macunaíma de Mário de Andrade."[3] ("Galvez is very much like our 'hero without a character,' Mário de Andrade's *Macunaíma*.") In *Galvez, Imperador do Acre*, absurdity evolves as an ontological given. Through his fiction Souza attempts to find meaning in "a disintegrating world without unifying principle, without meaning, without purpose; an absurd universe."[4] In this work the aesthetics of the absurd is a constant concern, not only in the novelist's vision of man, but also in the ironic structure which frames this vision.[5] A critical consideration of Márcio Souza's use of absurdist themes and tendencies is to be the central focus of this study.

I

In *The Dehumanization of Art*, José Ortega y Gasset observes that there exists an inclination for modern writers to consider art as ironical, a thing of no transcendent consequence.[6] Márcio Souza's absurdist vision contends that it is not only art, but life itself which is basically farcical. In *Galvez, Imperador do Acre*, one finds thematically and structurally the embodiment of Charles B. Harris's definition of absurdism.

> The absurdist vision may be defined as the belief that we are trapped in a meaningless universe and that neither God nor man, theology nor philosophy, can make sense of the human condition. . . . The "new" logic, with its acceptance of the illogical, and modern science, with its denial of causality and its concept of entropy, elevate chaos to the level of scientific fact.[7]

The act of interpreting absurdity as a theme is by no means a unique convention in modern literature. However, Souza's novel has gone beyond mere farce, parody, and black humor to produce something which is an amalgam of these elements, and which can well be termed "comedic terrorism."[8] His cutting wit attacks and debunks all that he perceives around him. He satirizes the preposterous and farcical events of Luiz Galvez's rise to power as the Emperor of Acre. His book is comprised of a series of offbeat adventures and absurd happenings conveying the novelist's vision of the ultimate absurdity: human existence. These happenings are, at times, portrayed as low comedy, as when Galvez, in leaping from his lover's window, inadvertently saves the life of his future mentor Dom Luiz Trucco (pp. 144–45) (pp. 139–40 English text).

Stylistically, Márcio Souza employs the technique of comic exaggeration, or burlesque, to expose the hypocrisy of Galvez's reign. "Os lances picarescos de Luiz Galvez formam um todo com o vaudeville político do ciclo da borracha" (pp. 195–96). ("The picaresque moments in the life of Luiz Galvez wholly conform to the vaudevillian politics of the rubber boom" [p. 190].) Souza's novel allegorically equates human existence to a traveling comic opera troupe appropriately named "Les Commediens Tropicales."[9] Politics, history, and ideals evolve within the work with the same third rate sense of staging as the ragtag troupe's portrayal of "opera buffa." An all-encompassing sense of the tawdry is portrayed by Souza in his iconoclastic role as social critic. Galvez's palace, which is emblematic of his reign, is conceived and described in grotesquely theatrical terms.

> O modelo vinha de uma caríssima cenografia para a Ópera "As Bodas de Fígaro," de Mozart, de forte sabor setecentista e recusada anos antes na Europa por ultrapassar o orçamento da Companhia. (P. 180)

> (Its model, the incredibly expensive set for *The Marriage of Figaro* by Mozart—hence the markedly eighteenth-century flavor—had been rejected years ago, in Europe, for exceeding the budget of the opera company.) (P. 174)

> O mármore raiado de rosa contrastava com a madeira escura do Palácio Imperial e em nada correspondia com as proporções do pardieiro de zinco enferrujado. Os lances de degraus majestosos não levavam a lugar nenhum, numa metáfora ao meu Império. (P. 191)

> (Its marble, streaked with pink, stood in awkward contrast to the muddy clapboard of Paixão's former property, and laughably malproportioned to its verandah of rusty zinc. The rise of majestic steps led nowhere, in one more metaphor of my Empire.) (P. 185)

The theme of politics as theater evolves as the book's primary object of satire as Galvez's political ideology also is described by another theatrical analogy.

> Uma coleção de pernas femininas bem ensaiadas, em meias de rendas. Alguns números de cancan, boas bebidas, eram tão bom argumento ideológico quanto qualquer outro. . . . A política nos trópicos é uma questão de coreografía. (P. 151)

> (A collection of well-rehearsed legs clad in lace stockings, a few cancan numbers, and plenty of good liquor proved to be as persuasive

an ideological argument as any other. . . . Politics in the tropics is really a question of choreography.) (P. 146)

Satire and burlesque allow Souza to debunk Brazilian attitudes and ideals through this narrative use of "dramma giocosa." While he exaggerates reality he seldom presents it in a non-recognizable form. Musical comedy and operatic productions form the backdrop for many of the novel's adventures.

> Entre as estrofes da delicada romanza do Barbeiro de Sevilha, "Ecco ridente in cielo . . .," esqueci os conselhos de Sir Henry e assumi o Império com um gesto napoleônico. Coloquei sobre minha própria cabeça a palma de folhas de seringueira lavrada em prata. (P. 169)

> (Somewhere between the strophes of a delicate *romanza* from *The Barber of Seville*, "*Ecco ridente in cielo*," I neglected the advice of Sir Henry and acceded to my Empire with a Napoleonic gesture. I placed upon my own head a wreath of rubber leaves molded in silver.) (P. 164)

In the "Dueto Bufo" scene (pp. 61–66) (pp. 59–64 English) Dona Irene vociferously accuses Galvez of rape after having just tried to ravish him on the ladies' room floor. The shrill voices of Radamés and Dona Irene coalesce as opera and life fuse, signalling Galvez's need to escape to the Amazon. "O terra, addio; addio valle de pianti" (p. 65). (Same text in English version.)

> Alcancei os bastidores e sem ao menos saudar algumas coristas que choravam na coxia, escapei pela porta dos fundos, como num folhetim. (P. 66)

> (I finally reached the wings, and without even a parting farewell to the chorus girls busy crying backstage, I made good my escape— through a back exit, naturally; as befits a *feuilleton*.) (P. 64)

Here life is mirrored in and forms part of the theatrical production, as later in the novel the comic opera will become equated to and commingle with Galvez's Amazonian empire. While the author accepts absurdity as a given within the narrative, he also views it as an offshoot of a bureaucratic and political process gone haywire.

> Do: Comandante Galvez.
> Para: Intendente Chefe.
> Prezado Senhor: Comunicamos que o Estado-Maior, em reunião de CFG.H5467, decidiu condenar a compra de cerveja da marca Heinekker, de origem teutônica, por se apresentar num sabor suspeito. . . . O Estado-Maior, outrossim, decidiu aumentar a cota

de champanha e uma caixa de xerez para uso exclusiv do Coman-
dante-em-Chefe.
Saudações Revolucionárias.
Viva o Acre Independente.
Galvez, Comandante-em-Chefe. (pp. 137–38)

(FROM: Commandant Galvez
TO: Chief Commissary Officer
Dear Sir: We wish to communicate that the General Staff, at a
meeting of CFG.H5467 and after due deliberation, has decided to
condemn the recent purchases of several cases of Heinekker beer,
a Dutch brand exhibiting a rather suspect taste. . . . And finally,
the General Staff has seen fit to increase the allotment of cham-
pagne, and to add one case of *jerez* for the exclusive use of the
Commandant.
Revolutionary Greetings,
Long Live Independent Acre!
Galvez, Commander-in-Chief) (P. 132)

In a series of special communiques, Commander Galvez's main concern seems to be with his allotment of White Horse whiskey and the
purchase of Lublin toilet water for his foul smelling Acrean regiments.
As his official communique III affirms: "Povo cheiroso é povo civilizado" (p. 132). ("A sweet-smelling people are a civilized people"
[p. 127].) Here language is shown to be a means of distancing people
from authority. The absurd formality with which these trivialities are
dealt conveys Souza's vision that all political and military institutions
use the opacity of language to obscure ineptitude and corruption.
These institutions are later portrayed as self-perpetuating examples of
structured chaos. The acidity of this observation and its direct reference to the then ruling military dictatorship was not lost to Souza's
readers nor to the country's censors, for soon after the work's publication Souza lost his job at the Ministry of Culture.
The slapstick vaudevillian aspects of the novel are many.

Um deulo de florete e guarda-chuva não era algo comum, ainda mais
travado entre uma coronela do Exército da Salvação e um maestro
de óperas. (P. 161)

(A duel between a rapier and a parasol is, even to this day, rather
uncommon—especially one pitting a lady colonel of the Salvation
Army against a gentleman conductor of Italian opera.) (P. 156)

In this same vein Souza's description of Galvez being deposed is rich
in vaudevillian black humor.

Burlamaqui entrou no Palácio e recebeu uma baforada de calor
e fumaça de charutos. Estava me procurando e queria a honra de me

depor pessoalmente. . . . Tentei uma posição mais confortável para meditar sobre o acontecimento e me apoiei nos braços dele, mas o esforço me fez o estômago virar e, para o meu pesar, vomitei copiosamente sobre a farda de meu depositor. (P. 194)

(Burlamaqui entered the Palace and was struck by a wall of fetid heat and cigar smoke. He began searching for me, bent on the honor of deposing me personally. . . . In an effort to find a more comfortable position to meditate upon the event, I fumbled my way further into the arms of my deposer, but the exertion turned my stomach and, to my regret, I vomited copiously onto his uniform.) (Pp. 187–88)

Aesthetically, Souza's use of absurdist humor is augmented by the fact that his novel's personages resemble comic strip characters. They are one-dimensional, and the author creates them in this manner to stress the caricature aspects of modern man. The novel holds that contemporary man's nature cannot be presented in its totality and that any novelistic attempt to do so is pure presumption. Thus, Souza indicates that man's being is too illusive to be fully portrayed through literature.

Since it can be argued that comic involvement voids emotional involvement, this cartoon aspect of Souza's art is meaningful as the reader will always remain detached from his purposefully thin characters. His characters personify ideals, much in the manner of a medieval allegory: Sir Henry Lust, Dom Pedro Paixão, Michael Kennedy, Justine L'Amour, and Joana Ferreira. Many American fiction writers of the sixties populated their novels with characters with names like Dr. Hilarious, Benny Profane, Billy Pilgrim, and Chief Halfoat, suggesting "the types of names given cartoon figures—Daddy Warbucks, Jughead, Flat-top, etc. As in comic strips, the names often suggest specific attitudes or ideas." [10]

Souza's creation of Sir Henry Lust is in this absurdist style of thinly textured comic book creations. Like a medieval allegory the abstract concept of "lust" is incarnated. However, it is anti-allegorical in intent since Souza's purpose is not to communicate a moral, but to depict a being who is totally amoral. Souza creates this one-dimensional character to better satirize Sir Henry as a scientist-Everyman, whose scientific knowledge leads him to conclude that the "Teatro Amazonas" was created by extraterrestrial beings. One senses the overt lampooning of Erich von Dänikens's successful book *Chariots of the Gods*.[11]

A concepção de que o Teatro Amazonas é um artefato espacial é exclusivamente racional, isto é, a intervenção no meio da jungle equatorial é produto de seres inteligentes. . . . (P. 87)

(Our concept of the Amazonas Theater as an artifact from space is a purely rational one; which is to say, this manifest intervention in the heart of the equatorial jungle must be a product of intelligent forces. . . .) (P. 84)

Science is again the object of Souza's parody as the reader soon discovers that Sir Henry's scientific research consists of collecting specimens of unusual male genitalia, which he proudly displays to his dinner guests.

Depois do jantar, Sir Henry me ofereceu uma completa visita ao camarote onde estavam guardadas as preciosas relíquias. E relíquias o eram na realidade, pois o meu caro cientista guardava, em vidros de formal, cerca de vinte amostras de genitálias masculinas. . . . (P. 122)

(After dinner, Sir Henry invited me to come have a tour of the cabin where the precious relics were being guarded. And precious relics they were, since my dear Dr. Lust was housing—in jars of formaldehyde—close to twenty samples of masculine genitalia. . . .) (P. 117)

In the novel's concluding chapters Souza seems to sustain the contention that Joana Ferreira, an ex-nun, is the work's only character to possess any sense of conscience. She is portrayed as the archetypal revolutionary. "Joana organizou um batalhão de seringueiros e comandava os homens com mão de ferro" (p.152). ("Joana had organized a battalion of latex workers and commanded her men with a fist of iron" [p. 147].) Then to this statement Souza wryly adds, "Ela tinha aprendido muito bem os ensinamentos da Igreja Católica" (p. 152). ("She had learned much from the teachings of the Catholic Church" [p. 152].) She is imbued with a fiery dedication to her new cause. "Joana continuava o seu trabalho, alheia aos delírios do Ministério. Reunia-se com o povo, organizava escolas e criava centros recreativos no interior do país" (p. 184). ("Joana was continuing with her work, irrespective of the deliriums of my Cabinet. She would meet with the people, was organizing schools, and set up recreation centers in the interior of the country" [p. 178].) To Joana's righteous concern Souza juxtaposes Galvez's sardonic comments regarding these same subjects. "Não me queixo; meu povo sempre evitou denegrir a imagem de seu país no exterior" (p. 184). ("I cannot complain—my people generally avoided denigrating the image of the nation abroad" [p. 179].) However, Souza's novel is not offering religious or political action as a means for social change. The characterization of Joana, as she passes from "Irmã Joana" to "Joana a Guerrilheira" and finally to "Joana d'Arc," evolves as the author's paradigm for the prototypical cause follower. Joana is the novel's only character to die while still young and vibrant.

> Soube que Joana foi abatida na tentativa de salvar o meu Império . . . O rosto estava sujo de sangue e de terra. A saia levantada permitia a visão de suas pernas morenas que pareciam pulsar iluminadas pelos fogos de artifício que explodiam no céu. (Pp. 194–95)

> (I learned that Joana was shot down in the attempt to salvage my Empire . . . her face encrusted with earth and blood. The lifted skirt offering one last glimpse of her tawny legs, which still seemed to throb, illuminated by the fireworks exploding across the sky.) (P. 188)

Her death affords Souza the opportunity to point out the tragedy of a life given over to following a vacuous, comic opera leader.

Michael Kennedy, the aforementioned American consul, is Souza's personification of an imperialistic United States. He is depicted as an ineffectual interventionist disgusted by his stay in the Amazon and constantly fearful for his health. Kennedy is appalled by the total lack of morality he sees around him but is willing to remain in order to obtain a favorable trade agreement for his country.

> E eu ouvia o velho Trucco sem remorsos confirmar a teoria de Kennedy sobre os latinos-americanos: um povo de péssimos negociantes e estadistas ingênuos. (P. 29)

> (And I listened as Trucco, with no qualms whatsoever, hopelessly confirmed Kennedy's opinion of Latin Americans: a people of questionable statecraft and lamentable business acumen.) (P. 27)

> Arrepiava os comerciantes e políticos pelos conchavos e promessas e arrepiava os nacionalistas pelas constantes ameaças que seu país costumava fazer contra a integridade da Amazônia. (P. 28)

> (Merchants and politicians shook in the face of his machinations and promises; and patriots shivered at the continual threats his country was wont to bandy against the integrity of the Amazon.) (P. 26)

These and a variety of other offbeat characters sail together on a ship named "O gaiola Esperança" (The S.S. Hope). The "Esperança" is ironically described as:

> . . . um daqueles ciganos dos rios, sem rota fixa, a pintura desgastada, tripulação incerta e sem nítida diferença entre a primeira e a terceira classe. (P. 140)

> (. . . one of those river gypsies without any fixed route: paint worn, crew uncertain, and no clear-cut distinction between first and third class.) (P. 135)

103

Here a comic description of the group's tawdry means of travel may have been the limit of Souza's humor. However, if one considers this work on a deeper, more metaphysical level, then one is led to believe that man's fragile sense of hope is also the object of this ontologically based satire.

Galvez, Imperador do Acre is a buoyant novel, a celebration by an artist looking through myth and history to present a jaundiced vision of both. Within the novel itself Souza's absurdist views are tempered and not overtly despairing regarding the meaninglessness of life.[12] He presents the facts of Galvez's life of greed, sexual excesses, and debauchery without judgmental commentary.

While there is little inherently innovative about the presence of satire and irony in contemporary Brazilian fiction, the novelty of Souza's use of these techniques is that they are employed on such a grand scale. More importantly, the novel's satire is self-directed and it is, by extension, a burlesque of all Art. Within the work the motive for publishing the manuscript, as expressed by the character identified only as "o brasileiro" (p. 14) ("the Brazilian" [p. 12]), is solely to attempt to recoup 350 francs.

> Espero pelo menos reaver os trezentos e cinqüenta francos que gastei nos manuscritos, enforcando entre outras coisas uma viagem de ônibus a Nice e um jantar no Les Balcans. (P. 15)

> (I hope to at least be able to recoup the 350 francs I spent on the manuscript, which was to have paid for, among other things, my bus trip to Nice and a dinner at Les Balcans.) (P. 12)

In another of the book's more satiric sections is detailed the life of an aspiring writer who venerates a strange literary fetish.

> ... Apolidório Tristão de Magalhães ... possuía um souvenir que tratava como relíquia santa: uma ceroula de Coelho Neto. ... Num momento de distração de Coelho Neto, furtou a peça íntima que, agora em moldura prateada, decorava a parede da biblioteca numa posição de destaque e veneração. (P. 27)

> ... Apolidório Tristão de Magalhães ... was also apparently in possession of a rather odd souvenir which he nonetheless revered as a holy relic: a pair of undershorts belonging to the prodigious Henrique Maximiliano Coelho Neto. ... Then finally—taking advantage of a propitious moment of grand, authorly distraction—Colonel Tristão had pinched, as it were, the intimate apparel in question, which now adorned the wall of his library, silver-framed, in a position of prominence and veneration." (P. 25)

Here Souza's humor in treating Coelho Neto's "ceroula" ("under-shorts") as a type of mystical icon goes beyond lampooning. Implicit in this scene is the ridiculing of the sanctity of literature and the debunking of the writer's place in Brazilian society. This humor again turns inward, expressing a belief that nothing is beyond satire, including the creative process.

The themes of detachment and meaninglessness are presented by Souza without emotional charge. The novel's structure, the comic-strip flatness of the characters, the hyperbolic nature of the occurences, while they do not allow for reader empathy, nonetheless lead the reader to an acceptance of absurdity as a norm.

While the novel presents Galvez's picaresque reign as a meaningless comedic charade, its structural underpinnings also augment this absurdist vision. John S. Brushwood has outlined the work's involved narrative structure in the following manner. "... What we read consists of the presumed account and analytical comments by the editor-narrator. The manuscript-narrator is in an intra-narrative situation as far as the editor-narrator is concerned. However, the presentation by the editor-narrator is also part of the fiction . . ."[13] From Brushwood's synthesis the humorous topos of the assigning of outrageous, ironic, and quasi-erudite titles should be emphasized. This use and misuse of these chapter titles constitutes one of the novel's more irreverent anti-literary components. To underscore the theme of form superseding substance, Souza continually employs these playful, supercilious, and purposefully banal titles. These titles serve as ironic prefigurations and opportunities for tongue-in-cheek authorial commentary. A few examples will suffice: Eros e Látex (Of Love and Latex), Chá e Simpatia (Tea and Sympathy), O Eterno Retorno (The Eternal Return), Guia Michelin de Manaus (Michelin Guide to Manaus), O Grito do Acre (The Cry of Acre), Sexual Life Beyond Equator (sic), and Povo Bom e Ordeiro (A Good and Well-Behaved People).[14]

The work's pseudo-authentic framing (the motif of the lost manu-script, the final excerpt from a supposedly venerable but obscure historical text), the attempt of the editor-narrator to discredit the manuscript-narrator's writings, and the work's narrative complexities are all presented as an ironic attempt to place artistic order on chaos. In the ridiculing of fictional conventions, Souza undermines literature's pretension as a means of explaining life. Márcio Souza not only satirizes the human situation, but more importantly, his narrative evolves as a burlesque of the very vehicle he has chosen to present that satire: the novel itself.

II

Márcio Souza's mordant humor underscores his penchant for exposing real sociopolitical problems. The hyperbolic sense of sham, symbolized by Galvez's warehouse turned "papier-mâché" palace, affords the author an opportunity for tacitly expressed commentary. That which is implicit in his lampooning of institutions and attitudes is far more eloquently stated through comedy than through the traditional and straight-forward novel of social protest. In *Galvez, Imperador do Acre*, irony has replaced strident verbosity as a means of confronting man's existential dilemma.

As the reader is brought to a realization of the role of irony in the novel, the following assumption by Ihab H. Hassan regarding modern fiction aids in illuminating Souza's use of this novelistic technique.

> Irony selects from the tragic situation the element of absurdity . . . it takes from comedy the unlawful or quixotic motive, the savagery which is the other face of play, and the grotesque scapegoat rituals of comic expiation. . . . Irony . . . is, nevertheless, preeminently suited to the needs of the present situation. Irony, in fact, is the basic principle of the form which dominates our fiction. It is the literary correlative of the existential ethic; it implies distance, ambiguity, the interplay of views.[15]

Souza's fiction, in its use of irony to exaggerate and dramatize reality, provides a type of Aristotelian catharsis. Irony becomes a defense mechanism against man's sense of unrealistic hope. The reader must go beyond the novel's humor in intuiting the work's serious intent. Souza's *Galvez, Imperador do Acre*, while artfully conceived and entertaining, is aimed at bringing his audience to the truth of the absurd, both a sociopolitical and metaphysically based truth.

The essence of the novel's intent is encapsulated in the following passage which belies the work's comical facade.

> Morriam no Acre, anualmente, oito crianças entre vinte, nos primeiros dias de vida. 20% da população ativa sofria de tuberculose. 15% de lepra. 60% estava infestada de doenças típicas de carência alimentar. 80% da população não era alfabetizada. Não havia médicos no Acre. Um quilo de café custava 0$20. 40% da borracha fina do Amazonas vinha do território acreano. (P. 154)

> (In Acre, annually, eight out of twenty children died in the first days of life; 20% of the active population suffered from tuberculosis; 15% from leprosy. Another 60% were infected with diseases typical of an undernourished condition; 80% of the population was illiter-

ate. There were no doctors in Acre. A kilo of coffee cost twenty cen-
tavos. And 40% of the finest rubber in the Amazon came from
Acrean territory.) (P. 149)

There is nothing humorous in this brief paragraph. It is terse and
straight-forward, standing in violent opposition to Galvez's comic-
opera empire. Souza's satire expresses a sardonic attitude toward both
the salvationist ideals of political activists and the interventionist principles of international governments. Galvez's subjects are helpless in
the face of a political system that ebbs and flows with the absurd
whims of a distracted leadership. In this aspect of the novel can be
seen an extended metaphor with Galvez representing a profane and
uncaring God figure. "Afinal, nos trópicos, os políticos, como Deus,
sempre tinham razões insondáveis" (p. 163). ("In the end, in the tropics, the politicians—like God himself—had their own unfathomable
reasons" [p. 159].)

Souza's novel offers no facile solutions to counteract the absurdity
of existence. His absurdist humor evolves as a means of confronting
life and creating a world view that makes this existence bearable. His
use of irony actually forms part of a novelistic process that commits
itself to right that which it criticizes.

> The writer, in picturing the absurdity of the human condition, is in
> effect protesting against it. Life must be lived, even though the search
> for ultimate meaning is foiled.[16]

Márcio Souza's comic vision expresses what Wylie Sypher refers to as
post-existentialist humanism.

> As long as man is aware of the void at the center of things . . . and
> the absurdity of his position in it, there is some locus for a sort
> of humanism, even if it be unlike any kind of humanism held in
> the past.[17]

In *Galvez, Imperador do Acre*, one finds that this newly defined
humanism permeates the novel.

> The absurdity of the human condition, if faced squarely, can be
> viewed as a cosmic joke . . . the dignity of man lies in his ability to
> face reality in all its senselessness; to accept it freely, without fear,
> without illusions—and to laugh at it.[18]

Souza's role as a satirist is not merely to destroy the myths of our time.
His overt pose is that of an iconoclast, but beneath this ironic posture
is a sense of quest. If Souza believed existence to be truly absurd, then
art would be merely a meaningless projection of consciousness and all
attempts at creation would be fruitless.

Hence, to maintain that life is a nightmare of absurdity and to do so within the controlled framework of art, is paradoxically a way of triumphing over it.[19]

Artistic creation becomes a positive gesture, one which affirms Souza's faith in art as a salutary and liberating force. Márcio Souza's *Galvez, Imperador do Acre*, is in itself a revolt; it is a quest to comprehend man's relationship to his universe. This attempt at comprehension ultimately evolves as an ennobling effort to better know the meaning of existence.

NOTES

[1] Oswald de Andrade, *Obras completas II* (Rio de Janeiro: Civilização Brasileira, 1971), p. 132. The English edition is *Seraphim Grosse Pointe*, trans. Kenneth D. Jackson and Albert Bork (Austin: New Latin Quarter Editions, 1979), p. 4.

[2] Haroldo de Campos essay quoted from Andrade's *Obras completas*, Andrade, p. 102, trans. Jackson and Bork, p. 113.

[3] Irving Howe, *Literary Modernism* (New York: Fawcett, 1967), p. 16.

[4] Andrade, p. 132, trans. p. 3.

[5] Ignácio de Loyola Brandão, *O beijo não vem da boca* (*The Kiss Doesn't Come from the Mouth*) (São Paulo: Global Editora, 1985), p. 12.

[6] Loyola Brandão, p. 6.

[7] Flávio Moreira da Costa, *O desastronauta: OK, Jack Kerouac, nós estamos te esperando em Copacabana* (Rio de Janeiro: Expressão e Cultura, 1971), p. 19.

[8] Kurt Vonnegut, Jr., *Breakfast of Champions* (New York: Dell Publishing Co., Inc., 1973), p. 210.

[9] Bruce Jay Friedman ed., *Black Humor* (New York: Bantam, 1965), p. vii.

[10] Friedman, p. 10.

[11] Sérgio Sant'Anna, *Confissões de Ralfo* (Rio de Janeiro: Civilização Brasileira, 1975), p. 23.

[12] Joseph Campbell, "The Need for New Myths," *Time* 17 Jan. 1972, p. 51.

[13] Campbell, p. 50.

Mad Maria Study

The first epigraph is from Carl Gustav Jung, *Psychological Reflections*, ed. Jolande Jacobi (New York: Harper, 1961), p. 189.

The second epigraph is from Márcio Souza, *Mad Maria* (Rio de Janeiro: Civilização Brasileira, 1983), p. 75. The English translation is taken from *Mad Maria*, trans. Thomas Colchie (New York: Avon, 1985), p. 81. All subsequent citations will be taken from these editions and page numbers will be entered directly into the text.

[1] Adnan K. Abdulla, *Catharsis in Literature* (Bloomington: Indiana University Press, 1985), pp. 115–16.

[2] The Editora Civilização Brasileira edition begins with this section as part of the main text, while the English edition uses it as an epigrammatic separate page.

[3] See Roberto Drummond, *A morte de D. J. em Paris* (*The Death of D. J. in Paris*) (São Paulo: Ática, 1983), pp. 3–7.

[4] Roberto Drummond, *Sangue de Coca-Cola* (Rio de Janeiro: Nova Fronteira, 1985), p. 22.

[5] Abdulla, p. 116.

[6] See also Abdulla, pp. 45–67.

[7] Kenneth Burke, "The Criticism of Criticism," *Accent* 15 (1955): 292.

[8] Abdulla, pp. 118–19.

[9] David William Foster, *Alternate Voices* (Columbia: University of Missouri Press, 1985), p. 60.

[10] Charles B. Harris, *Contemporary American Novelists of the Absurd* (New Haven: College & University Press, 1971), p. 72.

[11] Charles I. Glicksberg, *The Self in Modern Literature* (University Park, PA: Pennsylvania State University Press, 1969), p. 175.

Galvez Study

The first epigraph is from Irving Howe, *Literary Modernism* (New York: Fawcett, 1967), pp. 39–40.

The second epigraph is from Márcio Souza, *Galvez, Imperador do Acre* (Rio de Janeiro: Marco Zero, 1983), p. 181. The work was published in English as *The Emperor of the Amazon*, trans. Thomas Colchie (New York: Avon, 1980), p. 176. Further citations will be made by page numbers in the text.

[1] See John Barth, "The Literature of Exhaustion," *On Contemporary Literature*, ed. Richard Kostelanetz (New York: Avon, 1969), pp. 622–75.

[2] Carlos Felipe Moisés, "Crazy Galvez & Mad Maria," *Escrita: Revista de Literatura* 8, no. 32 (1983), p. 67.

[3] Moisés, p. 68. Novels like *O desastronauta* by Flávio Moreira da Costa and *Zero* by Ignácio de Loyola Brandão also fall within this category. For a further amplification of the evolution of anti-literature in twentieth-century Latin America, see Fernando Alegría, "Antiliteratura," *América Latina en su literatura*, ed. César Fernández Moreno (Mexico City: Siglo XXI, 1972), pp. 243–58.

[4] Charles B. Harris, *Contemporary American Novelists of the Absurd* (New Haven: College & University Press, 1971), p. 17.

[5] In a brief study of recent fiction the historical aspects of the rubber boom were discussed and brought forward as the major thematic consideration for this novel. Gilbert Perez, "These Days in the Holocene," *The Hudson Review* 33 (1980), 587–88. "Souza offers us the brief shoddy days of Galvez's story as emblematic of that whole fantastic episode in the Brazilian past" (p. 58). It will be the contention of this study that Souza's satire also transcends historical reality acquiring political, ontological, and metaphysical significance.

[6] José Ortega y Gasset, *The Dehumanization of Art* (Garden City, NY: Doubleday Anchor Books, 1956), pp. 45–58.

[7] Harris, p. 17.

[8] Comedic terrorism is a denomination used to note the intensity and pervasiveness of Souza's satiric intentions. In referring to American novelists of the sixties like John Barth, Kurt Vonnegut, Jr., Thomas Pynchon, and Joseph Heller, critics have used various terms to categorize their fiction. While these writers all share a basic absurdist vision of reality, the specific terms of classification varied. Among these classifications were "Black Humor," "Epicurean comedy," "the psychic novel," and the "novel of disintegration." Harris traces the derivation of these terms in an extensive note, p. 135.

[9] Michael Wood, "In the Latino Americano Mirror," *The New York Review of Books* 28, 16 (Oct. 22, 1981), p. 53. In writing of Souza's novel and other Latin American fiction, Wood observes that "Images of France, for example, stalk Latin American fiction like the ruins of some empire of the mind." This indeed is a valid observation, but it does not take into account that Souza's novel turns on this truism to mock it, burlesquing the whole Parnassian ethic and mind set. Also implicit in this aspect of Souza's satire is the Brazilian acceptance of all things French as culturally superior to the "cultura popular brasileira."

[10] Harris, p. 26.

[11] Erich von Däniken, *Chariots of the Gods? Unsolved Mysteries of the Past* (New York: Putnam, 1969).

[12] It is precisely this attitude of playful nonchalance, this detached and off-handed authorial posture that undercuts literature's pretensions and parochialism, placing *Galvez, Imperador do Acre* in the company of absurdist novels like *A Confederacy of Dunces* by John Kennedy Toole, *Little Big Man* by Thomas Berger, and *Catch-22* by Joseph Heller.

[13] John Brushwood, "Recent Translations of Latin American Fiction," *The Missouri Review* 5, no. 2 (1981–82), 98.

[14] Wood, p. 55, observes that these proliferating titles "suggest a universe of interminable comment, which recalls some of Joyce's jokes in *Ulysses*, and the similar earlier tricks of Machado de Assis."

[15] Ihab H. Hassan, "The Character of Post-War Fiction in America," *On*

Contemporary Literature, ed. Richard Kostelanetz (New York: Avon, 1969), p. 43.

[16] Charles I. Glicksberg, *Ironic Vision in Modern Literature* (The Hague: Martinue Nijhoff, 1969), p. 223.

[17] Wylie Sypher, *Loss of the Self in Modern Literature and Art* (New York: Vintage, 1964), p. 7.

[18] Harris, p. 30.

[19] Glicksberg, p. 13.

ASPECTS OF CONTEMPORARY JUDEO-BRAZILIAN WRITING

In Brazil. . . . Fresh breezes wafted scents of tropical plants and fruits for which I had no name in Yiddish.

Isaac Bashevis Singer

Judeo-Brazilian writing is not an easily defined concept. Mark Shechner points out in his essay "Jewish Writers," "Neither 'Jewish writer' nor 'Jewish fiction' is an obvious or self-justifying subdivision of literature, any more than Jewishness itself is now a self-evident cultural identity . . . (However) it is not unreasonable to invoke 'the Jewish writer' as a convenient shorthand for a feature of the literary census that we want to examine but are not yet prepared to define."[1] Bearing in mind this cautionary note, a study of Judeo-Brazilian writing merits consideration from a socioliterary perspective. An analysis of the role of minorities in any culture is a critical approach whose validity contributes to a broader understanding of existing literary forms.

Jewish history in Brazil dates directly back to the voyage of discovery by Admiral Pedro Alvares Cabral in 1500. His personal secretary in charge of the provisions ship was a Spanish Jew who, before his capture by the Portuguese, had served Sabáyo, the Arabian ruler of Goa. The secretary's Hebrew name has been obscured by conflicting histories, but he was given the name of Gaspar da Gama when he was forcefully converted to Christianity. Fluent in several languages, the former chief captain of Sabáyo's Indian fleet became a favorite of the court and King Manuel I. While he was regaled with gifts such as horses, servants, and a sizable monthly allowance, "the king and the chroniclers of his era continued to refer to him as the 'Jew' even after he had undergone baptism."[2]

Arnold Wiznitzer's *Jews in Colonial Brazil*, 1960, underscores the tensions and triumphs of this early history of Brazil's Jewish community:

> On their migrations through the world during the millenia of their dispersion Jews came also to Brazil. . . . Those who immigrated to the Portuguese colony in Brazil were called New Christians: Jews and their descendants who had been converted to Catholicism by force in Portugal. Most of them observed Jewish rites in secret, always afraid of being discovered by agents of the Inquisition. . . . Historiography has quite neglected the romantic and fascinating history of the underground and free-professing Jews in colonial Brazil, who formed the earliest Jewish community in America and became the "Jewish Pilgrim Fathers" of New York, as well as of Jamaica, Barbados, and other Jewish communities in the Caribbean area.[3]

It was not until Emperor Dom Pedro proclaimed Brazilian independence from Portugal in 1822 that the first official Jewish congregation was established in the northern coastal city of Belem. In time, well-organized communities were founded by Sephardic Jews from Syria and North Africa. Early congregations, such as Shaar Hashamaim (Porta do Céu), gave way to larger congregations in cities like Rio de Janeiro, Bahia, Manaus, and Ceará. Later, Jewish agricultural colonies were organized in the southern states of Santa Catarina and Rio Grande do Sul. Between the first and second world wars, 30,000 migrants arrived from Bessarabia, Rumania, and Poland, and in 1937, 8,000 more refugees came from Nazi Germany. However, late in 1937 a new law barred immigrants without at least 12,000 dollars deposited in a Brazilian bank. In 1940 the Vatican helped circumvent this law, and 3,000 more German Jews were settled that year.[4] Recent historical research has unearthed documents that officially corroborate these obstructionist and anti-Semitic policies that comprised the philosophical underpinnings of Vargas's Estado Novo.[5] From 1945 to 1965, Brazil received twenty million immigrants, including large numbers of Jewish settlers from Hungary, Syria, Lebanon, Egypt, and Turkey. In 1987 the unofficial estimated Jewish population ranged between 130,000 and 150,000.

In *Diaspora: An Inquiry into the Contemporary Jewish World*, 1985, Howard M. Sachar concludes that, "The nation's cultural life has been as widely influenced by the Jewish leaven as in any Western land, from the conductor of the national symphony orchestra to directors of state academies and institutes to deans of universities."[6] The assimilation process even included six Jewish generals in the armed forces in 1966. Sachar interviews Benno Milnitzky, president of the Confederation of Jewish Communities, on the Brazilianization of the Jewish experience. Milnitzky's views make for an interesting prologue to this chapter:

> I don't mind that Brazilian society is open. . . . Heaven forbid. I *do* mind that the openness of society here has undermined our Jewish integrity. . . . There's no strong leadership here, . . . certainly no rabbis worthy of anyone's attention. If only someone could instill in our people a feeling for the old Jewish ethical values, not the fake materialistic values of the Brazilian elite. Our people simply are too attracted by Brazilian materialism.[7]

Sachar's contention throughout *Diaspora* is that, "A California-like hedonism and self-satisfaction rarely generate the intellectual tensions that have been unique to Jewish creativity."[8] This observation leads to a discussion of why this Jewish community has not contributed to the development of its country's literature to a greater extent, certainly not in a degree equal to the literary accomplishments of the Italian, Argentine, and Canadian Jewish communities.[9] Diana Katcher Bletter in discussing the 50,000 member community of Rio de Janeiro characterizes it as "reflecting the melting-pot ethic . . . Jewish life in Rio tends to be more recreational and beach-oriented and less religiously observant. . . . The Jews in Rio are like those in Tel Aviv: on Shabbat, they go to the beach."[10]

This tropicalization of the Jewish experience is reflected literarily by Francisco Dzialovsky in his 1987 novel, *O terceiro testamento* (*The Third Testament*). His book chronicles the passing of old ways and traditions, and the rapid assimilation into an easy going Brazilian way of life.

> O calor dos trópicos, a abundância de sol e chuva, que faz tudo nascer com vigor, enchendo o mundo de vida, parecem ter efeito contrário em alguns casos onde só se vê o efeito da decrepitude. Em casa assistia além do fenecer dos pais e do idioma, o enterro de uma cultura que se manifestava cada vez menos, na medida em que a mãe

esquecia a receita de pratos típicos e na medida em que na conversa entre os velhos se introduzia cada vez mais palavras em português.[11]

(The tropical heat, the abundance of sun and rain, causes everything to be born vigorously, filling the world with life. This same tropical heat, in some cases, seems to have a contradictory effect, as only the effect of decrepitude is observed. At home, along with the slow demise of our parents and our language, there could also be observed the interment of a culture, a culture that daily manifested itself less and less, as our mother forgot recipes for traditional dishes, and as an ever-growing number of Portuguese words were introduced into the conversation of the old folks.)

To tell of the lives of a people in the hard light of historical fact is one way to get to know a community; however, through the literature created by that people a deeper, more meaningful presentation can be achieved. Moacyr Scliar is fast becoming the literary voice of Brazil's Jewish community, chronicling their history and myths. Scliar, apart from being a highly respected author, remains a practicing physician in his native city of Porto Alegre. To date he has fashioned an impressive corpus of award winning fiction that continues to be critically well received both within Brazil and abroad.

His book, *A estranha nação de Rafael Mendes* (1983: *The Strange Nation of Rafael Mendes*) is an amalgam of historical fact, mysticism, and illusion. Rafael Mendes is a successful businessman who learns that both his private life and company's future are in crisis. He then becomes aware of the existence of a series of genealogical notebooks in which he discovers he is Jewish. Mendes is the descendant of Portuguese *Marranos* who were forced to affirm Christianity in 1497 when the entire Jewish community was converted en masse. Through these notebooks Moacyr Scliar traces the history of Rafael's ancestors, a lineage that dates back centuries.

Scliar presents his private vision of Rafael Mendes's nation, a magical vision that is told in brief quasi-historical vignettes. There is a story of the prophet Jonah recounted with some interesting twists; a tale of Maimonides; relatives who bravely faced the rack and the Grand-Inquisitor; a mapmaker to Columbus; early pioneers to Brazil; farmers, actors, and soldiers; poets, physicists, and lawyers; and a relative who befriends Father Bartolomeu Lourenço, the supposed inventor of the airship (the subject of Portugese novelist, José Saramago's modern masterwork *Memorial do convento* [1982: *Baltasar and Blimunda*]). All these Rafael Mendeses are part of the "nation," and most tried to maintain their ties to their religion even in the worst of times. Scliar's novel universalizes the Jewish-Brazilian experience.

❉ ❉ ❉

Within the Brazilian "Romance Novo" there exists a long procession of anti-heroes and heroines whose lives are chronicled by a wide range of writing styles. One notable exception to the anguished and selfless heroes who populate these Brazilian works is Guedali Tartakovsky. Guedali Tartakovsky is a character whose life is full and joyous. He is one of the many original characters who narratively comprise Scliar's "mundo mágico," magical world. The following chapter will highlight *O centauro no jardim* (1980; *The Centaur in the Garden*), exploring the literary and social consequences of spiritual affirmation, ethnicity, and the work's inverted mythic structure. The novel underscores life's simple pleasures: friends, traditions, and family. Guedali Tartakovsky imagines himself to be a centaur in a world of men and women, always an outsider, a sensuously magical being having to disguise his true identity.

Earlier works, *O carnaval dos animais* (1968; *The Carnival of the Animals*) and *A guerra no Bom Fim* (1972; *The War in Bom Fim*) are other fine examples of Scliar's use of fantasy, magical realism, and poignant recollection. Bom Fim is a traditional Jewish neighborhood in Porto Alegre and has the flavor and feel of Saul Bellow's Napoleon Street in Montreal, or the "Barrio Once" in Argentine fiction. Moacyr Scliar's books are permeated with a strong sense of "mentshlekhkayt," a Yiddish term that roughly translates as an obligation for humanistic compassion, ultimately stressing the mutual interdependence of God and man. While employing many of the current technical innovations of post-modern anti-realist fiction, Scliar's writings thematically proffer a joyous and magical reality that is rooted in the values and traditions, myths and mysticisms of the Jewish people.

The writings of Moacyr Scliar, Carlos Heitor Cony, and Samuel Rawet are representative works of the literary production of Brazil's Jewish community. While Scliar's fiction is drawing a great deal of international attention with conferences at major foreign universities, the work of Clarice Lispector, until the publication of her final novel, showed little sign of her ethnic and religious heritage. Sociologically, the nationalism of the Brazilian experience placed great value on the assimilationist aspect of its culture. The Judeo-Brazilian experience had been—until the present age—an unlikely literary subject within the dominant Catholic culture. However, Lispector's *A hora da estrela* (1977; *The Hour of the Star*) reflects upon the author's use of Biblical and historical themes from the heritage of her youth.

While the fiction of Moacyr Scliar, like that of American author Cynthia Ozick, strongly expresses both traditional and mystical Jewish elements, Lispector's utilization of Jewish motifs or even a recognition of her Jewishness is less evident. The author has almost always been described as of Ukranian or Russian descent, when in fact her parents were impoverished Jewish immigrants to the northern Brazilian city of Recife. *A hora da estrela* will be analyzed in a later chapter dealing with narrative technique in the Brazilian contemporary novel.

Ethnic groups within Brazil itself are well represented as characters within the broad spectrum of the narrative. Like Isaac Goldemberg in Peru, Mordecai Richler in Canada, Guiseppe Abiuso in Australia, and Syria Poletti in Argentina, the members of Brazil's Italian, Japanese, Arabic speaking, and Jewish communities have not focused on the subject of ethnic subcultures to the extent that one would have expected in one of the world's most prominent multiethnic countries.

In the United States mentioning the term Jewish-American writer can call to mind a wide circle of critically acclaimed authors, while in Brazil one has difficulty finding but a handful. Fortunately, two of these novelists have produced a body of literature that is of high literary quality. One of the best examples of those works is Moacyr Scliar's *O centauro no jardim* which will be the subject of the following analysis.

Moacyr Scliar's
O *centauro no jardim*:
Ethnicity, Affirmation,
and a Unique
Mythic Perspective

*We know that every good idea and all creative
work is the offspring of the imagination, and
has its source in what one is pleased to term
infantile phantasy. . . .*

Carl Gustav Jung

*And inside—something, something, happi-
ness . . . I am pretty well satisfied to be, to be
just as it is willed, and for as long as I may
remain in occupancy. (Moses Herzog)*

Saul Bellow

Moacyr Scliar's and, to a lesser extent, Samuel Rawet's and Carlos
Heitor Cony's narratives are generally cited to exemplify "ethnic fiction" and "Jewish writing" in present day Brazil.[1] To date Moacyr
Scliar has produced an impressive body of prize winning novels and
short stories. He has long been an influential and innovative literary
force within his home country. His works express a rare poetic imagi-

nation fused with a wry sense of the ironic. While it is undeniably true that Scliar's writings reflect strongly upon his cultural heritage, it is hoped that this present study will reveal also that his narratives are deserving of increased international attention for reasons other than their exploration of ethnic themes.

I

Brazilian critics seem to be in unanimous agreement that Scliar's *O centauro no jardim* is one of the major works of the present period. Bella Jozef observes: "O novo romance de Moacyr Scliar mostra seu domínio na arte de narrar. Denso e complexo, possibilita ao leitor vários níveis de captação."[2] (Moacyr Scliar's new novel is proof of his domination of the narrator's art. Dense and complex, it affords the reader many levels of hidden meaning.) Finally, Cora Rónai, writing in the *Folha de São Paulo*, sums up the universality of the work's scope by stating, "Pode ser que, no fundo, todos nós, judeus ou não judeus, sejamos centauros, sacrificando as nossas peculiaridades e as nossas características individuais para sermos aceitos por uma sociedade onde não há pecado maior do que a originalidade."[3] ("It could be that, in the final analysis, all of us, Jews and non-Jews, are centaurs, sacrificing our own peculiarities and our own individuality in order to be accepted by a society where there is no greater sin than originality.")

Moacyr Scliar forms part of a group of modern writers who have combined a scientific education with a successful literary career. Among those immediately coming to mind are Portugal's Antônio Lobo Antunes, author of *Os cus de Judas* (*South of Nowhere*); Spain's Luís Martín-Santos, author of *Tiempo de silencio* (*A Time of Silence*); England's Oliver Sacks, the writer of *Awakenings*; Chile's Nicanor Parra, creator of the anti-poem; Argentina's Ernesto Sábato, author of *Sobre héroes y tumbas* (*Of Heroes and Tombs*); and Italy's Primo Levi, author of *Il sistema périodico* (*The Periodic Table*).

Scliar, who was trained as a physician, constructs a beautifully conceived myth, that of a surgeon capable of using his scientific knowledge and magical abilities to give human form to mythological beings. Within this same narrative is an insightful psychological analysis that is continually overlaid upon the narrator's personal myth. Scliar's central consciousness, Guedali Tartakovsky, tells of his life, giving it form and structure, from the seemingly aberrant perspective of a centaur living in a world of men. The dramatic tension of this work is rooted in the fact that the reality-fantasy polarity is so skillfully manipulated. Within the fabric of Guedali's myth the reader is able to gain insight concerning the psychological truths that lie just beyond the narration. The reader becomes an active participant in this psychic drama, an integral part of the structuring of the novel without whom Scliar's work would read as just another tale of "magical realism."

In *Mythology in the Modern Novel* John J. White observes that within this present mythological age of literature "myth can assume as many shapes as Proteus himself." He examines "various patterns of correspondences that contemporary novelists have chosen to establish between their subjects and classical prefigurations."[4] *O centauro no jardim* radically departs from the "mythical method" so popular in modern fiction. The innovative structuring principle of this text resides in the fact that instead of the author, Scliar, superimposing a mythic framework upon his plot or vice versa, he creates a narrator who mythologizes the events of his life. He confronts life by fictionalizing it, by escaping into the realm of his own myth. His is a constant battle with reality. "Talvez seja o caso de deixá-lo partir, de aceitar esta realidade que eles querem me impor: que sou um ser humano, que não existem os seres mitológicos que marcaram minha vida, nem os centauros, nem o cavalo alado." ("Maybe it would be better to let him go, to accept this reality they want to impose on me: that I am a human being, that the mythological creatures that so marked my life don't exist, neither centaurs, nor sphinxes, nor winged horses.")[5] Coincidently, the centaur is also a favored symbol in Primo Levi's vision of man.[6] Levi's works, like Scliar's, illustrate this essential duality inherent in the human condition. "Man is a centaur, a tangle of flesh and mind, divine inspiration and dust."[7]

The most fully articulated configuration of the centaur in classical mythology is the myth of Chiron. Chiron was the wise and noble hero who taught medicine to the Greek heroes. Asclepius, his prize pupil, was the god of medicine and healing. He became the physician to the Argonauts and possessed the ability to restore life. While Scliar's novel accommodates this classical myth, he doesn't utilize its structure thematically as did John Updike in his 1963 novel, *The Centaur*.[8] Updike's intricate retelling of the Chiron myth differs greatly from Scliar's work in tone and structure. Updike uses this well known classical myth as a contemporary prefiguration for the story of a teacher's search for redemption, while Scliar accommodates only its vague out-lines. Both works are artfully conceived and point to the pervasive and multifaceted uses of myth as a narrative framework in the modern novel.

II

O centauro no jardim is framed by a divided version of the same scene: that of a celebration in a São Paulo restaurant, the Jardim das Delícias (The Garden of Delights). The narration begins forcefully by creating an air of mystery and incongruity. "Agora é sem galope. Agora está tudo bem. Somos, agora, iguais a todos. Já não chamamos a atenção de ninguém" (p. 10). ("Now there's no more galloping. Now everything's all right. Now we're just like everybody else; we no longer attract any attention at all" [p. 1].) During this arresting introduction it is learned that Guedali and his wife Tita are out with their children and a group of friends. It is a seemingly happy occasion except for the references that Guedali makes to his troubled dreams. "São os meus sonhos que é preciso corrigir. É o meu cavalo que preciso pegar e despojar de todos os esquisitos apêndices. Ou então eliminá-lo com-pletamente dos sonhos. Há soníferos fabricados especialmente para este fim" (pp. 12–13). (My dreams are the ones I need to correct. It is my horse I must catch and dispossess of all its strange appendages. Or else eliminate it entirely from my dreams. There are sleeping pills pro-duced specifically for this" [p. 4].) The novel's various flashbacks are set in motion by Guedali's musings. "Melhor ficar calado. Melhor ra-biscar: *agora está tudo bem.* Apesar das letras grotescas, apesar do longínquo ruflar de asas. Apesar das cenas que agora me vêm à me-mória" (p. 15). ("It's better to stay quiet. Better to scribble, Now ev-erything is all right. In spite of the grotesque handwriting, in spite of the rustling of wings. In spite of the scenes that I am now remember-ing" [p. 6].) What we read throughout the novel is the intra-narrative account of the birth and life of a centaur recounted by the centaur himself. "É minha mãe quem grita: está dando à luz. Ajudam-na as duas filhas e uma velha parteira das redondezas" (p. 18). ("It's my mother who is screaming; she is having a baby. Her two daughters and an old midwife from the vicinity attend her" [p. 8].)

Scliar's novel is rich in background ambience as it portrays the daily lives of a small group of Jewish immigrants fleeing the pogroms to settle in Rio Grande do Sul. Their lives are the realization of Baron

Hirsh's life long dream of a rural religious community. Baron Hirsh is revered by these settlers and his portrait is always displayed in a place of prominence. It is carried from city to city like a mystical icon.[9] "O Barão não nos trouxe da Europa para nada. Ele quer que a gente fique aqui, trabalhando a terra, plantando e colhendo, mostrando aos 'góim' que os judeus são iguais a todos os outros povos" (p. 19). ("The Baron didn't bring us here from Europe for nothing. He wants us to stay here, working the land, planting and harvesting, showing the goyim that Jews are just like everybody else" [p. 8].)

The work richly portrays the strong sense of tradition, religion, and loyalty that binds these families. This ambience is sensitively presented, including the reluctant "mohel" who performs the youth's circumcision, the bar-mitzvah "aqui em casa. Só para a família" (p. 60) ("right here at home. Just for the family." [p. 46]), and the pain of an isolated boyhood spent among books and telescopes. This masterfully drawn Chagalesque montage forms the backdrop for Scliar's fable. In this aspect of the novel, Scliar is the consummate storyteller in the tradition of Isaac Babel and Sholom Aleichem. Because Guedali has experienced a lack of acceptance by others, he retreats into a solipsistic realm of his own making, taking refuge in literature and science. Scliar has created a character who lives within an extended metaphor, that of the centaur, the outsider, the swift-footed mythological being, an emblematic representation of the dream world of this handicapped child.

Guedali's emotional suffering is underscored in various episodes, for example, the incident in which his older sister Débora asks him to remain hidden so she can invite her present boyfriend to dinner. "Ele nem sabe de ti, não tive coragem de contar. Acrescentou que ainda não o trouxera à nossa casa justamente por minha causa, não queria pedir que eu me escondesse, para não me ofender" (p. 62). ("'He doesn't know about you, and I didn't have the courage to tell him.' She added that she hadn't brought him to our house yet precisely on account of me; she didn't want to offend me by asking me to hide myself" [p. 48].)

One of the keys to this artfully conceived narrative is that Scliar has created an open-ended allegory that is simultaneously interpretable on several different levels. From within Guedali's myth, Scliar's narration is able to explore the emotional reality surrounding the life of this special child. He creates a character whose being is set apart from the rest of society. As a centaur and a Jewish Brazilian, Guedali Tartakovsky feels himself to be an outsider who is never sure of the reactions of others. "Os anti-semitas bem poderiam ver no ocorrido uma prova da ligação dos judeus com o Maligno. Meu pai sabe que por muito menos seus antepassados torraram nas fogueiras . . ." (p. 27). ("The anti-Semites could very well use what had happened as proof of the Jew's connection with the Evil One. My father knew that for much less than this, his ancestors were roasted in ovens . . ." [p. 16].)

The work's structural artistry is based on the dialectical interplay between Guedali's perception of reality and the prosaic reality of others. Guedali views life as a continual search for the "cavalo alado" (winged horse) who exists just out of his reach. In this regard, his search can be symbolically viewed as an attempt to break the bonds of his earthly being, both physically and spiritually. Many times he senses the "ruflar de asas" (ruffling of wings) of the "cavalo alado" but only at the work's end does he achieve a sense of communion with the fabled winged horse.

While the young centaur is raised in an environment of love and caring, his family constantly seeks to isolate him. "Mas o carinho da família atua como um bálsamo; as feridas cicatrizam, as partes dispersas se unem, o sofrimento adquire um sentido" (p. 36). ("But my family's love acts as a balm; the wounds heal, the disparate parts unify, the suffering acquires a meaning" [p. 25].) He decides to leave home, seeking refuge in a small traveling circus, a place of magic and illusion. Within this ambience, not unlike that depicted in Lima Barreto's film *Bye Bye Brazil*, Guedali becomes the star attraction. After a disastrous love affair he returns to the family farm. Later he meets and marries another centaur whose past is as painful as his own. The couple hears stories of a surgeon who may be able to give them human form so that they will be outsiders no longer. Their hopes lie in the ability of "um cirurgião marroquino que fazia maravilhas" (p. 96). ("a Moroccan surgeon who performed miraculous operations" [p. 80].) The magical surgeon is the modern day embodiment of Asclepius and Chiron. "E as botas, naturalmente, que teríamos de usar muito tempo, talvez para sempre. . . . Nunca mais teríamos de ficar ocultos, nem no porão de um navio, nem em qualquer outra parte. Nunca mais galoparíamos" (p. 110). ("And naturally our boots, which we would have to wear for a long time, perhaps forever. . . . Never again would we need to be transported in trucks or wagons. Never again would we have to stay out of sight, in the hold of a ship or anywhere else. Never again would we gallop" [pp. 92–93].)

After the operation the pair returns to Brazil to begin a new life. Guedali's business flourishes and they are surrounded by a group of close friends. With their friends they plan for and construct a type of utopian urban commune called "Condomínio horizontal," the realization of Baron Hirsh's dream applied to a more contemporary setting. "Todo mundo começou a falar ao mesmo tempo: é um *kibutz*, gritava Bela, um verdadeiro *kibutz*! Uma colônia de férias, dizia Tânia" (p. 152). ("Everybody began to talk at the same time: It's a kibbutz, a real kibbutz! shouted Bela. A vacation colony, Tania said" [p. 132].) The couple's life progresses normally until the night of June 6, 1977, when Guedali believes that Tita is unfaithful with a youthful centaur. This impels him to return to the Moroccan surgeon. The surgeon has now fallen on hard times, and his clinic is in disrepair. Guedali's request is totally unexpected. "—O senhor ouviu, Doutor. Quero me tornar centauro de novo" (p. 182). ("'You heard me, Doctor. I want to become a centaur once again'" [p. 159].) Guedali does not go through with the operation, and he returns to the family's farm in Quatro Irmãos. "Era feliz o menino-centauro Guedali? Mais feliz que o Guedali bípede, ou menos feliz?" (p. 205). (Had Guedali the centaur boy been happy? Happier than the biped Guedali, or less happy?" [p. 180].) He returns to farming the land with the help of Peri, a hired hand, a type of shamanistic presence.

Within the tranquility of his boyhood home, Guedali attempts to come to grips with his life. In the following soliloquy he reflects upon his existence.

> Que diabos, onde estava o centauro em mim? . . .
> Por que não engolia meu orgulho, então? Por que não voltava para Tita, para meus filhos, para meus amigos?
> Não. Isso não faria. Não sem antes ter esclarecido as dúvidas que me atormentavam. Não sem antes descobrir quem eu era: um centauro aleijado, privado de suas patas? Um ser humano tentando libertar-se de suas fantasias? (Pp. 212–13)

> (Dammit, where was the centaur in me? . . .
> Why didn't I swallow my pride, then? Why didn't I go back to Tita, to my children, my friends?
> No. That I wouldn't do. Not without first clarifying the doubts that tormented me. Not without first finding out who I was: a crippled centaur, deprived of its equine body? A human being trying to liberate himself from his fantasies?) (Pp. 187–88)

As he confronts his dualist nature, the reader expects that Guedali will now reject his fantasy life. One anticipates an illuminating moment of Joycean epiphany in which mythic reality dissolves into objective reality. However, Moacyr Scliar, the eternal ironist, saves his literary creation from prosaic existence. The final frame of the novel is entered with Guedali on his thirty-eighth birthday, happy among friends and family and more sure than ever that he is truly a mythological being who has taken human form.

Scliar's narrative succeeds in organizing a private world in a manner that transcends immediate physical and psychological perception. The mysticism inherent in this work may not be doctrinally Cabalistic, but it does allude to the universe as the ultimate unreality. Both Tita and Guedali are familiar with the *Zohar*, the book that has formed the mystical undercurrent of Jewish life since the thirteenth century. "Guedali não sabe que Tita lê o *Zohar*, o texto misterioso a que os cabalistas recorrem em busca de respostas para as incógnitas do universo. Isto é: Tita pensa que Guedali não sabe que ela lê o *Zohar*; há segredos entre os dois" (p. 226). ("Guedali doesn't know that Tita reads the Zohar, the mystic text that the Jewish Cabalists examined in search of answers for the unknowable things of the universe. That is: Tita thinks that Guedali doesn't know she reads the Zohar; there are secrets between them" [p. 199].)

III

This mythological fantasy is replete with Freudian and Jungian overtones. The reader comes to realize that the events of Guedali Tartakovsky's life are those of the struggles of all men; however, his means of facing them are uniquely Freudian. From within the narrative itself Guedali alludes to Freud's teachings. "Li Freud. Ficou patente para mim a existência do inconsciente, dos mecanismos de defesa, dos conflitos emocionais. A divisão da personalidade, eu a compreendi bem. Mas, e patas? E cauda? Onde é que entravam?" (p. 57). ("I read Freud. The existence of the unconscious, the defense mechanisms, the conflict of emotions, became patently clear to me. I understand perfectly the division of the personality. But what about hooves? And a tail? Where did they come in?" [p. 43].)

In Freud's lecture entitled "The Paths of Symptom-Formation," he deals with the fantasy-reality polarity in the treatment of psychogenic symptoms. Freud relates "the origin and meaning of that mental activity called 'phantasy-making.' In general, as you know, it enjoys high esteem, although its place in mental life has not been clearly understood." [10] In a further discussion of the production of fantasies he observes, "In them is shown unmistakably the essence of imaginary happiness, the return of gratification to a condition in which it is independent of reality's sanction." [11] "In contrast to 'material' reality these phantasies possess 'psychical' reality, and we gradually come to understand that in the world of neurosis PSYCHICAL REALITY is the determining factor." [12] Finally, Freud makes reference to the role of fantasy in the creative process. "I should like to direct your attention for a moment to a side of phantasy-life of very general interest. There is, in fact, a path from phantasy back again to reality, and that is—art." [13]

In the writings of Anna Freud, *The Ego and Mechanisms of Defense*, 1937, she describes a syndrome which parallels that of Scliar's fictional creation. Among the ego defenses that Freud's daughter illustrates is "a falsification of what the person has actually experienced. He may deny the truth, either in fantasy or in word and act. . . . Denying the truth means simply pretending that something unpleasant is pleasant, and one often does this by means of fantasy." [14]

IV

In a very real sense, this novel's ending can be viewed as the culmination of Guedali's personal myth. While the final events of the work are never completely delineated in literal terms, there exists a symbolic interpretation that each reader must formulate concerning Guedali Tartakovsky's emotional response to the enigmatic young woman present at his birthday celebration. At the work's close, this beautiful woman is woven into his fantasies. "Antes mesmo que fale, antes que diga que esqueceu os documentos no carro, antes que me peça para acompanhá-la, já estou me levantando, já estou de pé. Antes mesmo que Tita, sorrindo e piscando o olho, me convide para ir para o hotel, já estou me levantando, já estou de pé" (p. 245). ("She opens her purse. Even before she speaks, before she says she left her credit cards in the car, before she asks me to come outside with her to get them, I am already getting up, I'm standing. Even before Tita, smiling and winking at me, can invite me to go back to our hotel room, I'm getting up, I'm standing" [p. 216].)

Symbolically, this purposefully unnamed woman becomes the synthesis of the various elements of Guedali's past. On her amulets is found the metaphorical fusion of Guedali's disparate religious, philosophical, and mythological tensions that have so divided his personality. In her presence Guedali will finally achieve his goals of finding, even being transformed into, the "cavalo alado" and of returning to the "seio de Abraão." Guedali will return to the "bosom of Abraham," to an Abraham-Abram who is revered as the founder of Judaism and as a symbol of devotion to God. "Ainda rindo, a moça inclina-se para apanhar a bolsa. Neste momento, a blusa entreaberta deixa ver um seio bem modelado, de contorno suave. E os colares, com mil penduricalhos: uma estrela-de-davi, indiozinhos; mais abaixo, já no desfiladeiro entre os seios, uma pequena esfinge em bronze; um cavalo alado, de asas abertas; o centauro" (p. 244–45). ("Still laughing, the girl leans over to get her purse. At that moment, her half-open blouse reveals a glimpse of her shapely breast. From her necklaces dangle myriad charms: a Star of David, little Indians. Farther down between her breasts, a small sphinx in bronze, a horse with outspread wings, and a centaur" [p. 216].) Guedali's flight of fantasy ends the narrative, but we must assume that he will go on believing himself to be a centaur in the Garden of Delights, which is how he has come to view life.

This reference to the "Jardim das Delícias" is a multi-faceted authorial suggestion alluding to both the "locus amoenus" of the holy Garden of Eden ("The Garden of Eden in some of the later mystical Jewish writings is the earthly counterpart of the heavenly Paradise")[15] and to Hieronymus Bosch's masterpiece, *The Garden of Earthly Delights*. Many art critics like Orienti and de Solier, following the lead of Wilhelm Fraenger, feel that Bosch was strongly influenced by the "underground learning" of his time. "On the evidence of his art, they regard Bosch as an adept, profoundly steeped in every hermetic discipline of the time from such comparatively accessible realms as astrology and the Tarot to the dangerously suspect lore of alchemy, Gnosticism, the Kabbala and other aspects of a reborn Jewish mysticism. . . ."[16]

There is a euphoric and mystical quality to the work's ending. Guedali has faced life's adversities and joys and now he is "prestes a alçar vôo, rumo à montanha do riso eterno, o seio de Abraão. Como um cavalo, na ponta dos cascos, pronto a galopar pelo pampa. Como um centauro no jardim, pronto a pular o muro, em busca da liberdade" (p. 245). ("About to take flight toward the mountains of eternal joy, the bosom of Abraham. Like a horse, hooves dancing, ready to gallop across the pampas. Like a centaur in the garden, ready to jump the wall in search of freedom" [p. 216].)

Moacyr Scliar's *O centauro no jardim* forms part of a process of self-discovery and self acceptance. It is a novel that ends in self-revelation. It is hoped that Scliar will continue to be appreciated and analyzed from a critical perspective that views him not solely as a Jewish-Brazilian writer, but rather, to paraphrase Philip Roth's complaint, a Brazilian writer who happens to be Jewish. In *O centauro no jardim*, Scliar dramatizes man's eternal yearnings, sufferings, and the inherent conflict born of his dualistic nature. For Scliar, the mystery of existence itself and the depth of feeling that resides in the mysticism of the life experience is central to his art.

O centauro no jardim is a highly structured novel which converges upon history, religion, and fantasy. What narratively appears to be a Chagalesque montage of illusion is, in point of fact, the private and poetic reality of a crippled youth who clings to his escapist fantasies well into manhood. The novel bristles with metaphors and ideas as Guedali's psychic projection of his being as a centaur in the garden of delights raises fantasy to the level of exuberant wisdom.

NOTES

The epigraph to this chapter is from Issac Bashevis Singer, *The Death of Methuselah* (New York: Farrar, Straus & Giroux, 1988), p. 131.

[1] Mark Shechner, "Jewish Writers," *The Harvard Guide to Contemporary American Writing*, ed. Daniel Hoffman (Cambridge: Belknap Press, 1979), p. 191.

[2] Arnold Wiznitzer, *Jews in Colonial Brazil* (Morningside Heights, NY: Columbia University Press, 1960), p. 4.

[3] Wiznitzer, p. vii.

[4] Much of this historical overview is based on information provided by the Latin American office of the Jewish American Institute for Human Relations' publication: José Isaacson and Santiago E. Kovadloff, *Comunidades judías de Latinoamérica* (Buenos Aires: Editorial Candelabro, 1970).

[5] See Maria Luiza Tucci Carneiro, *O anti-semitismo na era Vargas* (Rio de Janeiro: Brasiliene, 1988).

[6] Howard M. Sachar, *Diaspora: An Inquiry into the Contemporary Jewish World* (New York: Harper & Row, 1985), p.259.

[7] Sachar, p. 265.

[8] Sachar, p. 177.

[9] *Voices Within the Ark* (1980) which has the intention of "gathering together in one volume representative selections of the finest [Jewish] poetry since the turn of the century," the authors state. "No particular significant

Brazilian-Jewish poets appeared to have yet expressed themselves in Portuguese." See Howard Schwartz and Anthony Rudolf, *Voices Within the Ark* (New York: Avon, 1980), p. 847.

[10] Diana Katcher Bletter, "Rio de Janeiro," *The Jewish Traveler*, ed. Alan M. Tigay (Garden City, NY: Doubleday, 1987), p. 297.

[11] Francisco Dzialovsky, *O terceiro testamento* (Rio de Janeiro: Anima, 1987), p. 12.

Scliar Study

The first epigraph of this study is from Carl Gustav Jung, *Psychological Reflections*, ed. Jolande Jacobi (New York: Harper, 1961) p. 180.

The second epigraph is from Saul Bellow, *Herzog* (New York: Fawcett, 1965), p. 414.

[1] See Mark Shechner, "Jewish Writers," *Harvard Guide to Contemporary Writing*, ed. Daniel Hoffman (Cambridge: Belknap Press, 1979), pp. 191–239. Shechner's excellent introduction to this subject discusses the ambiguities that definitions engender.

[2] Bella Jozef is quoted from *O Globo*. The quote appears on the cover of L & PM Editores edition of *O centauro no jardim*, which will be cited fully in note five.

[3] Cora Rónai is quoted from the *Folha da São Paulo*, see also note five.

[4] John J. White, *Mythology in the Modern Novel* (Princeton: Princeton University Press, 1971), pp. 191–92.

[5] Moacyr Scliar, *O centauro no jardim* (Porto Alegre: L & PM Editores, 1983), p. 243. The English translation is from *The Centaur in the Garden*, trans. Margaret A. Neves (New York: Ballantine, 1984), p. 214. All subsequent citations will be taken from these editions and page numbers will be entered directly in the text.

[6] Primo Levi, *The Periodic Table*, trans. Raymond Rosenthal (New York: Schocken Books, 1984), p. 9. One of the other points of contact between Scliar and the writings of Primo Levi is that both authors reflect upon the disaccord that is brought about in the assimilation process. Levi states, "The Jewish people, after the dispersion, have lived this conflict for a long time and dolorously, and have drawn from it, side by side with its wisdom also its laughter" (p. 9).

[7] Levi, p. 9.

[8] John Updike, *The Centaur* (New York: Bantam, 1963).

[9] Aaron DiAntonio, "The Genesis and Demise of the Jewish Agricultural Movement," unpublished paper submitted for A–25, 3–26–85, Harvard College. "The Am Oylam (eternal people) movement . . . advocated emigration to the West and the establishment of socialistic, utopian, agricultural communes. . . . With dreams of becoming American farmers, these few thou-

sand idealists joined countless other Jews fleeing political persecution and economic disadvantanges in a mass exodus from Russia. . . . Later, the Jewish philanthropist Baron de Hirsh gave two million pounds sterling for the establishment of the Jewish Colonization Society and 2.4 million dollars for the Baron de Hirsh Fund which sponsored agricultural resettlement throughout the Americas."

[10] Sigmund Freud, *A General Introduction to Psychoanalysis*, trans. Joan Riviera (New York: Washington Square Press, 1968), p. 380.

[11] Ibid., p. 381.

[12] Ibid., p. 378.

[13] Ibid., p. 384.

[14] Anna Freud, *The Ego and the Mechanisms of Defense*, trans. Cecil Barnes (New York: The Hogarth Press, 1973), pp. 72–73.

[15] Maria Leach, *The Standard Dictionary of Folklore, Mythology and Legend* (New York: Funk & Wagnalls, 1972), p. 441.

[16] Peter S. Beagle, *The Garden of Earthly Delights* (New York: Rosebud Books, 1982), p. 26.

DYSTOPIAN
FICTION

In two novels of Ignácio de Loyola Brandão,
Zero (1974) and *Não verás país nenhum* (1982;
And Still the Earth), an avowedly absurdist portrayal of Brazilian dystopias is created in the tradition of Yevgeny Zamyatin's *We* (1924), Karel
Capek's *R.U.R.* (1921), George Orwell's *1984*
(1949), and Kurt Vonnegut's *Player Piano* (1954).
Loyola's dystopian novels evolve as a fictional
warning. His visionary writings are composed of
the same cautionary anti-utopian tones and futurist jargon as Anthony Burgess's *A Clockwork
Orange* (1962). Also, like Burgess, Loyola re-
flects upon the individual's relationship to the modern state. He creates
his own futurist slang, a high-tech "patios" in the manner of Burgess's
inventive Nadsat. Like Burgess, his futurist vision of São Paulo is
firmly rooted in the social, political, and environmental failing of the
present.

From within the international science fiction genre, Italy's Stefano Benni's *Terra* (1983) uses an inventively comic approach to comment upon the nature of contemporary society. During a protracted nuclear war, the earth's three political alliances search for a non-polluted home. They eventually discover Terra, a virginal planet that is actually the earth of an earlier era, and the voyagers evolve as Erich von Däniken's ancient astronauts. In much the same comic vein as Benni's work, and appearing at roughly the same time, Márcio Souza's *O ordem do dia, folhetim voador não identificado* (1983; *The Order of the Day, An Unidentified Flying Opus*) spoofs both the science fiction and espionage genres, making acrid comments concerning the state of politics and society in present day Brazil. Souza's broad focus includes CIA and KGB intrigues and bizarre bloodsucking aliens called the Chupa-chupa. There are unexplained cases of spontaneous combustion and as always large doses of Souza's own brand of biting political satire. In the chapter "Num cárcere privado, em algum lugar de Manaus" ("In a Private Cell, Somewhere in Manaus"), the satire and humor turn serious as Souza offhandedly links the methods used by the Brazilian torturers to their American instructors from Fort Bragg, who in turn had learned their lessons from the British. This is all done narratively in a very matter of fact tone, with the narration mirroring the torturer's methods.

René Wellek and Austin Warren have stated that "literature is no substitute for sociology or politics. It has its own justification and aim."[1] Fully bearing in mind this warning, Brazilian writers of the last two decades have tended to fuse the aesthetic experience with legitimate sociopolitical concerns. In response to a repressive government's attempt at sustaining itself, Brazilian novelists have centered upon the drama of innocent victims confronting graphically depicted torture. Ignácio de Loyola Brandão, along with writers like João Ubaldo Ribeiro, Ivan Ângelo, Moacyr Scliar, Márcio Souza, Roberto Drummond, and Antônio Callado, has worked at understanding and interpreting this aberrant human drama. As observed, in Brazil animal imagery and zoological metaphors are frequently used to translate this political horror into aesthetic terms.

The influence of the "conto do bicho" (the animal story), along with African animal stories like *Anasi Tales*, may well be the seminal inspiration for the Brazilian preference for this metaphorical analogy. Hélio Pólvora and Cyro de Mattos have observed that in Brazilian fiction "o bicho é uma presença marcante, umas vêzes intencional e outras acidental—mas sempre poderosa. . . ."[2] ("insects and animals are an important presence, sometimes intentional and other times accidental—but almost always powerfully employed. . . .") In this regard critic Charles I. Glicksberg affirms, "The zoological image . . . is frequently employed in modern literature as a means of symbolizing the degrading absurdity of human existence . . . (and) the total insignificance of the human species when considered biologically."[3]

Several novels serve as a type of epistemological collage of this grotesquely pervasive motif. João Ubaldo Ribeiro's 1971 classic, *Sargento Getúlio*, recounts the brutality and gratuitous violence of an ex-militiaman. The novel draws upon the zoological metaphor of the bull to equate the dominant presence of Getúlio with the spirit of the "sertão." In Ivan Ángelo's *A festa* (1975), the sexual blackmail scene of Cremilda de Tal portrays two corrupt policemen who are narratively equated to cockroaches. In Antônio Callado's *Bar Don Juan* (1972), a simian analogy is used to describe an overzealous police torturer. In Loyola Brandão's *Zero*, the characters of José Gonçalves and Carlos Lopes are equated to confused rodents overwhelmed by an inescapable labyrinth. To this same end, the instrument of torture itself, the "pau-de-arara," the parrot's perch, even serves as a title for France's Michel Rio's best selling novel, *Le perchoir de perroguet* (1983).

In *Hitler manda lembranças* (1984; *Hitler Sends His Regards*) Roberto Drummond evokes the emotional tenor of the times, directly incorporating it into the flow of his narrative. Drummond, like so many other writers, seems obsessed with analyzing the events of the "ditador de olhos azuis como miosótis"[4] (the dictator with blue eyes the color of forget-me-nots"). "O medo, a insegurança, a inútil revolta, o desespero, a tristeza, a angústia, e a sensação de que tudo ia durar a vida inteira. . . . Todas as resistências, armadas ou não, tinham sido liquidadas e seus líderes estavam mortos, banidos, exilados, cassados, presos ou emudecidos. A censura silenciava o Brasil."[5] ("The fear, the insecurity, the fruitless revolt, the despair and the feeling that everything was going to last an entire lifetime. . . . All the resistance, armed or otherwise, had been put down, and its leaders were dead, deported, exiled, quashed, imprisoned or silenced. Censorship silenced Brazil.") Critic Jack Zipes has highlighted the importance of the role that the sociopolitical present plays in the philosophical development of today's science fiction. "Perhaps it is endemic to academic criticism of science fiction to talk in abstractions. . . . Questions of rhetoric, semiotic codes, structure, motifs, and types take precedence over the historical context of the narrative and its sociopolitical implications."[6] Like Márcio Souza's writing, Loyola Brandão's novels also call into question the worth of the rational process itself.

While sociopolitical concerns are continually utilized as background, the parodistic aspect of Loyola's works allows violent and even humiliating political repression not to be internalized but externalized as farce. These satires even become self-directed, debunking the pretension of the novel itself to explain reality. His novel *Zero* embraces meaninglessness as a point of departure for political action. Harold L. Berger affirms, "Anti-utopian science fiction more than any other literary genre, reflects the monumental problems of our age. Its dystopias well reveal to posterity the crisis of confidence man now faces."[7] While Loyola shares with Márcio Souza an absurdist vision of the modern world, he stands out as one novelist who has continually attempted to explore the issue of technology's negative influence on Brazilian society. "Isto me vem à cabeça, ao ver estes velhos carros, talvez os últimos do grande sonho brasileiro. Logo depois do Notável Congestionamento, as fábricas foram fechadas e milhares de pessoas ficaram nas ruas." ("That's what came into my head looking at those old cars, maybe the last survivors from the time of the great Brazilian dream. After what was known as the Notable Congestion, the automobile factories closed down and thousands of the jobless poured into the streets.")[8]

Zero is a milestone in the history of the Brazilian novel. This iconoclastic narrative underscores the dislocation of time and space to such an extent that non-rational behavior becomes an accepted norm. The narrative voices within the novel swing wildly from playful badinage to strident preaching. Here the line between novelist, artist, journalist, and propagandist coalesces. *Zero* is filled with humorous non-sequitors, ambiguous happenings, and radical personality changes. It is the contention of this study that *Zero*'s importance is primarily historical, setting new directions and synthesizing various formal and narrative trends.

While the term absurdist novel can easily be applied to *Zero*, and the obvious parallels with post-existentialist and post-modern black humorists like John Barth, Thomas Pynchon, Joseph Heller, and Kurt Vonnegut, Jr., can be drawn, there exists one major difference. Loyola's chthonic vision of contemporary man and society is nihilistically and ontologically damning. *Zero*'s humor is not part of a psychic defense mechanism nor is it part of a cathartic process. It does not chronicle the romp-through-contemporary-hell motif of a Billy Pilgrim, Ignatius J. Reilly, Yossarian, or a Benny Profane. The novel evolves as pure "littérature engagée." The work underscores the philosophical matrix of many Brazilian novels of this period. Along with *A festa*, *Bar Don Juan*, and *Sargento Getúlio*, *Zero*'s scope reaches beyond individual concerns. What in the absurdist literature of North America is an individual and existential crisis is expressed in Brazilian fiction as a hortatory call for social and political change. With the publication of *Não verás país nenhum*, Loyola's writings expressed an aesthetic evolution that parallels a political movement towards liberalization. This progression will be the subject of the following comparative analysis of Loyola's evolving dystopian vision.

The Evolution of Ignácio de Loyola Brandão's Dystopian Fiction: *Zero* and *Não verás país nenhum* as Brazilian Cultural Fantasy

*Dia virá, brasileiros, em que a brisa do Brasil
soprará . . . para anunciar ao mundo, que, aqui,
fica o paraíso sobre a face da terra. . . .*

*(Brazilians, the day will come when a breeze
will evolve from Brazil to tell the world that
here can be found a true earthly paradise.)*

Roberto Drummond

*O país despedaçado, os brasileiros expulsos de
suas terras, as ávores esgotadas. . . .*

*(The country torn to pieces, Brazilians expelled
from their own territory, the trees are gone. . . .)*

Ignácio de Loyola Brandão

Ignácio de Loyola Brandão has long been an important literary
force within Brazil. His writings tender a highly individual vision of a

dystopian future—a corrupt tomorrow in which society is viewed as controlled and subjugated by misguided technological and governmental systems. Loyola's futurological fantasies form part of an evolving aesthetic which envisions both *Zero* (1974) and *Não verás país nenhum* (1981) as hortatorily apocalyptic. However, the latter novel expresses an aesthetic passage paralleling a political movement towards liberalization.

The coalescent nature of the Brazilian literary experience tends to imbue international influences and genres with a distinctly Brazilian character. The "expressionistic fantasies of science fiction"[1] are one case in point. André Carneiro, José J. Veiga, Rubem Fonseca, Márcio Souza, and Loyola Brandão are all authors who have formulated a corpus of science fiction writings from a strong Brazilian perspective. Writer-critic Darko Suvin expresses the link between historical reality and the art of today's prophet-writers. "Never was it so necessary as it is today to illuminate this history of ours, with its works and dreams, triumphs and servitudes. The formalized daydreams of science fiction can be claimed as a privileged 'pars pro toto' or vibration of this history."[2]

Zero and *Não verás país nenhum* form part of a novelistic process through which Loyola has attempted to work out a statement of belief in the human experience. He filters his vision of man's historical and ontological status through a projection of an anti-utopian future. The following study is an analysis of *Zero* and *Não verás país nenhum* from the primary perspective of Loyola's evolving dystopian vision of contemporary society and its decaying social and political institutions.

I

Loyola's *Zero* set new and innovative directions for the Brazilian absurdist novel. Having won numerous awards, it is an iconoclastic work that has been plagued with publishing and censorship problems from its very inception. Originally finished in 1969, it was not until 1974 that the work was finally published. Ironically, the book first came out in an Italian translation by the prestigious publishing house of Editora Feltrinelli. Elizabeth Lowe observes that the "prohibition of Ignácio de Loyola Brandão's *Zero* . . . brought the crisis of Brazilian literature to a head, stimulating heated debate and written polemics in all sectors of Brazilian society."[3] Commenting on the thematic rationale for the work's difficulties, Emir Rodríguez Monegal states that "*Zero* is overwhelming in its relentless description of how the police, the army and special repressive forces collaborate to torture, rape, castrate or kill anyone foolish enough to oppose them." [4]

Attempting to reduce this complex novel to the level of plot alone tends to diminish its many innovative conventions, tones, and attitudes. The black humor and anti-novelistic style of *Zero* articulate a pervasive cynicism regarding the modern world. Within this work the author views the incongruities of life as if they were commonplace occurrences.

> DETERMINAÇÕES SAGRADAS
> Ninguém poderá usar tipo mocassim. O calçado oficial terá amarrilhos e as cores permitidas são o marrom e o preto.
>
> (HOLY RESOLUTIONS
> Loafers will not be permitted. The official footwear will have laces and the permitted colors are brown and black.) [5]

Satire and burlesque in *Zero* function as the structural underpinnings of a reality where discordance is the norm and harmony the exception. Thematically, the novel's primary concern is the brutal interplay between victim and oppressor. In *Zero* this oppressor is a harshly absurd political system and its victim, the novel's central consciousness, José Gonçalves, another nominally symbolic Brazilian Everyman.

> José mata ratos num cinema poeira. É um homem comum. 28 anos, que come, dorme, mija, anda, corre, ri, chora, se diverte, se entristece, trepa, enxerga bem dos dois olhos, tem dor de cabeça de vez em quando, mas toma melhoral. . . . (P. 11)
>
> (José kills mice in a dingy movie theater. He's an ordinary guy, age 28, who eats, sleeps, pisses, walks, runs, laughs, cries, has fun, gets sad, screws, keeps both eyes open, has a headache every now and then but takes Anacin. . . .) (P. 1)

An absurdist scenario is established in which José is portrayed as a truly disenfranchised member of an unspecified nation of América-Latíndia. While the author sets the work in an imprecise future "amanhã" (p. 10) ("tomorrow" [p. iii]), he also contradictorily proclaims that *Zero* is a "romance pré-histórico" (p. 3) ("a prehistoric novel," only in Port. ed.) José's life is metaphorically chronicled as a grim joke with this homunculian figure working in a dilapidated movie theater exterminating rodents. The meaninglessness of José's existence is underscored by his own realization that he will be put out of work if he does his job well. In an accommodation of the Penelope motif, José scratches out and perpetuates his meager existence.

> José tem uma cota diária de ratos. Ele sabe que no dia em que tiver exterminado todos os bichos, perde o emprego. Um dia, não tinha mais ratos. José foi à Várzea, pagou 50 centavos a dois moleques, cada um trouxe três ratos. Assim, José continuou trabalhando. (P. 12)

> (José has a daily quota of mice. He knows that when he's exterminated all of them he'll lose his job. One day there weren't any more mice. So he paid two kids 50 cents apiece and they each brought him three mice. That's how José kept on working.) (P. 2)

One of the metaphors that Loyola draws upon to structure this novel is that of a rodent lost in a maze. "Um labirinto. Dentro, querendo sair" (pp. 235–36). ("A maze. José: inside, wanting to get out" [p. 257].) The work's epigrammatic poem by Portugal's Alexandre O'Neill entitled "O poema pouco original do medo" ("A Slightly Original Poem of Fear") reinforces this theme. "O medo vai ter tudo / quase tudo / e cada um por seu caminho / havemos todos de chegar / quase todos / a ratos / Sim /a ratos" (p. 8). (Fear's going to have everything / almost everything / and we will all / almost all / each by his own road / become mice / yes / mice [p. i].) Loyola then goes on to draw the reader's attention to the bestial nature of the human condition by creating a graphic equation laden with pressing irony:

$$\frac{Homem}{Animal} = \text{EQUAÇÃO DE EQUILÍBRIO (P. 171)}$$

$$\frac{Man}{Animal} = \text{EQUATION OF EQUILIBRIUM (P. 183)}$$

He then conceives another equation to convey the inconsequence of man's place in the modern world. This is accomplished by portraying José as a crippled anti-hero who physically and spiritually limps throughout the novel. His importance in cosmic terms is shown to be exponentially infinitesimal.

> A TERRA: pesa:..
> 6.000.000.000.000.000.000.000. de
> toneladas.
> JOSÉ: pesa 70 quilos ou quilogramas. (P. 12)

> (THE EARTH: weighs: ....
> 6,000,000,000,000,000,000,000
> tons
> JOSÉ: weighs 154 pounds) (P. 2)

141

Within *Zero* government is portrayed as at odds with technology and science. In various sections entitled "Adeus, Adeus" ("Bye-Bye"), Loyola scathingly details the reasons for the country's brain drain. "Aqui, o professor Marcondes Reis começou perdendo a cátedra, teve sua casa invadida duas vezes pela polícia, confiscaram todos os livros de sua biblioteca, ameaçaram seus filhos" (p. 41). ("Here Professor Reis first lost his lecturer's chair, and then his house was ransacked twice by the police, who confiscated all the books in his personal library and threatened his children" [p. 34].) Then to this passage Loyola ironically adds, "O presidente deu uma declaração: 'Quando a ciência subverte o homem e corrompe, é melhor ter um país sem ciência, atrasado'" (p. 41). ("The President made a declaration: 'When science subverts and corrupts, it's better to have a country without science, a little backward'" [p. 34].)

Thus, the entropic vision in Loyola's *Zero* is hastened to its final state by this government's anti-intellectual and anti-scientific bias. Within this environment *Zero* inquires into the dimensions of society's potential for self-destruction.

The novel is a veritable montage of communication: diagrams, newspaper clippings, slogans, popular songs, aphorism, etc. It is possible to consider the structure of the narrative as yet another labyrinth in which Loyola frames and reflects his thesis statement regarding the human condition. The narrative's focus is continually varied by commingling pseudo-historical references with prosaic observations. These fall under headings like "Pensamento do Dia" ("Thought for the Day"), "Visão" ("Vision"), and "Livre Associação" ("Free Association"). An example is "Perca um minuto na vida / e não perca a vida num minuto" ("It's better to lose a minute in life / than to lose your life in a minute"). Narratively, the fragmentation of chronology serves to blur the distinction between reality and illusion. At the same time, it mirrors the novel's thematic concerns. Reality is as fleeting and deceptive as the authorial presence within this work. Self-referential commentary within the intra-narrative situation at times countermands the truths of the main narrative, while at other times it simply takes the form of a droll aside. "*E aqui me despeço esperando ter a sua atenção nas próximas páginas. Espero tê-lo agradado. Recomende-me a sua família e a todos os seus*" (p. 21). ("*And here I take my leave, awaiting your attention in the following pages. I hope to have pleased you thus far. Greetings to you and yours*" [p. 13].)

II

Everywhere within this Latin American dystopia are signs of superficial consumerism. It is a spiritually exhausted society, replete with bureaucratic incompetence, urban terrorism, hunger, bigotry, and governmental repression. *Zero* evolves as an encyclopedic narrative that delineates the anti-aesthetic values of a culture that expresses itself in graffiti philosophy, commercial advertising wisdom, and pop theories. José and the rest of Latíndian society are drowning in superficiality. Knowledge is marketed and conveyed on Coca-Cola bottlecaps. "Na Coca-cola estão precisando de gente pra fazer as tampinhas" (p. 64). ("At Coca-Cola they need people to write bottlecaps" [p. 61].) Loyola, along with other artists as diverse as Roberto Drummond, film maker Gláuber Rocha, and Clarice Lispector, suggests the excessive influence of Brazil's multinational business community. "Coconut milk or Coca-Cola?" becomes the catch phrase to highlight this pervasive foreign influence.

Against the inane scenarios of Latíndian society is juxtaposed a futile attempt by Carlos Lopes to obtain help for his sick child. Again, Loyola depicts another vole astray in a societal maze:

> Não esquecemos Carlos Lopes.
> ? Lembra-se.
> O homem que levou seu filho ao Instituto. Aqui está ele de volta, mais sensacional que nunca. No último capítulo, o funcionário do Instituto tinha pedido uma lista de documentos e o Carlos Lopes foi providenciar. (P. 90)

> (Let's not forget Carlos Lopes.
> Remember him? The man who took his son to the clinic? Here he is back again, more sensational than ever. In the last chapter, the employee at the clinic told him to bring in all of his documents and Carlos went off to get them.) (P. 91)

Lopes is continually turned away from clinics by a tangle of bureaucratic regulations:

> . O pessoal de baixo anda louco, isso é caso para o 567.
> 765, não, sim 435, é mais em cima, desce, sobe para a direita. . . . (P. 91)

> (—The people downstairs are crazy, this case belongs at 567.
> 765, no it's 435, yeah, it's further on, go down, go up, turn to the right. . . .) (P. 92)

As his child dies in his arms, he is unable to help. This already plaintive scene turns even bleaker as Carlos is then sent to jail and tortured. The president of this country is acerbically depicted as a proto-typical and studied father figure who is more show business than substance. He sanctions torture and killing as he blesses his people in Pope-like fashion. "'Durma bem, minha boa gente.' A população fez o sinal-da-cruz, e agradeceu" (p. 190). ("'Sleep well, my good people.' The populace made the sign of the cross and thanked him" [p. 206].) He is well aware of the effect of publicity on the world community. Events are manipulated to maintain his regime. "Sequestremos nós os diplomatas. Depois, resistimos ao pedido de troca. Mais tarde, liber-tamos os diplomatas. Isso enfraquece a imagem dos Comuns, eles per-dem pontos" (p. 257). ("You'll kidnap a diplomat. My administration will refuse the demands, and then you'll set the diplomat free. This little scenario will make the Communs look bad, they'll lose points" [p. 283].)

III

One of the major themes of *Zero* is failed communication. Loyola's role as novelist is that of a semiologist for this atrophic society, inter-preting objects, signs, slogans, jokes, and graffiti. "HÁ SINAIS PARA VOCÊ" (p. 282). ("THERE ARE SIGNS FOR YOU TO READ" [p. 314].) True communication is nonexistent; it is all façade and sham. "*Há sinais*, por toda parte e ninguém percebe. Em tudo. Abra a vista, com largueza, para o presente" (pp. 28–29). ("*There are signs* all around and no one sees them. Signs and symbols everywhere. Open your eyes, wide, to the present" [p. 21].)

The eschatological drama of Carlos and José serves to underscore the harsh and indiscriminate brutality of this police state and its "se-cret war" against its own subjects. "Ternurinha era intransigente numa coisa: dava prazo para que o detido começasse a falar. Dali para a frente, aplicava os Métodos" (p. 261). ("But Ternurinha was intran-sigent about one thing: he set a time limit for the detainee to begin talking. After that, he applied the 'methods'" [p. 288].) The novel's vivid presentation of torture draws the reader directly into the scenes of human degradation. "Penduraram Átila no pau de arara. Envol-veram seus pulsos com panos e amarraram as mãos bem juntas uma da outra. Fizeram com que Átila se sentasse e passasse os braços em volta dos joelhos" (p. 262). ("They hung Átila on the 'perch': With cloth wrapped around his wrists and his hands bound together, they made him get in a sitting positon, his hands behind his knees" [p. 290].) The interplay between police interrogator and captive is described in terms of a methodical chess game. Loyola's novel, like Julio Cortázar's *Libro de Manuel* (1978; *A Manual for Manuel*), describes methodologies of torture in concise terms. What transpires in *Zero* is a litany of horrors with each "method" given a sadistically ironic name: "Churrasquinho" ("The Little Barbeque"), "Manicuragem" ("Manicure"), and "espanta cavalo" ("scare-the-horse"). Into these scenes of torture is inserted a brief chapter, "O Som e a Fúria" (p. 269–70) ("The Sound and the Fury" [p. 299–300]), composed entirely of advertising slogans promoting get-rich-quick schemes for private investors. Again, the reader is reminded of the failed vision of this society through its inverted use of communication. "Trabalhando para você: Fundo Biafra: Tradição secular de segurança: Fundo de Investimento e Participação / Suba na Vida / Subindo a Sobreloja da Av. XV, 67 com a Corretora ILLB/" (p. 270). ("Working for you: Biafra Finance Co. / a secular tradition in / Security / Investment / and Participation / Move up in life / Moving up to the 2nd floor shop at 67 Fifteenth Ave. / Corretora Brokers / Don't delay" [p. 300].)

In "Enganando o Mundo" (p. 266) ("Tricking the World" [p. 295]), society's hypocrisy is again exposed. Loyola, the mimetic author, refuses to allow anyone to escape guilt-free. "—Limpe as prisões. Esconda ou mate os presos. Arranje subversivos dispostos a colaborar, assinando declarações a nosso favor. Encha os hospitais com gente nossa e diga que são feridos pelos terroristas" (p. 266). ("—Clean up the prisons. Hide or kill the prisoners. Arrange for subversives willing to collaborate, have them sign declarations in our favor. Fill the hospitals with our people and say they were wounded by terrorists" [p. 295].) He then footnotes this passage with a piece of folk wisdom that places the onus of responsibility back on the reader. "(1) Alcides, meu amigo, diz: Só se engana o mundo, quando o mundo quer ser enganado" (p. 266). ("[1]My friend Alcides always used to say: you can only trick the world when the world wants to be tricked" [p. 295].) José wanders through the existential labyrinth of América-Latíndia awaiting its apocalyptic collapse. Everywhere are signs of a cultural and spiritual wasteland, a true vision of an age of Apocalypse.

IV

At the work's inception, Carlos and José are portrayed as pure victims. Unlike other novelists of the absurd, Loyola does not offer an analgesic for confronting the absurdities of the modern world, for *Zero* directly stresses a need for social and political change. "Pegaram todos, vão continuar a pegar até que possa descobrir um modo de lutar e organizar. E então, inverter" (p. 284). ("They got everyone, and they'll keep on getting everyone until we find a way to fight and organize. And turn things around" [p. 317].)

In *Zero* man and society are left to drift into total chaos. Loyola's entropic vision offers existentially a no-exit situation. His novel is not tendering humor as a spiritual defense mechanism. The work becomes a lament for a continent that he perceives as having lost its sense of reason. One of the book's enduring images highlights this point.

> ?MAS A CABEÇA
> ONDE ESTÁ A CABEÇA
> DA AMÉRICA
> QUE EU NÃO VEJO (P. 284)
>
> (BUT WHAT ABOUT THE HEAD?
> WHERE'S AMERICA'S HEAD?
> I DON'T SEE IT.) (P. 316)

To this thought is then added in the form of a warning sign, a strident political call to violence popular at the time.

> BURN, BABY BURN (P. 284) (P. 316 Eng.)

In *Zero* the narrative concatenation of all manner of futile, comic, and brutal episodes leads the reader to a recognition of man's zooidal and absurd nature. However, the novel's conclusion transcends absurdism, employing it only as a narrative technique. At the work's finale, it is a feeling of commitment to change that is durable in the reader's consciousness.

> &
> ouve-se uma prece
> desta gente audaz
> que não teme as guerras
> mas deseja a paz
> DEUS, SALVE A AMÉRICA (P. 285)

(&
hear the prayer
of this bold people
who don't fear war
but desire peace
GOD SAVE AMERICA) (P. 317)

The reader has been brought full circle from humorous empathy for a nebbish exterminator overwhelmed by his circumstances, to being challenged and threatened by this very same personage. José's metamorphosis has been completed. Through his association with the quasi-mythical, quasi-historical figure of Gê, he has been magically transformed into a self-confident and feared urban terrorist. Loyola postulates that while the rodent may not be able to escape the maze, he still possesses the potential to destroy it from within. José is now a threat to the very system that spawned and repressed him. Loyola's anti-hero has limped throughout the first half of the novel as a "Christ manqué" in his fruitless search for redemption. On a note of desperation, a call to arms and a prayer, the novel moves to its conclusion tendering an apocalyptic vision of an entire era of political repression.

V

The evolution of Loyola's narrative vision moves from a portrayal of a repressive dystopia in *Zero* to an even more menacing dystopian fantasy in *Não verás país nenhum*. In this latter novel, technology is viewed as having a greater negative impact upon society. Loyola attempts to persuade his readers of the importance of lessening government's hold on the individual and the environment. Like other science fiction writers, Loyola is reacting to a sociopolitical present as he conceives his futurological São Paulo. In *Não verás país nenhum* he even pays tribute to his literary contemporaries. "—Lembra-se quando líamos os livros de Clark, Asimov, Bradbury, Vogt, Vonnegut, Wul, Miller, Wyndham, Heinlein?" ("—Remember when we were all reading books by Clarke, Asimov, Bradbury, Van Vogt, Vonnegut, Wul, Miller, Wyndham, Heinlein?"[6]

There exist some interesting thematic parallels between Loyola's São Paulo and Robert Bloch's Chicago in *This Crowded Earth*.[7] Both novels portray insufferably overcrowded cities. In this fictive São Paulo all life is controlled by the civilian police, the "Civiltares." "São Paulo fechado, dividido em Distritos, permissões para circular, fichas magnetizadas para água, uma superpolícia como os Civiltares, comidas produzidas em laboratórios, a vida metodizada, racionalizada" (p. 100). ("São Paulo is a walled city, divided into districts with magnetic passes to get from one area to another, superpolice like the Civil Guard, food produced in laboratories—a thoroughly systematized, regulated, rationalized life" [p. 98].)

Politically, the government, "o Esquema," is as harsh as it is efficient. Loyola's São Paulo is ruled by a non-functioning leadership. It seems that the "system" now runs on inertia. "—Às vezes, duvido que exista gente por trás do Esquema. Esquema, Esquema, ouvimos falar. Há muito que o velho Caldeira está inválido, e continua como presidente" (p. 102). ("—Sometimes it's hard to believe there are actual people behind the System. The System, the System, that's all we hear. Old Caldeira's been an invalid for years, and still he's president" [p. 100].) The military and the technocrats have merged to keep the System operating. The Kafkaesque topos of the empty castle is effectively presented as an unfathomable "System" attempts to dehumanize society.

Events and perceptions are filtered through the novel's main character, Souza. As a former history professor, he attempts to recall the past; however, all memories are being technologically suppressed. The distinction between history and propaganda has become so blurred that Souza himself is never truly sure exactly who is controlling his life and what is left of Brazil. "Na universidade, muitas vezes, os alunos de ciências políticas queriam que eu destrinchasse a estrutura do poder. . . . Mas não adiantava, nos faltavam os elementos" (p. 219). ("Often the university students studying political science asked me to explain the structure of power. . . . But I couldn't help them— we lacked the basic information on which to build any theory" [pp. 230–31].)

After being dismissed from the university, Souza's days have become regimented. He is incapable of fully experiencing life, and his job is abhorrently meaningless. Loyola establishes an absurdist scenario in which the nation's propaganda ministry works at pacifying and manipulating the populace. The Amazon Region was totally deforested and has since turned into a vast desert. As a result, temperatures are rising, and the heat is oppressive. The book's mordant humor now portrays the Propaganda Ministry as having created a campaign to promote this ecological disaster area as the pride of Brazil, the ninth wonder of the world.

This use of burlesque to expose hypocrisy is presented through this seemingly complacent citizen, Souza. Loyola's work suggests that the reader, like Souza, needs to be shaken into a realization of the ecological and political failings of our age. In this cultural fantasy Souza's acceptance of the status quo fades in direct proportion to his will to question and act. "Mas ainda acredito em cada homem, em particular" (p. 158). ("But I still believe in the importance of the individual man" [p. 159].) His ontologic status is enhanced as he questions authority. Souza is now able to break free from the security of his past life. He and an old friend set out on a journey across the wasteland of São Paulo to discover what is left of Brazil.

Stylistically, the novel's use of symbolism is direct and forceful. One of the work's dominant symbols is the hole that slowly begins to appear in the center of Souza's hand. Pereira, his friend, suggests that the hole must have a prophetic purpose.[8] "—Tenho certeza que representa. E é mensagem" (p.103). ("'—But I'm sure it must represent something. It's got to be a message of some sort'" [p. 102].) Souza evolves as the messiah of anti-futurism. He is a throwback to an era when it rained, when food had taste, when children were allowed, and when government did not control all facets of society. The novel has an Orwellian impact that, like its precursor *Zero*, is created to critique an existing social system.

Souza's vatic presence views a society spinning toward total chaos. Entropy takes hold, and humanity is winding down toward annihilation. The root cause of much of this ecological and political difficulty is ironically attributed to the "Abertos Oitenta." Very much the ironist, Loyola leaves it up to the individual reader to fill in his or her interpretation of the ills of the "wide open eighties." "A aceleração histórica prejudicou tudo, a dinâmica se assumiu em sua concepção total, ou seja, contínua transformação, a cada instante, hora, dia. —Essa nova ordem tem um nome. Caos" (p. 169). ("The acceleration of history changed everything, the dynamics are totally different now, the dynamics are everything, total conception—or else transforming constantly, minute by minute. —This new order has a name. It's called chaos" [p. 173].)

The leitmotif of motion pervades the novel. Souza tells of a relative, Sebastião Bandeira, who attempted to develop a perpetual motion machine. Souza then saves and befriends a young woman who continually and inexplicably spins and enchants him. He discovers her name is Elisa, the Greek word for freedom. "—Bonito, sim! Vem do grego. Quer dizer libertada" (p. 274). ("—No, it's pretty.! It's from the Greek. It means 'free' " [p. 285].) The implication of this magically symbolic scene suggests that movement, action, and rebellion are all antidotes and analgesics to counteract and stave off the entropic process.

As his odyssey progresses, Souza and millions of other Brazilians are moving en masse to obtain miraculous silk umbrellas that are rumored to ward off the sun's killing rays. This is all part of a governmental scheme to relocate the populace under the "marquise extensa," a giant shelter. "A marquise" is promoted as a marvelous project conceived by the technocrats to save the nation. Ironically, technology's response to the threat to the earth is merely to create a colossal carport-like structure, shaped to spell BRASIL when viewed from the moon. One senses the overt lampooning of the Brazilian Transamazonian highway project with its attendant promotion and its tie to nationalistic feelings.[9]

Loyola's black humor is particularly biting in this passage. Governmental technology offers mankind salvation from certain annihilation by constructing a ridiculous concrete structure under which millions of Brazilians jostle for positions of survival. "A falação foi uma característica que os Esquemas souberam capitalizar, introduzindo na psicologia popular. Fizeram com que a falação se transformasse numa cortina de fumaça, encobrindo tudo que fosse possível" (p. 322). ("Rhetoric was a national trait the System knew how to capitalize on, with the invaluable help of popular psychology. They turned rhetoric into a vast and eminently exploitable smoke screen" [p.332].) While the concept is as absurd as it is nightmarish, it can also be viewed as an acerbic metaphor for present day society.

> O ESQUEMA ESTÁ ENTREGANDO AS MARQUISES, A GRANDE SOLUÇÃO PARA OS DIAS DE CALOR—NINGUÉM MAIS AO DESABRIGO—ESPLÊNDIDA REALIZÇÃO DO MINISTÉRIO SOCIAL. (P. 311)

> THE SYSTEM PROUDLY PRESENTS—THE MARQUEE—THE ULTIMATE SOLUTION TO THE HEAT WAVE—THE SHELTER FOR EVERYONE—ANOTHER SPLENDID ACHIEVEMENT FROM THE MINISTRY OF SOCIAL WELL-BEING. (P. 322)

The novel gives satirical form to the demythification of the sacrosanct totems of modern culture and the belief that technology will necessarily enhance man's future. While Loyola uses irony and burlesque to dramatize the work's serious intent, his absurdist posture is actually a means of exploring the existential abyss of contemporary reality. "Pegar um lugar longe da borda. Não é mais possível, as pessoas se atropelam, se empurram, gritam, dão rasteiras, esfaqueiam, entram em pânico. Ainda bem que não tem crianças, ia ser um massacre" (p. 331). ("I try to spot a place away from the edge. Impossible. People are pushing and shoving, climbing on top of each other, clawing wildly in utter panic. It's a good thing there aren't any children, they'd be trampled for sure" [p. 343].) "Estamos vivos. . . . Agora, trata-se de saber quem resistirá menos. Nós, ou a laje?" (p. 328). ("We're alive. . . . Now it's just a matter of wondering who will last longer, us or this silly roof" [p. 340].)

VI

After the publication of *Zero*, Loyola's aesthetic vision no longer ascribed to the somewhat prepackaged wasteland outlook. Unlike many contemporary novelists who utilize apocalyptic visions of our age in a programmatic fashion, Loyola accommodates this somewhat clichéd convention. He now employs his vision of dystopia as background to develop his hortatory thesis statement. "Qualquer mudança tem de começar necessariamente dentro do homem. Para depois atingir o todo. A modificação externa, a alteração da sociedade, vem da transformação interior" (p. 295). ("Any real change necessarily begins inside us, and only later affects the whole. External modification, the alteration of society, is a result of interior transformation" [pp. 306–07].) He postulates that like Souza, all men must awaken from the depths of conformity to question all aspects of their existence. "Quantas chances o homem tem na sua vida?" (p. 240). ("How many chances does a man get in his life?" [p. 250].) The novel particularizes the importance of human relationships and personal freedom.

Technically, Loyola's use of the symbols of vegetation (the bush, the tree) can be viewed as one of the structuring principles of the work. Trees and vegetation have played an important role throughout the work, and in the concluding phase a small piece of vegetation emerges as a key symbol. The tree and bush are utilized as hierophany by Loyola. Mircea Eliade defines the religious mystery of hierophany as, "The manifestation of the sacred in some ordinary object, a stone or a tree."[10] Also, in this context Alfred Métraux chronicles the various folkloric traditions which "for many people of the world the tree is symbolic of immortality."[11]

At the bleakest point in the narrative, when Souza and millions like him are huddled under the giant slab, the novel holds out a sign as hierophany. A small piece of vegetation has returned to the heat scorched wasteland. "Contemplo o ramo. Nesta planície agreste, ele cresce, indiferente. Alheio à sua própria impossibilidade de crescer. Afirma-se, envolvido em sua negação. Como resiste, sem água, sob o sol que corrói até mesmo carne e ossos?" (p. 329). ("I stare at the plant. It's true, it's alive, it's growing, indifferent to the arid sand stretching to infinity. Alien to its own impossibility. Surrounded by negation, it asserts itself. How can it hold out, without a drop of water, against a sun powerful enough to consume flesh and bones?" [p. 342].) The existence of this plant offers hope. Souza is overwhelmed by the miracle of the presence of this simple plant. He equates it with man's will to survive and triumph. "Me ocorreu que isto é a liberdade. A capacidade de ressurgir continuamente, sob novas formas, revigorado. O processo de se recompor, tombar e erguer, nada mais é que tática, dissimulação. Um jeito de enganar a morte, derrotá-la. Que a morte é simples estágio superável" (p. 330). ("It occurs to me that's what freedom is—the capacity to revive continually in new forms, reinvigorated. The process of renewal, of hitting the bottom and coming back up again, is a tactic, a way of tricking death. Death, which is a simple, surmountable stage" [p. 342].)

VII

The evolution of Loyola's aesthetic vision moves from the creation of a novel of social commitment in *Zero* to a more complex work of an absurdist, yet deeply human nature. The novelist's aesthetic vision has evolved from a strident call for social change to an underscoring of the indomitable nature of the human spirit. Ignácio de Loyola Brandão has now individualized his social concerns, postulating that societal change must be born within each man and woman. "Mesmo a caminho do inferno há uma possibilidade de salvação, um atalho que termina te levando ao céu. . . . —Ponha na cabeça que não pode morrer. A vida está aí, é importante, uma só, inteira pela frente" (p. 283). ("Even on the road to hell there's a chance for salvation, a shortcut to heaven. . . . —Get it through your head that you can't die. Life is here in front of you, it's important, you only get one shot at it" [pp. 295–96].) *Não verás país nenhum* is an excellent example of Brazilian speculative literature, possessing an important Orwellian impact with regard to its environmental, sociopolitical, and ecological warnings. In creating a fictional world set within a dystopian future, Loyola has been able to elevate what are authentically national and Brazilian concerns to a universal level.

NOTES

[1] René Wellek and Austin Warren, *Theory of Literature* (New York: Harcourt, Brace and World, 1956), p. 103.

[2] Cyro de Mattos and Hélio Pólvora, *Antologia de contos brasileiros de bichos* (Rio de Janeiro: Block Editores, 1970), p. 9.

[3] Charles I. Glicksberg, *The Tragic Vision in Twentieth-Century Literature* (Carbondale: Southern Illinois University Press, 1962), p. 160.

[4] Roberto Drummond, *Hitler manda lembranças* (Rio de Janeiro: Nova Fronteira, 1984), p. 56.

[5] Drummond, p. 56.

[6] Jack Zipes, "Mass Degradation of Humanity and Massive Contradictions in Bradbury's Vision of America in *Fahrenheit 451*," *No Place Else*, ed. Eric Rabkin (Edwardsville and Carbondale, IL: Southern Illinois University Press, 1983), p. 182.

[7] Harold L. Berger, *Science Fiction and the New Dark Age* (Bowling Green, Ohio: Popular Press, 1976), p. 201.

[8] Ignácio de Loyola Brandão, *Não verás país nenhum* (São Paulo: Global Editora, 1985), p. 100. The English edition is *And Still the Earth*, trans. Ellen Watson (New York: Avon Books, 1982), p. 98–99.

Loyola Study

The first epigraph of this study is from Roberto Drummond, *Sangue de Coca-Cola* (Rio de Janeiro: Editora Nova Fronteira, 1981), p. 16.

The second epigraph of this study is from Ignácio de Loyola Brandão, *Não verás país nenhum* (São Paulo: Global Editora, 1985), p. 72. The English translation is *And Still the Earth*, trans. Ellen Watson (New York: Avon, 1982), p. 70.

[1] David William Foster, "Major Figures in the Brazilian Short Story," *The Latin American Short Story*, ed. Margaret Sayers Peden (Boston: G. K. Hall, 1983), p. 30.

[2] Darko Suvin, *Metamorphoses of Science Fiction* (New Haven: Yale University Press, 1979), p. XV.

[3] Elizabeth Lowe, *The City in Brazilian Literature* (Rutherford, NJ: Fairleigh Dickinson University Press, 1982), p. 116.

[4] Emir Rodríguez Monegal, *World Literature Today* 53, no. 1 (1979): 20.

[5] Ignácio de Loyola Brandão, *Zero* (Rio de Janeiro: Editora Codecri, 1982), p. 86. The translation is taken from *Zero*, trans. Ellen Watson (New York: Avon, 1983), p. 86. Further quotes will be from these editions and will be entered directly into the text.

[6] Loyola Brandão, *Não verás país nenhum*, p. 98–99. Watson, *And Still the Earth*, p. 98–99. Further citations will be from these editions and entered into the text.

[7] Robert Bloch, *This Crowded Earth* (New York: Ballantine, 1968).

[8] Contemporary academic criticism following the scholarship of Theodore Ziolkowski, *Fictional Transfigurations of Jesus* (Princeton, NJ: Princeton University Press, 1972) could well view the character of Souza as a fictional transfiguration of certain aspects of the life of Christ. Religious symbology abounds. "Cristã sou eu. A última cristã num mundo fodido" (p. 282). ("I'm a Christian. The last Christian in a fucked-up world.")

[9] See Francis Lambert, "Latin America since Independence," *The Cambridge Encyclopedia of Latin America*, ed. Simon Colleir (Cambridge: Cambridge University Press, 1985), p. 275.

[10] Mircea Eliade is quoted from *Seven Contemporary Short Novels*, eds. Charles Clerc and Louis Leiter (Dallas: Scott, Foresman, 1975), p. 707.

[11] Alfred Métraux, *The Standard Dictionary of Folklore, Mythology and Legend*, ed. Maria Leach (New York: Funk & Wagnalls, 1972), p. 1123.

NARRATIVE
STRATEGIES

The paradoxical nature of contemporary reality is the subject of much of modern Brazilian fiction, be it called anti-fiction, surfiction, postmodernist, postrealist, or metafiction. This writing evolves from an assumption that the author's role as moralist is no longer valid. Thus, Márcio Souza, in debunking the foibles of a self-serving sociopolitical system that allows an incompetent adventurer to rise to power as the Emperor of Acre, makes no judgmental commentary from within his narratives. Souza's work is suffused with a facetious and gamesome sense of the authorial irony. In a matter-of-fact narrative posture, Souza creates Galvez's comic empire, juxtaposing it to the poverty and illiteracy of its subjects. It is then left for each reader to draw his or her conclusions and analogies. That which some readers view as a thinly veiled parody of the existing military dictatorship others interpret as a scathing burlesque of the inept and self-serving nature of this same government.

As critic Philip Stevik observes regarding contemporary literature, "authorial postures of the writers—(are) innocent, and naive, flip, facile, in the manner of a stand-up comic. . . ."[1] Novelist Raymond Federman refers to this same narrative stance as "playgiarism." Marcos Rey in *Esta noite ou nunca* (1985; *Tonight or Never*) is one of the many Brazilian authors to employ this tongue-in-cheek ironic posture.

> —O que acha você do Brasil? —perguntou-me.
> —Acho que a população daqui devia ser transferida para outros continentes—disse. —A América Latina cumpriria melhor a sua função como uma grande reserva ecológica habitada apenas por guardas florestais.[2]

> ("What do you think of Brazil?" he asked me.
> "I think the entire population from here ought to be transferred to other continents," I said. "Latin America will be able to achieve its true destiny as a grand ecological reserve inhabited only by forest rangers.")

As seen in the works of Rey, Souza, Moreira da Costa, Drummond, and Loyola Brandão, examples of authorial intrusion and playfulness reach an almost obsessive level. It is one of the unique and endearing traits of postmodern Brazilian fiction. Brazilian authors feel at ease commenting directly to the reader or parenthetically footnoting a text. While the parodying of political institutions, persons, and attitudes is pandemic, a digression in the form of a direct remark to a reader to deflate another national foible is as important as any fixed story line. The oral tradition is still very much in evidence in Brazil and could be the inspiration for the pervasiveness of this narrative convention. In *Stories on a String* (1982) Candace Slater has observed the influence of the popular versed stories called "folhetos" or "literatura de cordel" on the writings of contemporary authors concluding, "Today not only intellectuals and artists but a larger middle class looks to popular art forms such as the 'folheto.' For some, these stories are simply a novelty. For others, they are indicators of profound social and economic changes within both the Northeast and Brazil as a whole."[3]

Contemporary writers enlist the reader as a confidant. The author's role is no longer perceived as that of a purveyor of truth. Both writer and reader have shared an intense historical moment. In an era of philosophical and political paradoxes, truth seems as illusive as the plot line in any of Raymond Federman's novels.

The concept of self-referentiality is a prevalent one in most postmodernist art forms. Vivid Brazilian examples abound: Flávio Moreira da Costa's inclusion of his own photograph in *O desastronauta*,

Chico Buarque and Francis Hime's musical greeting to their listeners in "Meu Caro Amigo" (My Dear Friend) (1976) and Jorge Amado's narrative posture in *Tenda dos milagres* (*Tent of Miracles*) (1969) and *Tereza Batista, cansada de guerra* (*Teresa Batista, Home from the War*) (1972).

Authors like Roberto Drummond, Márcio Souza, Ivan Ângelo, and Rubem Fonseca in *Bufo & Spallanzani* (1985) make little attempt at projecting or portraying reality per se for their reader. They create texts that augment and are aesthetic extensions of reality. One of the most important functions of this hyperreal narrative is its anti-conventional attitude towards both metaphysical and novelistic conventions. Italian critic Alide Cagidemetrio has concisely defined the very texture of contemporary experimental fiction. "The self reflective novel aims at detecting its own nature and its own making, at exposing that which is concealed in its illusion."[4]

There exists much technically innovative fiction in modern Brazilian literature. This type of literature seeks its own validity, attempting to exist as an independent art form. Four cases where technical innovation in writing forms part of an artfully fashioned narrative are Roberto Drummond's *Sangue de Coca-Cola* (1983; *Coca-Cola Blood*), Loyola Brandão's *Zero* (1974), Rubem Fonseca's *Bufo & Spallanzani* (1985), and Ivan Ângelo's *A festa* (1976).

Roberto Drummond's *Sangue de Coca-Cola* is a pop fantasy that is structured on the high emotional pitch of the yearly Brazilian carnival. This narrative Mardi Gras evokes a series of military dictatorships, naming names, and in essence, frenetically rewriting the history of the past two decades in pop terms. Contemporary Brazilian novelists in an effort to explore the national consciousness could have quite simply placed a mirror up to reality to reflect the political and economic struggles of the times; however, Drummond's *Sangue de Coca-Cola* stands out for its innovative textual strategies and structural originality. It evolves as a narrative event, a verbal carnival. As occurs in the plastic arts with "Action Painters" and "Happenings," this work is almost pure performance. It is a virtuoso improvisation by Roberto Drummond. The novel is more energy than plot, a fiction that flows from the mind of its author. It is a kaleidoscope of events, symbols, myths, fantasies, and ironies. In anti-traditional fashion it is the verbal performance of the novelist, his highly abstract and personal imagination that is placed in high relief. Ronald Sukenick, the author of *Blown Away* (1986), and one of the masters of the postmodern American novel, states: "Improvisation liberates (the novel) from any a priori order and allows it to discover new sequences and interconnections in the flow of experience."[5]

What Günther Grass attempted to achieve through a complex set of paradigms, anti-paradigms, and ambivalent symbology in the Danzig trilogy, Drummond strives to convey through his ongoing narrative carnival: the acceptance of the reader's ethical and moral responsibility to insure that the events of the past twenty years will never be repeated. Through this carnival of the mind, Drummond assesses the events, people, and national consciousness that allowed Brazil to pass through its long night of political repression. Behind the process of the carnival and the process of narrative creation is a playful sense of performance, of living out fantasies, and engaging the reader in the chaos of the novel. The carnivalesque fantasy that Drummond provides for his reader is laced with paradox and an ironic realization that all art, like life, is merely a game, a charade, an illusion of reality.

Ivan Ângelo's masterpiece of experimental writing, A festa, is a metafictional work in which the reader ultimately interprets and pieces together the mosaic of Ângelo's postmodernist vision of official history. By rejecting the constraints of merely portraying history, Ângelo recreates a new reality which allows the reader to relive it. His is an open-ended reader-centered text. The reader becomes a coparticipant in the work's evolution. It is left to each reader to discover personal truths concerning "the year of Misfortune." Arthur M. Saltzman in writing on the general tendencies of contemporary experimental fiction and on William Gass's postrealist fiction in particular states, "Forsaking a descriptive function, the novel asserts itself as a competing reality, a new object to be contended with—in Gass's words, a world of words."[6]

Rubem Fonseca also creates a novel whose playful narrative posture, exploration of the creative process, and metafictionality are dominant elements in the work's plot and structure. From within the text, the novel's author-narrator Gustavo Flávio concerns himself with, discusses, and resolves the problems of completing the very text the reader is presently reading. Episodes are discarded; ideas are proposed and rejected. Other characters even discuss the novel with the author. In an effort to reinvent reality, Fonseca's novel converges on science, literary theory, and pulp fiction to create a playfully ingenious amalgam of all three. Spallanzani is, of course, Lazzaro Spallanzani (1729–1799), the founder of modern experimental biology and "Bufo," the frog, is one of the objects of his experiments. The experiment focused upon in the novel affirms that the sex urge is stronger than the will to live. This then becomes a metaphor for the narrative. "O pé de Bufo estava todo carbonizado, mas ele mantinha Marina fortemente agarrada entre seus braços. O cientista continuou queimando a perna e a coxa de Bufo até incinerá-las completamente."[7] ("Bufo's foot was all carbonized, but he held on to Marina pressing strongly with his arms. The scientist continued burning the leg and thigh of Bufo until both were completely burned off.")

Fonseca has often explored the Eros-Thanatos polarity in his novels. Of late he has concentrated on the mystery and detective genre. In *Bufo & Spallanzani* his style has crystallized, as this genre has evolved as an art form. The murder-suicide of a Rio socialite meshes with the story of a strange and compulsive writer who effortlessly turns out novels on his beloved TRS-80. The novel is gravid with social commentary and literary parody. The writer, who is working on the same *Bufo & Spallanzani*, is also the prime suspect in the murder investigation. A key to the work's composition is found in one of the many digressions to discuss literary theory. In this maze of truths and half truths is found this statement on the role of the writer. "O escritor deve ser essencialmente um subversivo e a sua linguagem não pode ser nem a mistificatória do político (e do educador), nem a repressiva, do governante."[8] ("The writer should be essentially a subversive and his language can neither be mystifying like that of the politician [and that of an educator], nor repressive, like that of a governmental administrator.")

Perhaps the most interesting aspect of the novel, apart from its unique narrative perspective, is the characterization of "Guedes, o tira," Guedes, the detective. Inspector Guedes is depicted as a loner living in a roach infested flat, dressed always in the same sweaty and stained jacket. Fonseca employs this aspect of his characterization as a comic "retornello." "Guedes estava com o seu uniforme, o blusão seboso e a camisa encardida de colarinho aberto."[9] ("Guedes was there in his usual uniform, a filthy jacket and a grimy shirt with an open collar.")

In Brazil after the "ditadura," Fonseca has created a character, an authority figure who is not only scrupulously honest, but intelligent, street wise, and appealing. The reader wants to know more about Guedes, but in true grade B fashion we only see him in profile. The narrator-author observes, "Guedes era um tira honesto, tenho que reconhecer isso, e havia muitos outros tipos honestos, o que não deixa de ser uma coisa extraordinária num país em que chega a ser incalculável o número de corruptos em todos os níveis da administração pública e privada."[10] ("Guedes was an honest cop, I've got to admit it, and there were many other guys like him. However, this fact doesn't cease to be amazing in a country where the number of corrupt people in all levels of the private and public sector is incalculable.")

Like Dashiell Hammett's oddly named detective, the Continental Op, Guedes symbolizes the man of virtue whose life is lived out amid the corruption and amorality of contemporary society. It is Guedes whose personal life is a shambles, who is intent on righting in some small way the immorality and dishonesty that he confronts daily. However, Guedes is a loner, and, at times, his sense of personal morality and intuitive judgement supersede the rigidity of judicial law.

The text is a constant interplay of atmospheres, erudition, and mystery. Fonseca in the guise of the hack-writer-protagonist-narrator is able to freely and, at times, facetiously expound upon literature, science, society, and sex. The novel is a veritable thesis of information and misinformation. It is footnoted in scholarly fashion while its love story is the equal of any TV soap opera. This entertaining narrative, perhaps Fonseca's best to date, ends with a direct appeal to the reader to resolve the loose ends of the story.

Sérgio Sant'Anna's short story collection *O concerto de João Gilberto no Rio de Janeiro* (1982; *João Gilberto's Rio de Janeiro Concert*) is in the tradition of *Rolling Stone* journalism. The work is composed of a series of quick takes, all under pop, ironic, or playful titles. This narrative convention of employing a running commentary on the text is an updated pop version of a convention that Machado de Assis used effectively at the turn of the century.

While the sociopolitical reality of the "ditadura" is translated into artistic terms by the hyper-real recreations of history by Ivan Ângelo in *A festa*, others like Dalton Trevisan (1925) employ the form of the microtext. Roberto Drummond has shown a marked preference for pop fantasy. In a work that stands as one of the touchstones of this modern period, "A morte de D. J. em Paris" (1975; "The Death of D. J. in Paris"), Drummond creates a narrative microdrama that explores Brazilian reality by developing a Minas-Paris polarity, a type of reality end game. "Na hora D. J. sentiu um gosto de Minister no seu Gauloises, sua Paris virou uma capa do "Paris Match:" era de papel."[11] ("D. J. at that moment sensed the taste of Minister in his Gauloises, his Paris became a *Paris Match* magazine cover: it was all only paper.") The inclusion of prosaic elements and atmospheres that reflect Brazilian life is particularly strong in those novels set in the refugee communities of New York, Paris, and Berlin. Again, this aspect of the contemporary narrative forms part of a sharing and exploration of Brazilianism; in brief, it is an assiduous identity search and affirmation of national selfhood in a time of political uncertainty.

Literary theorist Richard Gilman asserts that there will always be a recognizable avant-garde literature. For this reason, every decade or two, there occurs a conscious attempt to redirect the expression of existing values. What Fred P. Elison called the "New Brazilian Novel" in 1954 is now conservatively ensconced as part of the established old garde. The "Romance Novo" of the 1970s and 1980s expresses the same futurist concerns that Gilman ascribes to all avant-garde works. Gilman strongly places experimental fiction within a political context: "If avant-garde art is civilization itself or the principle on which civilization can go forward to be renewed . . . then something a great deal broader than aesthetic issues is clearly in question. In this idea of the redemptive or socially propulsive power of art . . . one can discern a fusion or at least affinity of political and social energies, values and aspirations with literary and aesthetic ones." [12]

Clarice Lispector's *A hora da estrela* (1977; *The Hour of the Star*) exemplifies the Brazilian postmodern, reader centered text. Lispector's aesthetic vision has evolved over the seventeen years since the publication of *Laços de família*, and the following study proposes to point out the surprising and unexpected direction that one of Brazil's most respected writers has taken. This novel elaborates upon the artist's role, the creative process, and the place of women in contemporary Brazilian society. These thematic concerns are emphasized through postmodernist narrative techniques. Lispector's well-crafted sentences, assiduous use of vocabulary, and deliberate choice of symbols are present as always; however, this novel conveys a new dimension, a passionate involvement in the sociopolitical present.

Clarice Lispector's
A hora da estrela:
The Actualization
of Existential, Religious,
and Sociopolitical Paradoxes

> *One woman's agony in her room is something*
> *so insignificant that it casts no shadow across*
> *the great universe.*
>
> Elsa Morante

> *Sentavam-se no que é de graça: banco de praça*
> *pública. E ali acomodados, nada os distinguia*
> *do resto do nada. Para a grande glória de Deus.*
>
> *(Sitting there, they were indistinguishable from*
> *the rest of the nothingness. For the greater glory*
> *of God.)*
>
> Clarice Lispector

> *At her most introspective, Clarice is willfully*
> *capable of tying herself and her reader into*
> *metaphysical knots.*
>
> Giovanni Pontiero

In his study of contemporary political novels Robert Boyers observes that "the tendency of many recent critics to ignore a book's sense of itself, has led them also to be indifferent to what it is. Confounding the construction of a book with the book itself. . . ."[1] The following study, while falling far from an analysis that could be considered political in the traditional sense, exists in the margins of this genre.

Ivan Ângelo's narrative preoccupation with questions of social morality and culpability were masterfully expressed in his 1976 novel *A festa*. This highly political work highlighted the plight and poverty of a group of refugees from Brazil's impoverished Northeast. The very next year saw the appearance of Clarice Lispector's novel *A hora da estrela* (*The Hour of the Star*). Lispector had previously been known as Brazil's premier philosophical writer, the one author who could be linked to and compared favorably with the French novelists of the "nouveau roman."

The surprising aspect of this work is the book's unrestrained passion. After producing novels and short stories of "high art," ontological narratives detached from basic human and social concerns, Lispector returned with her final novel to focus upon the social paradoxes of contemporary Brazil.

The work is based upon Lispector's subjective and autonomous perception of existing reality. It is a personalized text that charts the private realm of her own and her country's consciousness. The work's essence, its "sense of self," in Boyer's words, is made manifest directly through its "construction." Thus, Lispector is able to tender thematic concerns through the work's uniquely devised narrative structure.

As a short story writer and novelist, Clarice Lispector's reputation continues to grow as her works are assiduously studied and interpreted world wide. Nancy T. Baden "places her with the best of Brazilian stylists—a complex, original author who remains at the forefront of contemporary letters."[2]

Certain tendencies and currents in literary history evolve collectively, almost simultaneously, as a reflection of the times or as a reaction against status quo literature. Lispector, like Ivan Ângelo, Elsa Morante in Italy, and Christa Wolf in East Germany, has created a text that reflects a desire for greater reader involvement. *A hora da estrela* like Wolf's *Nachdenken über Christa* (1979; *The Quest for Christa*) "emphasized the validity of the writer's relying on his [or her] own subjective experience of reality and encouraging the reader to do likewise."[3]

From an avowed post-structuralist perspective, Wolfgang Iser's theories of literature stress the importance of a narrative process in which a reader actively participates in the production of textual meaning. Iser's phenomenology of the reading process contends that the literary work is "actualized," not only by the author's mode of experiencing the world and the structural properties of that work, but— just as importantly—by an active reader who co-participates in the production of textual meaning. Jane P. Tompkins stresses in chronicling Iser's theories, "The text's intentions may be manifold, they may be infinite, but they are always present embryonically in the work itself, implied by it, circumscribed by it, and finally traceable to it."[4]

This study purposes to analyze Clarice Lispector's *A hora da estrela* from both its ingenious "construction" as a reader-centered text and its "sense of self" as a pessimistic vision of contemporary philosophical, religious, and sociopolitical paradoxes.

I

In 1964 in *A legião estrangeira* (*The Foreign Legion*), Clarice Lispector discusses the subject of literature and social justice. "Muito antes de sentir 'arte', senti a beleza profunda da luta. . . . O que não consigo é usar escrever para isso, por mais que a incapacidade me doa e me humilhe." ("Long before I ever felt 'art,' I felt the profound beauty of human conflict. . . . What I cannot do is to exploit writing . . . however much my incapacity pains and distresses me.")[5] Perhaps in the ensuing years the political and social failings of the "ditadura," or more simply a desire to portray societal as well as metaphysical dilemmas, turned Lispector to a literature of social engagement. Her novel, *A hora da estrela*, is a questioning work in which she reflects upon not only her role as a writer, but also on the plight of a single pitiable young woman, Macabéa. Lispector links Macabéa's story to the lives of the many other faceless women who have come to find a better life in Rio de Janeiro. "Como a nordestina, há milhares da moças espalhadas por cortiços" (p. 20). ("There are thousands of girls like the girl from the Northeast to be found in the slums of Rio de Janeiro" [p. 14].)

The book highlights Macabéa's story, a being so spiritually and physically impoverished that she possesses no sense of selfhood. "Nem se dava conta de que vivia numa sociedade técnica onde ela era um parafuso dispensável" (p. 36). ("She wasn't even aware that she lived in a technological society where she was a mere cog in the machine" [pp. 28–29].) From within the narrative Macabéa is presented as a product of poverty and a male-dominated society. There is no room for her to even dream of a better life. Lispector's narrator burns to tell his tale, for he states, "—E preciso falar dessa nordestina senão sufoco" (p. 23). ("And I must write about this girl from the Northeast otherwise I shall choke" [p. 17].) While he has a compulsion to tell this simple story with "no melody," this "canticle," the task of writing it is presented as overwhelming. One feels a new fervor and intensity in Lispector's style. "E dever meu, nem que seja de pouca arte, o de revelar-lhe a vida. Porque há o direito ao grito. Então eu grito" (p. 19). ("It is my duty to confront her with her own existence. For one has a right to shout. So, I'm shouting" [pp. 13–14].) Lispector's narrator wants to share the girl's pain, to take some kind of action. That action is perceived as inherent in the act of writing. "Já que palavra é ação? . . ." (p. 21). ("For surely words are actions?" [p. 15].) The girl's ensuing characterization is succinctly presented by Giovanni Pontiero.

> Her humdrum existence can be summarized in few words: Macabéa is an appallingly bad typist, she is a virgin, and her favorite drink is Coca-Cola. She is the perfect foil for a bullying employer, a philandering boy friend, and her workmate Glória, who has all the attributes Macabéa sadly lacks. (P. 90)
>
> She seems incapable of meeting the real world on its own terms. The society in which she finds herself has little use for "the pure happiness of idiots." (P. 94)

Lispector universalizes the plight of her anti-heroine by equating her story to the many other faceless "nordestinas," northeastern women, like her. She narratively and artfully takes up the cause of the disenfranchised, and, late in her writing career, the theorizing and intellectualizing that characterized her earlier works have been replaced by an involvement in contemporary events. "Tenho a tentação de usar termos suculentos: conheço adjetivos esplendorosos, carnudos substantivos e verbos tão esguios que atravessam agudos o ar em vias de ação . . ." (p. 21). ("I have at my command magnificent adjectives, robust nouns, and verbs so agile that they glide through the atmosphere as they move into action" [p. 15].) "Só eu, seu autor, a amo. Sofro por ela" (p. 34). ("I am the only person who finds her charming. As the author, I alone love her. I suffer on her account" [p. 27].) Even the work's title page is unique. It has a colloquial quality, a postmodernist, anti-novelist nonchalance. She offers several titles which form a component definition of her intention. "A CULPA É MINHA OU A HORA DA ESTRELA OU ELA QUE SE ARRANJE OU O DIREITO AO GRITO . . . ELA NAO SABE GRITAR . . . ASSOVIO NO VENTO ESCURO . . ." (p. 15). ("The Blame is Mine or The Hour of the Star or Let Her Fend for Herself or The Right to Protest . . . or She Doesn't Know How to Protest . . . or Whistling in the Dark Wind . . ." [p. 9].) Again, in the fashion of the post-modernists, she enters her own narration. In the book's dedication she links herself directly to the narrator-author (DEDICATÓRIA DO AUTOR [Na verdade Clarice Lispector] (p. 7) (The Author's Dedication [alias Clarice Lispector] [p. 7]) addressing her readership and challenging them to turn the "action" of her words into reality.

It would seem that Lispector even picks up the catch phrases and the gauntlet of fellow writers like Roberto Drummond and filmmaker Gláuber Rocha whose ideological questioning refers to a choice between national identity or foreign influence, coconut milk or Coca-Cola. From within the novel, quite unexpectedly, the narrator rails against the foreign incursion of a multi-national soft drink company even into the remote backlands of the Northeast.

> —O registro que em breve vai ter que começar é escrito sob o patrocínio do refrigerante mais popular do mundo e que nem por isso me paga nada, refrigerante esse espalhado por todos os países. Aliás foi ele quem patrocinou o último terremoto em Guatemala. Apesar de ter gosto do cheiro de esmalte de unhas, de sabão Aristolino e plástico mastigado. (P. 30)

> (—The record that is about to begin is written under the sponsorship of the most popular soft drink in the world even though it does not earn me anything; a soft drink that is distributed throughout the world. It is the same soft drink that sponsored the recent earthquake in Guatemala. Despite the fact that it tastes of nail polish, toilet soap and chewed plastic.) (P. 23)

Never in her long literary career has Lispector's narrative been so charged with irony and an understated use of the grotesque. In *A hora da estrela* Lispector's acerbic vision turns on those Brazilian women (and by extension includes those men like Olímpico who express preference for this standard) who assume or ape an ideal of beauty that is derived from foreign influences. The character with the nominally ironic name of Glória exemplifies this point:

> Tinha um cheiro esquisito. Porque não se lavava muito, com certeza. Oxigenava os pêlos das pernas cabeludas e das axilas que ela não respava. Olímpico: será que ela é loura embaixo também? (P. 73)

(Her body exuded a peculiar smell, and it was quite obvious that she didn't wash much. She bleached the hairs on her legs and under the armpits without bothering to shave them. Olímpico wondered: was she bleached down below as well?) (P. 63)

Glória tinha um traseiro alegre e fumava cigarro mentolado para manter um hálito bom nos seus beijos intermináveis com Olímpico. (P. 74)

(Glória wiggled her bottom in an inviting way and she smoked mentholated cigarettes to keep her breath fresh for those interminable kissing sessions with Olimpíco.) (P. 64)

Even Macabéa dreams of a non-Brazilian ideal of beauty. "O que ela queria, como eu já disse, era parecer com Marylin" (p. 74). (What Macabéa wanted most of all, as I've already said, was to look like Marilyn Monroe" [p. 64].)

The novel is rich in symbolism. Macabéa's name is a highly unusual one in Brazil. "Eu preferia continuar a nunca ser chamada em vez de ter um nome que ninguém tem . . ." (pp. 51–52). ("I'd have preferred to go on being called nothing instead of a name that nobody has ever heard of . . ." [p. 43].) Lispector traditionally took great care in her use of nominal symbology. Here the name makes direct reference to the Biblical personage of Judah Maccabee, a patriot and symbol of strength of the Jewish people. Macabéa is as passive as her Biblical namesake is aggressive. The Biblical correspondence at once points to an ironic juxtaposition of frailty and strength and again confuses the male-female role as in the case of Lispector's choice of a fictional narrator, Rodrigo S. M. Lispector is suggesting that Macabéa should acquire some of the strength that allowed the ancient Maccabees to rebel and triumph against overwhelming odds. Like her younger contemporaries, Lispector's novel is a responsive work, one that addresses social problems through crafted narrative strategies. Perhaps Lispector, who herself immigrated to Brazil as a young Jewish girl from the Soviet Union, felt herself to be an outsider (as a woman writer of Jewish descent) like her frail heroine Macabéa and the many undereducated and disenfranchised Brazilians whom she now depicts. Lispector presents us with a tragic main character who is unable to, or fearful of, imagining a better life. Lispector shares her cause and anguish. "Não cobiçou o bombom pois aprendera que as coisas são dos outros" (p. 84). ("She did not covet Madame Carlota's chocolates for Macabéa had discovered that things belonged to others" [p. 73].) "(Ela me incomoda tanto que fiquei oco. Estou oco desta moça. E ela tanto mais me incomoda quanto menos reclama. Estou com raiva)"

(p. 33). ("[The girl worries me so much that I feel drained. She has drained me empty. And the less she demands, the more she worries me. I feel frustrated and annoyed]" [p. 25].) In this regard Ponteiro, who has long chronicled and translated her works, makes a significant observation. "As in all her previous narratives, Clarice Lispector narrates *from within*. In *The Hour of the Star* her own unmistakable presence often merges with that of Macabéa" (p. 92).

II

Wolfgang Iser's phenomenological theory of the reading process "lays full stress on the idea that, in considering a literary work, one must take into account not only the actual text but also, and in equal measure, the actions involved in responding to the text."[6] Iser discusses the "discovery of the unformulated, which can then be taken over by the active imagination of the reader . . . giving him or her a 'chance to formulate the unformulated.' "[7] Lispector's *A hora da estrela* is the quintessence of a reader-centered text.

As eminent a critic as Brazil's Eduardo Portella reads this novel as "a alegoria da esperança possível," an allegory of possible hope,[8] while this present study—quite to the contrary—sees little hope, either from a religious, philosophical, or sociological perspective.

The work makes direct reference to social class differences, differences that exist as a backdrop to the novel, but differences that Macabéa is unable to fathom. "O título era 'Humilhados e Ofendidos'. Ficou pensativa. Talvez tivesse pela primeira vez se definido numa classe social. . . . para que lutar?" (p. 48). ("The book was entitled *The Shamed and the Oppressed*. The girl remained pensive. Perhaps for the first time she had established her social class. . . . Why struggle?" [p. 40].)

> Vez por outra ia para a Zona Sul e ficava olhando as vitrines faiscantes de jóias e roupas acetinadas—só para se mortificar um pouco. É que ela sentia falta de encontrar-se consigo mesma e sofrer um pouco é um encontro. (P. 42)

> (Occasionally she wandered into the more fashionable quarters of the city and stood gazing at the shop windows displaying glittering jewels and luxurious garments in satin and silk—just to mortify the senses. The truth is that she needed to find herself and a little mortification helped. (P. 34)

Macabéa is linked to her four roommates who share her plight. "Quando as quatro Marias cansadas foram trabalhar, ela teve pela primeira vez na vida uma coisa a mais preciosa: a solidão" (p. 49). ("When the four weary Marias set off for work, she could enjoy at last the greatest privilege of all: solitude" [p. 41].) Note also that the other girls are not delineated within the novel and all share the Christian and typically Brazilian name, Maria. This is contrasted to the Old Testament, Biblically inspired name Macabéa.

In "DEDICATÓRIA DO AUTOR (Na verdade Clarice Lispector")" (p. 7) (Author's Dedication [alias Clarice Lispector] [pp. 7–8]) Lispector not only links herself directly with her narrator, Rodrigo S. M., but also dedicates the work to the power, beauty, and majesty of music and to classical composers like Beethoven, Chopin, Bach, and Strauss. The novel then marks its long passage from sound to silence. The importance of music in the author's life is juxtaposed to the total absence of sound at the work's close. "Os sinos badalavam mas sem que seus bronzes lhes dessem som" (p. 97). ("The bells were ringing without making a sound" [p. 85].) Furthermore, the dedication also tells us that the author, alias Clarice Lispector, has taken into account the political difficulties that Brazil faced in the mid-seventies. "*Esta história acontece em estado de emergência e de calamidade pública*" (p. 8). ("This story unfolds in a state of emergency and public calamity" [p. 8].)

Lispector's novel ends with the narrator reminded of the immediacy of death. "Meu Deus, só agora me lembrei que a gente morre. Mas—mas eu também?!" (p. 98). ("Dear God, only now am I remembering that people die. Does that include me?" [p. 86].) She then balances that thought by stating that it is the "tempo de morangos" (p. 98) ("the season for strawberries" [p. 86].) The text's final word is an emphatic and simple, "Sim" ("Yes"). Always a minimalist regarding language, Lispector leaves it up to each reader to interpret the "Yes." Is it accepting or remorseful, consoling perhaps? Is it emphasizing the immediacy of death or the fact that one of nature's pleasures is here to stave off the realization of that death? Lispector has filled this simple word and this brief dialogue with a lifetime of philosophical interpretations regarding life's essential questions.

A hora da estrela signals a change in Lispector's tone and aesthesia, not in style, for the work still exhibits all the power and subtleties of language and narration. Her present text is, however, more openly designed so that each reader can enter its ambiguities, filling out its pauses and unspoken dictates. To those critics who have seen in the author's previous works a mystical longing for a union with God, this text offers no indication in that direction. "Ela não pensava em Deus, Deus não pensava nela" (p. 33). ("She did not think about God and God did not think about her" [p. 26].) "Depois pediu perdão ao Ser abstrato que dava e tirava. Sentiu-se perdoada. O Ser a perdoava de tudo" (p. 76). ("She then asked to be forgiven by the Abstract Being, the Giver and Taker of all things. She felt she had been forgiven. The Abstract Being had shown mercy" [p. 66].) The reader is then made aware of the ironic implications in this scene, that of a true innocent needing to seek forgiveness. The scene is laden with ironic implications, from the use of the term "Abstract Being" to the juxtaposition of little Macabéa and the personification of the "Ser abstrato".

In the characterization of Madame Carlota—the crass priestess of occult powers, ex-prostitute, brothel keeper, and clairvoyant—is one of the work's most challenging embryonic symbols. This symbol is open to a wide spectrum of interpretations: false religiosity, government corruption, religion in general, God or a grotesque parody of all authority. Carlota is linked many times within the narrative to Jesus; she even proselytizes on his behalf. "Meu amigo Jesus" (p. 86). ("My friend Jesus" [p. 75].) Her being is equated to that of Jesus. "Porque quem está ao meu lado, está no mesmo instante ao lado de Jesus" (p. 83). ("Anyone at my side is also at the side of Jesus" [p. 72].) She seeks to make Macabéa a "fã de Jesus" (p. 83) ("fan of Jesus, too" [p. 72]). Madame Carlota lives in garish elegance. "Você notou que Ele até me conseguiu dinheiro para ter mobília de grã-fino?" (p. 83). ("You have seen how Jesus even provides me with money to buy all this expensive furniture?" [p. 73].) "Até tinha cheiro de igreja" (p. 85). ("The brothel used to smell like the inside of a church" [p. 74].)

Macabéa, the virginal innocent, faces this syphilitic toothless presence, and it is Madame Carlota who sends her to a foreseen death. She, like the holocaust victims, was deceived and led to her death. Macabéa is killed by a yellow Mercedes as big as an ocean liner, driven by a blond foreigner named Hans. In an almost minimalist text, each character, each name, each symbol was chosen with great care. In the strangely magical and embryonic presentation of the Madame Carlota motif can be found resonances of the Holocaust. "Embora a moça anônima da história seja tão antiga que podia ser uma figura bíblica" (p. 38). ("The anonymous girl of this story is so ancient that she could be described as Biblical" [p. 30].)

As Macabéa leaves Madame Carlota's, her life is described as transformed. "Sua vida já estava mudada" (p. 90). ("Her life had been transformed" [p. 79].) This mention of transformation, narratively, is a direct link back to the Dedication, to the author's (alias Clarice Lispector's) mention of Strauss's *Tod und Verklärung*. "À '*Morte e Transfiguração*', *em que Richard Strauss me revela um destino?*" (p. 7). ("To *Death and Transfiguration*, in which Richard Strauss predicts my fate" [p. 7].) Thus, the novel concludes, ironically comparing Strauss's visions of redemption with the illusionary and false promises of Madame Carlota.

Instead of a glorious transformation, attention remains inordinately long on Macabéa's agony as she lies on the pavement with "um fio de sangue inesperadamente vermelho e rico" (p. 90) ("a trickle of blood . . . surprisingly thick and red" [p. 79]). "Ela sofria? Acho que sim" (p. 92). ("Was she suffering? I believe she was" [p. 80].) In a poetic and surreal presentation, a Chagallesque presence accompanies her death, a frayed old violinist, a vision of the narrator's youth (and Lispector's) in Recife. There are also references to Biblical promises of salvation that comprise this scene. "Terá tido ela saudade do futuro? Ouço a música antiga de palavras e palavras, sim, é assim" (p. 96). ("Did she crave a future? I hear the ancient music of words upon words. Yes, it is so" [p. 84].) "E mudada por palavras—desde Moisés se sabe que a palavra é divina" (p. 90). ("Transformed, moreover, by words—since the time of Moses the word had been acknowledged as being divine" [p. 79].) An implicit sense of narrative irony is achieved by linking the phrase "had been acknowledged" to a scene of death, suffering, falsehood, futility, and false hope.

The sense of disillusionment in this scene is overwhelming. From within the scene itself the narrator confides in the reader. "O que queria dizer que apesar de tudo ela pertencia a uma resistente raça anã teimosa que um dia vai talvez reivindicar o direito ao grito" (pp. 90–91). ("What I wanted to say was that despite everything, she belonged to a resistant and stubborn race of dwarfs that would one day vindicate the right to protest" [p. 79].) The use of the phrase "what I wanted to say" and yet another reference to "protest" again underscore the work's sense of outright futility. Lispector, the master stylist, is utilizing irony and understatement to transfer her concerns to her reader. The entire posture of expressing the difficulty of getting this simple story on paper is an ironic narrative device. The true difficulty was in creating a novel that would generate reader response. Lispector makes the reader part of this hopeless sociopolitical, religious, and philosophical situation and then turns to that same reader and pleads, "Trata-se de livro inacabado porque lhe falta a resposta. Resposta esta que espero que alguém no mundo ma dê. Vós?" (p. 8). ("It is an unfinished book because it offers no answer. An answer I hope someone somewhere in the world may be able to provide. You perhaps?" [p. 8].)

A hora da estrela exists in the margins of the genre of the modern political novel, "palavra é ação" (p. 21) ("words are actions" [p. 15]). "Esqueci de dizer que tudo o que estou agora escrevendo é acompanhado pelo ruflar enfático de um tambor batido por um soldado. No instante mesmo em que eu começar a história—de súbito cessará o tambor" (p. 29). ("I forgot to mention that everything I am now writing is accompanied by the emphatic ruffle of a military drum. The moment I start to tell my story—the noise of the drum will suddenly cease" [p. 22].) It is a quiet work whose conception and presentation as a reader centered text evolves as a muted call for compassion and change. The very same year A hora da estrela appeared, Italy's Elsa Morante published her masterpiece La storia (History, A Novel). While there exist differences in style and technique, both works reflect upon the role of contemporary women within male dominated societies. Both novels delve below larger moments of historical unrest to focus upon faceless victims whose lives define true history.

In A hora da estrela a Brazilian woman is presented as both creator and victim of contemporary history. Lispector depicts a being, like the "milhares," the thousands of others, who have had no voice in their country's history. Historical reality, the relentless flood of refugees from the Northeast, is an unmasterable presence in this novel. Macabéa is but one of the many "nordestinas," one of the many faceless women who are unaware that they exist in a world and a political system that is at best indifferent to them. The central and unstated problem of Lispector's reader centered text, as it is with much of the fiction of this period, is society's ethical and intellectual responsibilities.

NOTES

[1] Philip Stevik, Alternate Pleasures: Postrealist Fiction and Tradition (Urbana: Univ. of Illinois Press, 1981), p. 37.

[2] Marcos Rey, Esta noite ou nunca (São Paulo: Ática, 1985), p. 162.

[3] Candace Slater, Stories on a String: The Brazilian Literatura de Cordel (Los Angeles: The University of California Press, 1982), p. xiv.

4 Alide Cagidemetrio, "The Real Thing," *Critical Angles*, ed. Marc Chénetier (Edwardsville and Carbondale: Southern Illinois University Press, 1986), p. 7.

5 Ronald Sukenick, *In Form: Digressions on the Art of Fiction* (Edwardsville and Carbondale: Southern Illinois University Press, 1985), p. 212.

6 Arthur M. Saltzman, *The Fiction of William Gass* (Edwardsville and Carbondale, Ill.: Southern Illinois University Press, 1986), p. 9.

7 Rubem Fonseca, *Bufo & Spallanzani* (Rio de Janeiro: Francisco Alves, 1985), p. 174.

8 Fonseca, p. 147.

9 Fonseca, p. 63.

10 Fonseca, p. 31.

11 Roberto Drummond, *A morte de D. J. em Paris* (São Paulo: Ática, 1983), p. 98.

12 Richard Gilman, "The Idea of the Avant-Garde," *Writers and Politics*, eds. Edith Kurzweiland and William Phillips (Boston: Routledge & Kegan Paul, 1983), p. 70.

Lispector Study

The first epigraph of this study is from Elsa Morante, *Arturo's Island*, trans. Isabel Quigly (New York: Knopf, 1959), p. 187.

The second epigraph is from Clarice Lispector, *A hora da estrela* (Rio de Janeiro: Nova Fonteira, 1984), p. 56. The English translation is *The Hour of the Star*, trans. Giovanni Pontiero (Manchester, England: Carcanet, 1986), p. 47. All subsequent citations will be taken from these editions and entered directly into the text.

The third epigraph is from Giovanni Pontiero's "Afterward," p. 219 as quoted above.

1 Robert Boyers, *Atrocity and Amnesia: The Political Novel since 1945* (New York: Oxford University Press, 1985), p. 3.

2 Nancy T. Baden, "Clarice Lispector," *A Dictionary of Contemporary Brazilian Authors*, eds. David William Foster and Roberto Reis (Tempe: Arizona State University, Center for Latin American Studies, 1981), p. 74.

3 Neil Jackson, "Christa Wolf," *Contemporary Foreign Language Writers*, eds. James Vinson and Daniel Kirkpatrick (New York: St. Martin's Press, 1984), p. 37.

4 Jane P. Tompkins, "An Introduction to Reader-Response Criticism," *Reader-Response Criticism*, ed. Jane Tompkins (Baltimore: The Johns Hopkins University Press) p. xv.

5 Clarice Lispector, *A legião estrangeira* (Rio de Janeiro: Editora do Autor, 1964), p. 149. The English translation is *The Foreign Legion*, trans. Giovanni Pontiero (Manchester, England: Carcanet, 1986), p. 124.

[6] Wolfgang Iser, "The Reading Process: A Phenomenological Approach," trans. Catherine Macksey and Richard Macksey, *Reader-Response Criticism*, p. 50.

[7] Iser, p. 68.

[8] Eduardo Portella, "O grito do silêncio" as quoted from the Portuguese edition of Clarice Lispector's *A hora da estrela* (Rio de Janeiro: Nova Fronteira, 1984), p. 9.

NARRATIVE DIRECTIONS AND CRITICAL CONCERNS

The contemporary Brazilian narrative in its search for new forms freely incorporated many "Cinema Novo" techniques such as flashbacks, quick cuts, framing scenes, montage, and, most importantly, its predilection for exploring and exposing social issues and inequities. The relationship between the Brazilian film world and the narrative is a symbiotic one. Several classic movies have evolved from established novels: *Vidas secas* (*Barren Lives*), *Tenda dos milagres* (*Tent of Miracles*), and *Amar, verbo intransitivo* (*Love, An Intransitive Verb*). Mário de Andrade's rhapsodic novel *Macunaíma* (1928) is a seminal text in the development of today's postmodern novel. According to Randal Johnson, the film version by Joaquim Pedro de Andrade (1969) set the tone for the radicalization of the novel in the 1970s. He describes *Macunaíma* as "the first Cinema Novo film to be formally innovative, politically radical, and immensely popular with the Brazilian masses."[1] This film, like the modern novel, attracted a mass audience, explored the national character, and did all this by employing and exploiting folkloric and mythic tendencies. Just as many of the innovative aspects of Bertold Brecht's "epic theater" were inspired by the avant-garde cinematic conventions of his times (in particular the works of Eisenstein, Keaton, and Chaplin), the Brazilian novel of the '70s freely accommodates narrative techniques from the "Cinema Novo" and vice-versa. For critic Keith Cohn the dynamics of exchange between the cinematic experience and the modern novel are significant:

> For the cinematic experience included, among its most significant effects for the novelists, a spatial configuration of the flow of time, an innate relativity and perpetual shifting of point of view, and a vivid discontinuity of the narrating material by means of montage . . . the most dynamic aspects of the new novel form were *simultaneity*, or the depiction of two separate points in space at a single instant of time, *multiperspectivism*, or the depiction of a single event from radically distinct points of view, and *montage*.[2]

In recent years the Brazilian film industry, which once showed such promise, has degenerated into producing mostly pornographic films. Very few titles have emerged of late that are of an artistic nature. With exceptions like Hector Babenco's O beijo da mulher aranha (The Kiss of the Spider Woman), Suzana Amaral's A hora da estrela (The Hour of the Star), and Memórias do cárcere (Memories of Imprisonment) by Nelson Pereira dos Santos, the end of censorship has unleashed a flood of sexually explicit films. In the International Film Guide 1986, Luis Arbex observes, "101 features were made in 1984— 51 softcore, 20 hardcore. As for the remaining 30, only 6 had any artistic value. . . . At this writing only three non-pornographic films were screened in 1985 within the domestic industry."[3] Marcos Rey addresses this sorrowful fact by humorously and grotesquely fictionalizing the world of William Ken Taylor, an aspiring Brazilian writer who assumes an Anglo Saxon name to be able to sell his work. Taylor ends up writing for the "cinema pornô" and becomes passionately obsessed with Eliana Brandão, the reigning queen of São Paulo's tawdry world of the "pornochanchada." Rey's Esta noite ou nunca turns a narrative strobe light on all facets of this get-rich-quick industry. Malcolm Silverman considers this work to be "incessantly parodying parody."[4] While the book's main focus is the Brazilian movie industry, Silverman states that "Rey succeeds in ridiculing the hypocrisy surrounding numerous [other] Brazilian social and institutional ills."[5]

In their search for new directions, contemporary Brazilian authors have looked to popular forms of art and literature: science fiction, pulp novels, murder mysteries, and adventure narratives. Many of these works have a social and proletarian immediacy. These popular art forms are all freely adapted by the novelists of the period. John G. Cawelti has studied the art of formula stories and concludes, "The world of formula can be described as an archetypal story pattern embodied in the images, symbols, themes, and myths of a particular culture."[6]

In general terms the Brazilian novel is aimed at a mass audience. One case in point is crime fiction or the detective genre which has been elevated to an art form by Rubem Fonseca. *A grande arte* (1983; *High Art*), while appealing to the mass audience, is still able to involve and challenge an intellectual elite. *O caso Morel* (1973; *The Morel Case*) is another inventive work in which Fonseca accommodates the format of a murder mystery. This novel is composed of varying narrative devices: depositions, oral and written accounts, and diary entries. All these narrative techniques are needed to uncover the truth of a sexually deviant relationship that may have led to murder, and to forward Fonseca's views on the illusionary and fragmented nature of life and art.

Many authors' satires and social commentaries of popular culture are couched in these supposedly subliterary genres. It is a difficult task to ascertain if in the selection of genre the individual author wishes to burlesque the popular form or is merely using it as a means of wider communication. Fonseca's *A grande arte*, rather than parodying the crime story and the detective genre, is paying homage to it. In a sense, he is reinventing it in the Brazilian mode, creating a genre that can cut across all strata of Brazilian society. He populates this fictional world with a melange of characters through whom he is able to comment freely on the political present. "A história atual do Brasil pode ser resumida nestas palavras—poder desenfreado, medo, estupidez e corrupção. . . . Se me permite um circunlóquio, no Brasil o Poder cria corruptos e a corrupção cria poderosos." ("The recent history of Brazil can be summarized in five words—unbridled power, fear, stupidity, and corruption. . . . If you'll permit me a circumlocution, in Brazil power creates the corrupt and corruption creates the powerful.")[7]

Fonseca's crime fiction has a "film noir" quality about it, a hint of

Raymond Chandler, and even a tribute to B-movie dialogue, but always with a Brazilian twist and sense of the ironic. Like American author Andrew L. Bergman's Jack LaVine series, Fonseca seems to stop just short of parodying the genre.

> "Sou advogado no Rio de Janeiro. Criminalista."
> "No Rio não deve faltar cliente, não é? A cada minuto, ou será a cada segundo? um crime de morte."
>
> ("I'm a lawyer. Criminal practice. In Rio."
> "Must be plenty of clients there, huh? What is it—every minute or every second somebody's killed?")[8]

In *A grande arte* he creates the character of Mandrake, a womanizing lawyer who investigates the ritualistic murders of two prostitutes. Mandrake's investigation leads him on a sensuous journey through Rio's underworld of killers, knife fighters, and drug dealers to the highest levels of Brazilian society. Rubem Fonseca's innovative writing becomes more involved and fascinating with each new work.

II

There is a general tendency to be overly enthusiastic regarding the literature of a period that one sets out to study. However, as is the case with all national literatures, the vast majority of the works were at best derivative and lacking in imagination. For the studies in this book there was an attempt to choose narratives that represented a movement toward excellence. Other works, many by these same authors, did not measure up aesthetically. A case in point is Ivan Ângelo's *A casa de vidro* (1979; *The Glass House*) which doesn't compare to *A festa* in narrative technique, thematic management, or in the force of its presentation. Márcio Souza has yet to duplicate the ingenuity of his *Galvez, Imperador do Acre* and *Mad Maria*. His prolific writings are always interesting, but his new works have yet to transcend that which is merely readable to that which is artistic. *O ordem do dia*'s confused and confusing plot is merely a means by which Souza's satiric vision can again examine the Brazilian sociopolitical system. The humor is, as always, acerbic and not without its Rabelaisian moments. However, even an average novel like *A condolência* (1984; *The Condolence*) makes for an enjoyable read and contains large doses of Souza's satiric sense of invective. In his use of description, he is unable to resist characterizing a shirt as having more mends than the national constitution, a phrase that brought about—even in 1984—sharp criticism from many factions.

After a distinguished career that has engendered a wide national and international following, it was hoped that Jorge Amado's *Tocaia Grande* (1986) would be a work of such outstanding merit that it would ensure its author a Nobel Prize in literature. Many Brazilian critics believed that Amado's work, like Brazilian writing in general, has never received the kind of critical attention and international exposure that it deserves. Ironically, these same critics were soon to be overwhelmed by the attendant publicity that accompanied the January, 1988, publication of *Showdown*.

Steve Paul, book editor of the Kansas City Star, is one of the many reviewers who was compelled to comment on the work's extensive publicity campaign. "Bantam Books bought *Showdown* for $250,000, reportedly an American record for hard-cover rights to a foreign novel. The publisher invited him [Amado] to New York for a week late last month to help launch its considerable promotion of the book. One Fifth Avenue bookstore devoted an entire window to it. And Amado's itinerary was filled with dozens of media interviews."[9] *Tocaia Grande* (*The Big Ambush*), the book's Portuguese title, sold phenomenally well in Brazil; however, aesthetically it never quite lived up to its advance notice. Its mythically populist recreation of historical reality is mired in a forced and predictable utopianism. "Organizaram uma espécie de ponte humana: sobre cada uma das doze toras de madeira um homem se equilibrou, em pé. Assim, mudando de mão em mão, os nenéns cruzaram o rio." ("They organized a kind of human bridge: one on each of the twelve wooden beams, balancing himself, standing. In that way, going from hand to hand, the children crossed the river.")[10] "Em lugar de ir-se embora, o povo juntara-se solidário. Virou uma família, explicou em Ilhéus o coronel Robustiano de Araújo, testemunha idônea." ("Working night and day, in a spontaneous collective effort paid for by a curious bartering of produce and animals, where possible, and by money when God brought good weather, the inhabitants had remade the topography of the village.")[11]

Tocaia Grande still exhibits Amado's great gift for storytelling. The novel is peopled with a host of good hearted prostitutes, local gunmen, voodoo rites, a paternal cacao Baron, and another lovable Lebanese merchant. However, the book suffers from a sense of déjà vu for anyone who enjoyed his previous works. *Publishers Weekly* calls it an "unfocused and somewhat maudlin epic . . . a busy patchwork that lacks pattern and direction."[12] *Time* magazine's Stefan Kanfer, in discussing Amado's use of the metaphor of the big ambush, states, "It is an overriding metaphor, not only for events in Jorge Amado's novel but also for those outside it. There the ambushees are bookstores, critics and the public. The firepower comes from an arsenal of hype."[13] He goes on to add, "But it seems fair for consumers to receive accuracy in advertising. The awestruck promotion implies that *Showdown* is the work of a potential Nobel laureate. The book itself suggests Louis L'Amour with a Portuguese accent."[14] This work's appearance coincided with the publication of two outstanding novels: Aharon Appelfeld's *The Immortal Bartfuss* and José Saramago's *Baltasar and Blimunda*, and from an aesthetic perspective, it pales in comparison.

Since experimentation with new forms of expression is a major component of the literature of the time, there is always a high risk for failure as well as success. Many works of the period will remain only as expressions that captured a strident moment in time or examples of the Brazilianization of international trends. Loyola Brandão's *Zero* was finished in 1969 and presented its victimized hero overpowered by a sense of helplessness and impotence. This nebbish anti-hero's life, in the late sixties, was conveyed in what for the times were avant-garde narrative techniques. His odyssey through a surreal chthonian reality was as innovatively presented as any of John Barth's or Thomas Pynchon's novels. However, by the time the work appeared in Brazil, after its detour through Italian translation and Brazilian censorship, it no longer had the same innovative impact.

Today João Ubaldo Ribeiro's *Sargento Getúlio* continues to be appreciated. It can be said that its reputation as literature has grown exponentially since its appearance. Darcy Ribeiro's *Maíra* is still an underrated masterpiece, as are Antônio Torres's *Essa terra*, and Ivan Ângelo's *A festa*. In Darcy Ribeiro's case this is perhaps due to his standing as a noted scholar, statesman, and anthropologist, so the work is considered more fact than fiction, a literary documentary. However, as often occurs for a writer who comes to literature late in life, she or he brings to the craft of fiction a lifetime of well thought-out ideas and concerns. For Ribeiro, these concerns and ideas were presented through narrative strategies that are of the most avant-garde and imaginative nature. The book was written with emotional depth and powerfully presented.

Other fine works are found in the form of short fiction collections: *O pirotécnico Zacarias* (1974; *Zacarias, The Pyrotechnist*) by Murilo Rubião; *A morte de D. J. em Paris* (1975; *The Death of D. J. in Paris*) by Roberto Drummond; *Abraçado ao meu rancor* (1984; Embraced to My Hatred), *Paixões* (1984; *Passions*) by Domingos Pellegrini; *O último verão de Copacabana* (*The Final Summer of Copacabana*) by Sônia Coutinho; and Edilberto Coutinho's *Maracanã, adeus* (1980; Good-Bye Maracanã). The latter will be judged as a landmark piece of fiction for its brilliant demythification of populist Brazilian ideals and fantasies.

III

There was a time when Brazilian authors and intellectuals looked to Europe, in particular Paris, as a cultural center. However, this present generation, like the "modernists," questions and at times burlesques the Brazilian penchant for the acceptance of things foreign as culturally superior to the "cultura popular brasileira," popular Brazilian culture. Examples abound: Márcio Souza's acerbic wit underscores this point throughout his many novels; Rubem Fonseca in "Lúcia McCartney" explores the vapid existence of a young woman who apes foreign culture to the point of renaming herself after a member of a British rock band; Roberto Drummond's *A morte de D. J. em Paris* on one level of meaning deals with an escapist mentality and a return to an appreciation of the simple elements in his own culture.

A significant number of writers of the present generation have lived and studied in the United States. In particular, many have attended the University of Iowa to take part in its International Writing Program. Among those who come to mind are João Ubaldo Ribeiro, Carlos Filipe Moisés, Roberto Reis, Luiz Vilela, Flávio Moreira da Costa, Julio Cesar, Monteiro Martins, and Sérgio Sant'Anna. For this and other reasons the image of the North American is, for the most part, an accurate one in regard to exterior categorization. There are doctors from St. Louis and Johns Hopkins University, ubiquitous missionaries, secret agents trained at Fort Bragg, Harvard students, a gang of Rio youths who assume the styles and attitudes of a classic American movie, and a beautiful French-Canadian drug smuggler.

Foreign reflections are generally utilized as mere emblematic or metonymic correspondences even though they are usually drawn with an unerring accuracy with regard to specific details. One exception to this generalization is Silviano Santiago's 1985 novel *Stella Manhattan*. The atmosphere and events of New York in the '60s and '70s are totally incorporated into the work. "Por não a ter levado a Woodstock naquele verão, Stella proibira Eduardo de ir ao cinema por um mês . . . Stella ameaçara Eduardo com uma visita ao consulado." [15] ("For not having taken her to Woodstock that summer, Stella had forbidden Eduardo to go to the movies for a month . . . Stella had threatened Eduardo with a visit to the Consulate. . . .") The novel is also interspersed with Spanish and English. Stella, the transvestite aspect of Eduardo's personality, is oblivious to Brazilian political events. "E para Stella a substituição do presidente Costa e Silva pela tróica militar entrava num ouvido e saía pelo outro." [16] ("And for Stella the substitution of President Costa e Silva by a military troika had gone in one ear and out the other.")

The world of intrigues that Eduardo da Costa e Silva in his Brooks Brothers tie inhabits at the Brazilian Consulate in Rockefeller Center and the homosexual world of Stella Manhattan, his effusive alter ego, are drawn with precision. As Stella vamps behind her apartment window, the author, in English, ironically captures the reaction of her American neighbors. "'He's nuts.' 'Who's nuts?' 'The Puerto-rican who lives in the building across the street.'" [17]

IV

As previously stated, a dominant aspect of recent Brazilian fiction is its desire to combine innately Brazilian societal attitudes, elements of popular culture, subliterary art forms, and the political paradoxes of the moment with a constant experimentation with the narrative as an art form. The particularly theoretical and innovative nature of postmodernist works like *Maíra*, *A festa*, *A hora da estrela*, and *Sangue de Coca-Cola* suggests that this generation of writers has attempted to expand existing aesthetic and narrative traditions. However, it must be reaffirmed that an obligation to reach a wide spectrum of readers, conveying ideas and supporting ideals, is more prevalent than in most countries. A loose parallel can be drawn between this generation of writers and the post-World War II German novelists, in particular the works of Günther Grass.

In a 1966 Princeton seminar on German literature, Grass claimed to have resolved the age old dilemma of separating art from politics by dividing himself in two, professing to be able to be both writer and political activist. In the Brazilian novelists' personalization of recent history it is often hard to distinguish between the voice of the writer and that of the political activist. One aspect of the modern Brazilian novel that stands out is the close interaction between art and politics. Like Grass's symbol of the tin drum as a fusion of both artistic expression and political protest, the Brazilian novel itself is a true fusion of aesthetic and political concerns.

With exceptions like Osman Lins's masterwork *Avalovara* (1973) and Nelida Piñon's novels, the writers of this period can be compared to the post-World War II generation of German authors whose works were obsessively absorbed in analyzing the historical and social process that brought about the rise of the Third Reich.

Peter Handke, at the same Princeton conference where Grass spoke, coined the term "description-impotence" to refer to the excessive concentration on, and portrayal of, modern German history by his literary contemporaries. Of late, a new Brazilian generation of writers has emerged who are exploring the eternal problematics of man's and woman's destiny within a totally apolitical context. Like Handke's now famous Princeton pronouncement, many authors have reached the saturation point with a literature of social engagement. As the sociopolitical facet of the Brazilian novel is drawing to an end, at least the intensity and pervasiveness of it, younger authors are searching for new themes and forms. They are trying to find a voice and subject matter to suit their times. In the literary supplement of *O Estado de São Paulo*, novelist Márcia Denser, in discussing her book of short stories, *Diana caçadora* (1986; *Diana the Huntress*), states that her work is purposefully the antithesis of those writers who pass out political, ideological, and religious messages. The story "Tigresa," "Tigress," from this collection is narrated by a young author, Diana Marini. Marini's brashness, arrogance, and sense of self-assurance expose the hypocrisy of a group of São Paulo jet-setters. Diana, the huntress, enters the world of the superficial party goers and appears to be the sexual prey of the hostess. Denser's post-modernist poetics eschews the sociopolitical to focus upon relationships and personalities. She portrays the sexual battlegrounds of contemporary Brazilian life, the parties, bars, and motels. This book has the texture and tone of Tama Janowitz's *Slaves of New York* (1986), especially the story "O animal dos motéis" ("The Animal of the Motels"). Denser's writing blends elements taken from popular culture like lyrics from Roberto Carlos and Caetano Veloso with allusions to the works of Hemingway and

Cortázar. Denser's narrative concludes with Diana humbling the hostess, Lila, at her own sexual end-game. In the mid-1980s Denser emphatically and colorfully states what might have been heretical ten years earlier. "Com proselitismo não se faz literatura. Quem comer desse peixe vai vomitar."[18] ("You can't make literature by proselytizing. Whoever eats of this fish is going to vomit.")

V

Márcia Denser's feeling may be a reaction to the overabundance of artlessly conceived sociopolitical narratives. However, it is perhaps time for the younger generation of writers to turn their attention to other areas to find new concerns. Even during the height of the "ditadura," there were those novelists who continued to create an inner-directed, ahistorical, and apolitical literature. However, for this reader, many younger writers will, in all likelihood, continue to explore and articulate themes related to social and political repression. It seems almost incumbent upon the Brazilian artistic community to periodically attempt to define the essential human weakness that allowed a repressive era to continue for such a long period of time, much in the way that the Holocaust, fifty years later, continues as a recurrent subject of modern fiction.

Popular acceptance of the works of this period is generated by the fact that they are an amalgam of contemporary styles and techniques. Caricature, magical realism, myth, and political intention freely fuse with fable, realism, and absurdist elements. Each writer makes an effort to find a voice that will resonate with the populous. Most of the narratives presented have the intention of communicating, politicizing, and creating reader awareness.

It would be a gross omission to imply that only the authors mentioned played important roles in the past twenty years. Other major writers have left an imprint on the period and deserve further study in a broader format: Lya Luft, Autran Dourado (1926), Raduan Nassar (1935), André Carneiro (1922), José J. Veiga (1915), Dinah Silveira Queiroz (1910), Ruth Bueno, Herberto Sales (1917), Tânia Faillace (1939), Víctor Giudice (1934), João Antônio (1937), Caio Fernando Abreu (1948), Orígenes Lessa (1903), Elda van Steen, Fernando Sabino (1923), Júlio Cesar Monteiro Martins (1955), Roberto Reis (1949), Márcia Denser (1949), Domingo Pelligrini (1949), Oswaldo

França Junior (1936), Marcos Rey (1925), Renato Tapajós(1943), Samuel Rawet (1929), Renato Pompeu (1941), and Ana Maria Martins. For the most part, Brazilian writers of this period moved away from the concept of the novel as an intellectual exercise. The Brazilian narrative from the time of Machado de Assis has, generally, attempted to delight, entertain, and instruct. The dense novel of "high" art was reserved for the intellectual elite, while writers like Jorge Amado have been phenomenally successful writing for a mass audience.

From a critical perspective within Brazil itself it is safe to study established writers like Guimarães Rosa and Mário de Andrade. However, as occurred in the United States with writers like Gilbert Sorrentino, Donald Barthelme, Cynthia Ozick, Walker Percy, William Gaddis and Tim O'Brien, there had to occur a safe waiting period for them to be acceptable to the critical establishment, to be legitimately sanctioned. Much of what passes for literary criticism of this very recent period is of the superficial magazine review and literary supplement variety of presentation. In this type of criticism there usually occurs a broad overview of the work under consideration with little regard for the text as the central theme. In many cases the impressions of the critics are based on philosophical affinities, foreign influences, and even discussions of the numbers of volumes that a particular edition has sold. There also has been a general and continuing trend to equate the study of literature with philosophy. Thus, much academic criticism, however penetrating and illuminating it may be, is of such a theoretically philosophical nature as not to be of much help or interest to the foreign reader. Roberto Reis, who is a respected Brazilian critic and fiction writer himself, decries the traditionalism of current Brazilian literary criticism, its lack of openness to new forms, and its failure to utilize an ideological perspective.[19]

From a North American perspective, the study of Portuguese and its literatures is all too often inextricably linked to, and is often a weak appendage of, the study of Spanish and its literatures. Far more time and energy go into the "discovery" of obscure and mediocre Colombian poets than go into the entire field of Brazilian literature.

Whether the novels of this period constitute a "Brazilian boom" is for history to decide. It is interesting to note, however, that these works have been embraced not only by Brazilian, but also by English, American, German, and Italian readers. Readers far from academic circles welcome the novels of Souza, Ribeiro, Loyola Brandão, and Ângelo. The "irrevocably worldly and social"[20] aspect of Brazilian post-modernist literature, as Jerome Mazzaro defines the term, seems

185

to have struck a strong note of popular and international appeal. In brief, the New Brazilian novel's spontaneous popularity is derived from a truly international groundswell.

VI

The final study of this book concerns a writer who has long been an innovator in finding new forms of expression. Murilo Rubião's short stories, his metafictions, are a combination of magic, surrealism, fantasy, Biblical accommodations, and intricate philosophical conundrums. Rubião's stories will serve as an example of those writers who continued to write fiction as a mind game, an intellectual and philosophical exercise. It must be stated that Rubião has remained a vastly underrated presence in the field of Brazilian fiction. In the same manner that Rubião utilizes the world of Biblical stories, recasting them in a modern light, Borges adds his twists and bends to tales like Scheherazade's six hundred and second night, Julio Cortázar retells the Theseus legend in *Los reyes* (1949; *The Kings*), and John Updike retells the classical myth of the Centaur.

Rubião's short narratives are awash in ludic elements. His fiction underscores a sense of freedom, an aesthesia that is conceived without the rigidity of the writer's and reader's roles being clearly defined. This confrontation with traditional reality is achieved through the use of Biblical prefigurations, or in Jorge Luis Borges's terminology, "prophesyzing."[21] Rubião's writings employ Biblical resonances as foreshadowing to acclimate the reader, so that she or he will be prepared for the metaphorical exaggerations and magical realities that follow. The prophesyzing of his texts with Biblical accommodations lends a sense of credibility even to the most surreal occurrences. However, as one might expect, not all readers of this period wanted to enter Rubião's world of literary artifice, for these literary games—apart from those tied to strong sociopolitical messages, like those of Ângelo and Darcy Ribeiro—seemed like a superfluous imposition of fantasy upon a readership that was avidly seeking ideological and cultural definitions.

Biblical Correspondences and Eschatological Questioning in the Metafiction of Murilo Rubião

The idea of an all-powerful divine being is present everywhere, if not consciously recognized, then unconsciously accepted. . . .

Carl Gustav Jung

To Frazer, magic is compulsion; religion is propitiation; a combination of the two exists side by side since neither method proves fully successful alone.

Melville Jean Herskovits

Contemporary Brazilian fiction is beginning to receive the kind of critical attention that has previously been reserved for the "boom" years of Brazil's Spanish-speaking neighbors. Translations of important works are now internationally well received. Modern writers are intensely reviewed by both scholarly journals and the popular press.

However, one very singular writer, Murilo Rubião, has maintained a consistent tradition of personalism in his short fiction since the 1940s. His is a unique aesthetic focus related to the "metafictions" of Barth, Calvino, Kafka, and Borges, but still richly framed in the writer's personal vision and concerns.

It is generally the case that most discussions of Rubião's works underscore the surrealistic or magically realistic qualities of his writings. His fantastic visions and magical worlds are usually alluded to and described, but very rarely is there an attempt to analyze the underlying oneiric logic and thematic unity in his fiction.

A detailed exploration of two of Rubião's famous stories—two pieces that lend their names to collections—may offer an insight into the fictional world view of one of Brazil's most original writers. The evolutionary philosophical view that these two stories portray is an interesting one and worthy of further study. Bobby J. Chamberlain relates that Rubião was born in Silvestre Ferraz, Minas Gerais, in 1916 and worked as a journalist, government bureaucrat, and commercial attaché.[1] *O ex-mágico* (*The Ex-Magician from the Minhota Tavern*) was published in 1947, *O pirotécnico Zacarias* (*Zacarias, the Pyrotechnist*) in 1974. Although there exist parallels in style and structure, Rubião's thematic and eschatological focus during the passing decades has altered dramatically.

Raymond S. Sayers considers Rubião "one of the two or three outstanding writers of fantastic fiction, a genre that occupies a strong place in modern Brazilian writing."[2] Sayers observes that Rubião's characters are depersonalized and there is no real tension or empathy between reader and text. The reader "is forced to remain an outsider— that is precisely the effect which the author desires and which contributes to his originality."[3] Utilizing Sayers's reading of Rubião's fiction as a point of departure, the present study calls attention to the seminal importance of these short narratives in the development of contemporary Brazil's postmodern anti-realistic fiction. While underscoring the historical importance of this fiction, the study will also analyze Murilo Rubião's use of Biblical correspondences and inversions to tender an evolving vision of eternal eschatological questions.

I

The idea of creating or recasting a parallel religious text, one that complements and may even run contrary to traditional theological thinking, is not new. In sixteenth-century Portugal and Spain there existed an abundance of ascetic and mystical writings. "Jewish religious thought has had two major . . . aspects. One has been that of down-to-earth rationalism represented by the Talmud and its vast commentary literature. The other has been that of mysticism embodied in the literature of the cabala. While the Talmudists sought to apprehend God, wisdom, and righteousness by means of logic, the cabalists sought the same objectives by means of the 'hidden wisdom' and esoteric practices. . . . Denied the natural means for coping with reality they grasped at the magical."[4]

Rubião's fictive imagination constructs an ingenious parallel text that is, in essence, a parodistic inversion of important Biblical motifs and themes. The Biblical layer is especially strong in "O ex-mágico da Taberna Minhota." No element of Rubião's fiction is extraneous. He is a conscious and deliberate artist. Elizabeth Lowe states that "Murilo Rubião claims to have rewritten 'O convidado' for twenty-six years."[5] The author himself affirms, "I never worried about giving an end to my stories. Using ambiguity as a fictional means, I try to fragment my stories to the utmost to give the reader the certainty that they will go on indefinitely."[6] Thus, one must assume that the Biblical correspondences are consciously planned and that the creation of a magical reality is not merely an end in itself. Lowe's reading of these works stresses the theme of "the sentence to infinite repetition, or the condemnation to eternal life."[7] Jorge Schwartz also highlights the "theme of the infinite, rendered by repetitive and circular action, [which] reduces the alleged future to an eternal present. This, in turn, becomes the 'mask' of the Apocalypse."[8] The masterful aspect of Rubião's minimalist and carefully constructed fiction is that it is accomplishing exactly what the author has stated that he intended to accomplish: "using ambiguity as a fictional means," that is, to generate active reader participation and critical interpretation.

Theodore Ziolkowski, in discussing novelists like Günter Grass, Gore Vidal, and John Barth in his book *Fictional Transfiguration of Jesus*, states: "It is hardly surprising to find a strong strain of parody in . . . their . . . fictional transfiguration. . . . These sophisticated talents of the twentieth century with their jaded sensibilities, who know everything and have lost all naiveté, must agree with this modern Faustian view that all the devices of art 'are suitable today only for parody.' "[9] In the way that John Barth's *Giles Goat-Boy* "exploits the Bible for the sheer aesthetic fun of structural parody,"[10] Rubião's fiction is a parodic analogue of biblical occurrences. However, Rubião's use of fantasy and magicality has a deeper, more theological focus: a concern with the problematics of eschatology. Rubião's stories explore universal theological questions. Ziolkowski refers to "the vast neo-baroque splendor of Barth's zany cosmos;"[11] Rubião's aesthetic vision is anything but zany, for it is steeped in melancholy and anguish. He has created two companion pieces of short fiction wherein death has no finality and where the central question—even though presented in an anti-realistic and avant-garde manner—is the eternal relationship between the divine and the human.

II

Rubião's fiction blurs the distinction between illusion and reality, magic and religion, the human and the divine. The God figure's realization of his eternal nature and the subsequent burden that that discovery causes is the axis upon which both pieces turn. The ex-magician comes into existence abruptly, and his miraculous genesis is depicted in flat, colloquial, and prosaic terms: "Um dia dei com os meus cabelos ligeiramente grisalhos, no espelho da Taberna Minhota. A descoberta não me espantou e tampouco me surpreendi ao retirar do bolso o dono do restaurante." ("I found myself one day, with light gray hair, in the mirror of the Minhota Tavern, a discovery which in no way frightened me, any more than it astonished me to take the owner of the restaurant out of my pocket.")[12] The magician's story continues in a narratively detached fashion. It consciously accommodates and exploits the creation myth. The story's tone inverts biblical hyperbole and grandiloquence, for this modern day deity's manner is anything but godlike. Rubião's story tenders important metaphysical questions from the perspective of the God figure's inability to explain his capacity to create: "Ele sim, perplexo, me perguntou como podia ter feito aquilo. O que poderia responder, nessa situação, uma pessoa que não encontrava a menor explicação para sua presença no mundo?" (p. 53). ("He, rather perplexed, asked me how could I have done such a thing. What could I answer, given my situation, a person who lacked the least explanation for his presence in the world?" [p. 109].) This same ironically colloquial tone and an extreme openness of meaning is now found in much of the anti-realistic fiction of Ignácio de Loyola Brandão, Roberto Drummond, Marcos Rey, Moacyr Scliar, and Luiz Vilela: "Disse-lhe que estava cansado. Nascera cansado e entediado" (p. 53). ("I said to him that I was tired, that I was born tired and weary" [p. 109].)

Rubião's stories are tightly constructed analogues and purposefully vague allegories. A historical and sociopolitical dimension is added, as the magician is employed to entertain the customers at the very tavern where he was created: "E passei daquele momento em diante a divertir a freguesia da casa com os meus passes mágicos" (p. 53). ("So I began, from that time on, to entertain the clientele of the establishment with my magical activity" [p. 109].) In an overt accommodation of Jesus's first manifestation of his divine power at the wedding feast at Cana, Rubião burlesques the fact that in contemporary society the profit motive outweighs religious revelation:

> O homem, entretanto, não gostou da minha prática de oferecer aos espectadores almoços gratuitos, que eu extraía misteriosamente de dentro do paletó. Considerando não ser dos melhores negócios aumentar o número de fregueses sem o conseqüente acréscimo nos lucros. . . . (P. 54)

> (The man himself, however, failed to appreciate my habit of offering onlookers a variety of free lunches, which I would mysteriously draw forth from the inside of my own jacket. Judging it to be not the best of transactions merely to increase the number of customers—without a corresponding growth in profits. . . .) (P. 109–10)

The story continues to explore and exploit the brooding God figure's conception of himself. Although he possesses the ability to perform supernatural feats, he is not at peace for he is envious of others:

> Por que me emocionar, se não me causavam pena aqueles rostos inocentes, destinados a passar pelos sofrimentos que acompanham o amadurecimento do homem? Muito menos me ocurria odiá-las por terem tudo que ambicionei e não tive: um nascimento e um passado. (P. 54)

> (Why be moved, though, if those innocent faces, destined to endure the suffering inflicted upon any man's coming of age, aroused no pity in me, much less any anger, over their having everything I longed for but did not myself possess: birth, and a past.) (P. 110)

The contemporary irony of Rubião's inverted mythic perspective is that the God figure is not presented as all-knowing and all-powerful but is instead as racked with self-doubts as his human counterparts. His powers become a burden. "Com o crescimento da popularidade a minha vida tornou-se insuportável" (p. 54). ("As I grew more popular, my life became intolerable" [p. 110].) He longs to put an end to all the attention that he continually receives. In an act of self-mutilation he decides to try to remove the source of his anguish: "Numa dessas vezes, irritado, disposto a nunca mais fazer mágicas, mutilei as mãos. Não adiantou. Ao primeiro movimento que fiz, elas reapareceram novas e perfeitas nas pontas dos tocos de braço" (p. 55). ("On one of these occasions, completely furious, and resolved never again to practice magic, I cut off my hands. To no purpose. As soon as I moved, they reappeared, fresh and perfect, on the ends of the stump of each arm!" [p. 111].) Having failed, he merely wishes to die: "Urgia encontrar solução para o meu desespero. Pensando bem, concluí que somente a morte poria termo ao meu desconsolo" (p. 55). ("I had to resolve my despair somehow. After weighing the matter carefully, I concluded that only death would put a proper end to my misfortune" [p. 111].) Rubião then accommodates the motif of Daniel and the lions' den: "Firme no propósito, tirei dos bolsos uma dúzia de leões e, cruzando os braços, aguardei o momento em que seria devorado por eles" (p. 55). ("Steadfast in my decision, I took a dozen lions out of my pockets and, crossing my arms, waited for the moment when I would be devoured" [p. 111].) Here even the lions are filled with a parallel sense of anguished ennui. "—Este mundo é tremendamente tedioso—concluíram" (p. 55). ("'This world is tremendously tedious,' they declared" [p. 112].) Upon learning this, the magician turns violent and slays them in a grotesque manner: "Não consegui refrear a raiva. Matei-os todos e me pus a devorá-los. Esperava morrer, vítima de fatal indigestão" (p. 55). ("I failed to restrain my outright rage. I killed them all, and began to devour them myself. I had hopes of dying the victim of a fatal indigestion" [p. 112].) The magician comes to realize that he is immortal; he can find no way to kill himself. Theological inversions and ironies are sharply drawn.

> Puxei o gatilho, à espera do estampido, a dor da bala penetrando na minha cabeça.
> Não veio o disparo nem a morte: a mauser se transformara num lápis.
> Rolei até o chão, soluçando. Eu, que podia criar outros seres, não encontrava meios de libertar-me da existência. (P. 56)

(I pulled the trigger, expecting a loud report and the pain of the bullet tearing through my head.
There was no shot, and no death: the handgun turned into a pencil.
I rolled to the floor, sobbing. I who could create other beings had no means to liberate myself from existence.) (P. 112)

The story's most profanely ironic twist occurs as the magician-God figure finally does discover a means of dying, a quotidian form of death, so to speak:

Ouvira de um homem triste que ser funcionário público era suicidar-se aos poucos.
Não me encontrava em condições de determinar qual a forma de suicídio que melhor me convinha: se lenta ou rápida. Por isso empreguei-me numa Secretaria de Estado. (P. 56)

(From a sad man I heard that to be a civil servant was to commit suicide little by little.
I was in no condition to determine which form of suicide was best suited to me: slow or quick. As a result, I took a job in the Department of State.) (P. 112)

As in much of Brazilian fiction, sociopolitical reality is viewed with a fine sense of absurdist black humor.

1931 entrou triste, com ameaças de demissões coletivas na Secretaria e a recusa da datilógrafa em me aceitar. Ante o risco de ser demitido, procurei acautelar meus interesses. (P. 57)

(1931 began cheerlessly, with threats of mass dismissals in our department and a refusal by the typist to consider my proposal. Faced with the possibility of being discharged, I tried somehow to look after my own interests.) (P. 113)

Work, love, and friends are only a "distração momentânea" (p. 56) ("momentary distractions" [p. 113]). The magician is still racked with anguish. "Debatia-me em incertezas" (p. 56). ("I struggle with uncertainties" [p. 113].) He now wishes to remain at his trivial job and reverts to magic, attempting to deceive his supervisor; yet, when he most needs his magic, when it is intrinsically important to him, it fails. "Tive que confessar minha derrota. Confiara demais na faculdade de fazer mágicas e ela fora anulada pela burocracia" (p. 57). ("I was forced to admit defeat. I had trusted too much in my powers to make magic, which had been nullified by bureaucracy" [p. 113].) He now can only feign his "miraculosos dons de mago" (p. 57) ("miraculous gift of wizardry" [p. 113]). At the story's end he is left alone contemplating his existence: "Não me conforta a ilusão. Serve somente para aumentar o arrependimento de não ter criado todo um mundo má-gico" (p. 57). ("Of course, the illusion gives me no comfort. It only serves to intensify my regret not to have created a total magical world" [p. 114].)

The central symbols in the fiction of Rubião are color, light, and brilliance. Fireworks, important as an emblem of divine presence and knowledge, also constitute a motif that is underscored in both pieces of short fiction. In a poignant soliloquy the magician laments his ina-bility to cover the earth with magically polychromatic displays that emanate from his own being. He yearns for the love and attention of all men. In essence, he seeks the transcendence of divine affirmation:

> Por instantes, imagino como seria maravilhoso arrancar do corpo lenços vermelhos, azuis, brancos. verdes. Encher a noite com fogos de artifício. Erguer o rosto para o céu e deixar que pelos meus lábios saísse o arco-íris. Um arco-íris que cobrisse a terra de um ex-tremo a outro. E os aplausos dos homens de cabelos brancos, das meigas criancinhas. (P. 57)

> (At certain moments I imagine how marvelous it would be to extract red, blue, white, and green handkerchiefs from my body, fill the night with fireworks, turn my face to the sky and let a rainbow pour forth from my lips, a rainbow that could cover the earth from one extremity to the other. Then the applause from the old men with their white hair, and from gentle children.) (P. 114)

The tale ends on this note of pathos, with the God figure dreaming of radiant transcendental displays of color. Rubião's story evolves as an inverted spiritual quest, a theological enigma in which both God and man suffer and dream of revelation within the "Kenoma," the non-place of emptiness.

III

It is possible to view Murilo Rubião's fictional world as an aesthetic continuance of the absurdist and antilogical elements that were con-tained in the novels of Mário de Andrade and Oswaldo de Andrade. His fantasist's imagination has also inspired and influenced younger writers, laying the groundwork for the popularity of the Brazilian ab-surdist antinovel. In essence, his fictional poetics have expanded exist-ing Brazilian literary traditions while remaining firmly rooted in the collective spirit of the absurd that has constituted such a strong world view from colonial times to the present. His narrative obsession with metaphysical issues, the offhand, colloquial, and ironic presentation of his stories, and his characters' comic-strip thinness and quasi-allegorical nature are all antecedents of such present-day novels as Ignácio de Loyola Brandão's *Zero*. Rubião's serious metaphysical musing is presented in an absurdist narrative form. Inverted Biblical motifs evolve as contemporary "cabalistic" enigmas filled with magic, mystically ambiguous meaning, and evanescent flashes of pure metaphysical illuminations.

In his essay "The Christian Novel Now," Peter Prescott observes, "One need not profess the faith to recognize the mythic structure that Christian themes can lend a narrative, or the fine opportunities for moral perplexity that they afford."[13] Within the fictive world that Rubião creates are the stirrings of the "metafictional vogue" that was to occur some twenty years after the publication of "O ex-mágico." It was Robert Scholes and William Gass who defined the term "metafiction." Gass, the American philosopher, critic, and novelist, points out metafiction's affinity to antiliterature.

> The use of philosophical ideas in the construction of fictional works—in a very self-conscious and critical way, I mean—has been hastened by the growing conviction that not only do these ideas often represent conceptual systems of considerable complexity, they have the further advantage of being almost wholly irrelevant as accounts of the real world. They are, that is, to a great degree *fictional* already, and ripe for fun and games. . . .
> Indeed, many of the so-called antinovels are really metafictions.[14]

The more recent of the two narratives,"O pirotécnico Zacarias" (p. 13) ("Zacarias, the Pyrotechnist" [p. 87]), begins as do all of Rubião's stories, with a biblical epigraph, in this case from the Book of Job (11:17): "*E se levantará pela tarde sobre ti uma luz como a do meio-dia; e quando te julgares consumido, nascerás como a estrela d'alva*" (p. 13). ("And thine age shall be clearer than the noonday; thou shalt shine forth, thou shalt be as the morning star" [p. 87].)[15] Job, a contemporary emblem of suffering and anguish, gives voice to his strong faith in God and the future. His vision of divine revelation is expressed by the symbol of intense light. In *The Art of Biblical Narrative* (1981), the critic Robert Alter, while discussing the historical interweaving of Biblical events and characters, states, "The only evident exceptions to the rule are (Jonah and) Job, which in its very stylization seems manifestly a philosophic fable (hence the rabbinic dictum, 'There was no such creature as Job; he is a parable')."[16] Rubião's approach to his fiction is very much in the fabulist's tradition. He creates characters and situations that fall outside the realm of objective reality. His is a distorted, fantastical vision which his readers explore with the dedication of the ancient cabalists.

With the centrality of the symbol of light established, the story of Zacarias begins. The tension in the work is created from the opening query: "Raras são as vezes que, nas conversas de amigos meus, ou de pessoas das minhas relações, não surja esta pergunta. Teria morrido o pirotécnico Zacarias?" (p. 13). ("Rare is the occasion when, in conversations among friends of mine or people of my acquaintance, this question doesn't arise: was the pyrotechnist Zacarias actually dead?" [p. 87].) Zacarias recounts the events of his physical death. However, in death life continues. A physical paradox is tendered and an enigmatic fictional game is set in motion: "O indivíduo a quem andam chamando Zacarias não passa de uma alma penada, envolvida por um pobre invólucro humano" (p. 13). ("The individual whom they persist in calling Zacarias is nothing but a tormented soul wrapped in some pitiable human garb" [p. 87].) "Viver, cansar bem os músculos, andando pelas ruas cheias de gente, ausentes de homens" (pp. 15–16). ("To live, to get muscles good and tired, walking along streets filled with people, empty of men" [p. 89].) Every element in Rubião's polished works of fiction is conceived with endless care. His selection of the name "Zacarias" evokes the figure of the Biblical priest of the same name (Luke 1:5–67, 3:2), who was struck dumb by the angel Gabriel for his skepticism. He recovers his speech as his son John the Baptist is born; at that moment he praises God in an effusive blessing often referred to as the Benedictus. Another overt use of symbolism is the choice of the name "Estrada do Acaba Mundo" (p. 15) ("Acaba-Mundo Road [End-of-the-World Road]" [p. 89]). The apocalyptic connotation here is also employed to convey Biblical resonance instantly.

After Zacarias's (non)death, life's sensual pleasures continue: female companionship, alcohol, and particularly the presence of color. Zacarias calls his love of light and color a "polychromatic delirium," stating, "Sem cor jamais quis viver" (p. 15). ("I never want to live without color" [p. 89].) As the months pass, he grows to accept his state. With physical death has come an awakening and deepening of experiences. He now endures a heightened sense of anguish and compassion for all men. His anxiety also includes concern for his present state of being.

> Só um pensamento me oprime: que acontecimentos o destino reservará a um morto se os vivos respiram uma vida agonizante? E a

minha angústia cresce ao sentir, na sua plentitude, que a minha capacidade de amar, discernir as coisas, é bem superior à dos seres que por mim passam assustados. (P. 19)

(Only one thought really troubles me: what events will fate hold in store for a dead man, if the living breathe such agonizing lives? And my anxiety increases on sensing, in all its fullness, how my capacity to love, to discern things, is far superior to that of the many who pass me by so fearfully.) (Pp. 92–93)

In what can only be described as a very uncustomary vision for a contemporary writer, Rubião's narrative concludes, not on an anguished note, but with the hopeful vision that was reflected in the opening quote from the Book of Job. The ending is affirmative, joyous, and somewhat unexpected in a splenetic age of predominately alienated writings.

O dia poderá nascer claro, o sol brilhando como nunca brilhou. Nessa hora os homens compreenderão que, mesmo à margem da vida, ainda vivo, porque a minha existência se transmudou em cores e o branco já se aproxima da terra para exclusiva ternura dos meus olhos. (P. 19)

(Still, a clear day might dawn tomorrow, the sun brilliant as never before. And at such an hour men may come to realize that, even on the margin of life, I am still alive, because my existence has been transmuted into colors, and whiteness is already drawing close to the earth, to the exclusive delight of my eyes.) (P. 93)

Rubião brings together these two pieces of short fiction under the unifying images of light and color. The ex-magician, who two decades earlier lamented his inability to cover the earth with a rainbow of color, is fictionally reincarnated in the character of Zacarias, who can not "live without color" (p. 89). Zacarias, at work's end, attains an anthropomorphic diffusion of his being into cosmic and Divine Light.

Though much of contemporary literary criticism utilizes the term "apocalyptic" in the sense of a highly negative warning, the term in its original Greek meaning of "disclosure" or "revelation" in a positive sense is applicable to Rubião's metafiction. "Zacarias, the Pyrotechnist" prefigures the power and sensuous splendor of the Book of Revelation. Like Saint John before the blinding light of the New City descending to earth, Zacarias senses an existence in which his being will be "transmuted into colors." The intense rapture, delight, and hope of the Book of Revelation mirrors the narrative's final paragraph: "Ainda vivo" ("I am still alive"), "o sol brilhando como nunca brilhou" ("the sun brilliant as never before"), "Amanhã o dia poderá nascer claro"

197

("a clear day might dawn tomorrow"), "o branco já se aproxima da terra" ("whiteness is already drawing close to the earth") (Portuguese p. 19, English p. 93). Rubião is consciously constructing a correspondence with one of the world's most beautiful and influential pieces of literature to convey his contemporary gospel of hope.

Murilo Rubião's prose evolves as an existential rethinking of man's place in the universe. He attempts to engender a new fiction, one which continually seeks to define the unique nature of contemporary man's existence. He has moved beyond the now cliché-ridden concept of the encounter with nothingness to a metaphysical stance that stresses a strong element of faith. However, it is difficult to equate the metaphysical impulses in Rubião's writings to any traditional concept of religion. His metafictions ask his readers to actively participate in the creative process. Through his conscious and lyric accommodation of Biblical correspondences, he imparts to his narratives resonances of the universal literary experience, what Coleridge calls "the film of familiarity." In "Zacarias, the Pyrotechnist" he employs these correspondences to convey, in magically poetic terms, a hopeful vision of contemporary man's eschatological situation.

NOTES

[1] Randal Johnson, "Cinema Novo and Cannibalism: *Macunaíma*," *Brazilian Cinema*, eds. Randal Johnson and Robert Stam (Rutherford, NJ: Fairleigh Dickinson University Press, 1982), p. 178.

[2] Keith Cohn, *Film and Fiction* (New Haven: Yale University Press, 1979), p. 208.

[3] Luis Arbex, "Brazil," *International Film Guide 1986*, ed. Peter Cowie (London:The Tantivy Press, 1985), p. 79.

[4] Malcolm Silverman. Review of *Esta noite ou nunca* by Marcos Rey. *World Literature Today* 60, no.2 (1986): 296–97.

[5] Silverman. 296–97.

[6] John G. Cawelti, *Adventure, Mystery, and Romance* (Chicago: University of Chicago Press, 1976), p. 16.

[7] Rubem Fonseca, *A grande arte* (Rio de Janeiro: Francisco Alves, 1984), p. 203. The English edition is *High Art*, trans. Ellen Watson (New York: Harper & Row, 1986), p. 233.

[8] Fonseca, p. 106, Watson, p. 117.

[9] Steve Paul, "Bawdy in Brazil," a review of *Showdown* by Jorge Amado. *The Kansas City Star* 14 February 1988: 1E.

[10] Jorge Amado, *Tocaia Grande: A face obscura* (Rio de Janeiro: Record, 1986), p. 314. The English edition is *Showdown*, trans. Gregory Rabassa (New York: Bantam Books, 1988), p. 304.

[11] Ibid p. 321, and in English p. 312.

[12] Anonymous review of *Showdown* by Jorge Amado. *Publishers Weekly* 8 January 1988: p. 71.

[13] Stefan Kanfer, "Macho Days on the Cacoa Frontier," a review of *Showdown* by Jorge Amado. *Time* magazine 15 February 1988: p. 92.

[14] Ibid p. 92.

[15] Silviano Santiago, *Stella Manhattan* (Rio de Janeiro: Nova Fronteira, 1985), p. 21.

[16] Santiago, p. 20.

[17] Santiago, p. 12.

[18] Márcia Denser, "Esta é a musa dark da literatura brasileira," rev. of *Diana caçadora* O Estado de São Paulo 22 May 1986: 10.

[19] Roberto Reis, "Hei de convencer" *I & E Ideologies and Literature* 6 (1978) 120–27.

[20] Jerome Mazzaro, *Postmodern American Poetry* (Urbana: University of Illinois Press, 1980), p. viii.

[21] See Carter Wheelock, "Borges, Cortázar, and the Aesthetic of the Vacant Mind," *International Fiction Review* 12, no. 1 (1985), pp. 3–10. In this study Professor Wheelock discusses magical causality and Borges's use of prophesying which parallels Rubião's approach to writing.

Rubião Study

The first epigraph of this study is from Carl Gustav Jung, *Psychological Reflections*, ed. Jolande Jacobi (New York: Harper, 1961), p. 301.

The second epigraph is from Melville Jean Herskovits, "Magic," Maria Leach ed., *The Standard Dictionary of Folklore, Mythology and Legend*, (New York: Funk & Wagnalls, 1975), p. 660.

[1] Bobby J. Chamberlain, "Murilo Rubião," D. W. Foster and Roberto Reis eds., *A Dictionary of Contemporary Brazilian Authors* (Tempe: Arizona State University Center for Latin American Studies, 1982), p. 131.

[2] Raymond S. Sayers. rev. of *The Ex-Magician and Other Stories* by Murilo Rubião, *World Literature Today* 54, no. 2 (1980), 264.

[3] Sayers, 264.

[4] Nathan Ausubel, *Pictorial History of the Jewish People* (New York: Crown Press, 1984), p. 39.

[5] Elizabeth Lowe, *The City in Brazilian Literature* (Rutherford, NJ: Fairleigh Dickinson University Press, 1982), p. 196.

[6] Lowe, p. 196.

[7] Lowe, p. 149.

[8] Lowe, p. 154. Lowe is paraphrasing Schwartz's "Obra muriliana do

fantástico como máscara," *Minas Gerais Suplemento Literário*, 15 March 1975, p. 14.

[9] Theodore Ziolkowski, *Fictional Transfigurations of Jesus* (Princeton: Princeton University Press, 1972), p. 231.

[10] Ziolkowski, p. 257.

[11] Ziolkowski, p. 257.

[12] Murilo Rubião, *O pirotécnico Zacarias* (São Paulo: Ática, 1974), p. 53. The English edition is *The Ex-Magician and Other Stories*, trans. Thomas Colchie (New York: Avon, 1979), p. 109. All subsequent quotes will be taken from these editions, and page numbers will be entered directly into the text.

[13] Peter S. Prescott, *Never in Doubt* (New York: Arbor House, 1986), p. 83.

[14] William H. Gass, "Philosophy and Form of Fiction," in *Fiction and the Figures of Life* (New York: Knopf, 1970), p. 25.

[15] The biblical quotation actually ends with " . . . as the morning" and not "the morning *star*" included in the epigraph of the English version of the the story.

[16] Robert Alter, *The Art of Biblical Narrative* (New York: Basic Books, 1980), p. 33.

CONCLUDING
OBSERVATIONS

Since 1964, many Brazilian authors have attempted to transcend the passive and reactive role of the writer. Their literary works are seen today as responsive. While their literature is composed of its own internal and timeless rhythms, it is also highly sensitive to historical and political currents. Still adhering to many of the modernist ideals of the 1920s, these authors aspire to analyze the national consciousness while seeking to create a universal literature. In the process they have eternalized the lives of history's victims during an aberrant period of political repression. Along with the malevolent and ubiquitous Ford Falcon in contemporary Argentine literature, the "pau-de-arara," the parrot perch, will pass into literary history as an archetypal symbol of repression.

Many of the narratives studied in this book underscore the personal dramas and destinies of individuals living within an overwhelming and oppressive political and existential situation. The great abstractions of philosophical thought are shown to pale in relation to the modern heroes' and anti-heroes' desire to avoid victimization. With the fall of old myths and archetypes comes the creation of a new antihero, the "João-Ninguém," be he or she called José Gonçalvez, Souza, D. J., Cremilda, the prisoner, Macabéa, Nelo, Laurinha, Joe Caripuna, Zacarias, Alma, or the entire cast of characters that make up Márcio Souza's "floating opera." These anti-heroes form part of a remarkable spiritual autobiography. The world that they populate is maddeningly impersonal, inscrutably bureaucratic, and overtly violent. Out of this sociopolitical milieu, the New Fiction is able to articulate the ambiguities of the human drama. From this political and human drama Brazilian writers have created a responsive literature that is at once nationally oriented and, at the same time, truly universal.

While the documentation of repression is a strong component of the New Fiction, it is by no means the central point of most of the works. Generally, novelists manage to transcend the mangled corpse syndrome. The vast majority of the writings of this period attain a critical distance and focus that integrate aesthetic preoccupations with social intention. Jacques Ehrmann's synthesis of this aesthetic preoccupation seems truer than ever and bears restating; "The power of words over history, of history over words, such is the problem of our time . . ."[1]

The preceding studies have profiled many of the themes, energies, and voices that comprise the contemporary Brazilian narrative. There are the science fiction dystopias of Loyola Brandão; the metafictions of Lispector and Rubião; Vilela's, Drummond's, Sant'Anna's, and Moreira da Costa's novels of postmodern consciousness; the stylized detective fiction of Fonseca; the magical fantasies of Moacyr Scliar; Darcy Ribeiro's socially conscious archetypal fiction; the absurdist visions of Márcio Souza; the sociopolitical narratives of Callado, Antônio Torres, and Ivan Ângelo, and the singular genius of João Ubaldo Ribeiro.

Since the central focus of these studies directs attention to those contemporary authors whose major writings occur within this intense period of political repression, it is not surprising that much of the fiction of this era has dealt with issues of social morality, culpability, and cultural identity. This fiction exhibits all the experimental strategies, formal exploration, and aesthetic creativity that parallel the universal literary currents of our time. However, the thematic focus of these narratives is, for the most part, nationally oriented, assiduously exploring the reality that lies just beneath the accepted national myth.

In the mid-1980s writers continued to redefine and demythologize cultural and social myths and ideals. Jorge Amado published *Tocaia Grande*, a work that reflects and recreates Brazilian history in both mythic and antimythic terms. For as he states, "Quero descobrir e revelar a face obscura, aquela que foi varrida dos compêndios de História."[2] ("I want to discover and describe history's dark side, that which was erased from the textbooks.") João Ubaldo Ribeiro, whose international reputation now has been solidly established,[3] published his anti-history *Viva o povo brasileiro* in 1984.

Many writers of the era have responded to the inherent contradictions of the Brazilian myth of state by striving to transform it, or at least to cut through much of its cultural nationalism. In the New Fiction's attempt to reshape the collective consciousness, the vast majority of Brazilian writers have not remained indifferent to historical perspectives. In their fiction the dynamism of an "idealized national future" that characterized the Kubitchek years has been juxtaposed to the reality of the ordinary and, often times, desperate lives of Brazilians living under a succession of repressive governments.

Over the past two decades fiction writing in Brazil has constituted, in a symbolic sense, an act of national catharsis. Ultimately, it is the aesthetic quality of this new fiction that should be stressed. In Brazil a corpus of fiction has been produced that is, in many ways, as fascinating as, and the aesthetic equal of, its much heralded Spanish speaking neighbors.[4] The contemporary Brazilian narrative is only now beginning to receive the kind of critical attention that had previously been reserved for the "boom" years of the Spanish-American novel. Translations of important works are internationally well received and this fiction is beginning to be reviewed by professional scholars in the field of comparative literature. This fiction is both an ideological stance and an artistic creation that values craftsmanship, originality, and the ability to tell a good story. Brazilian fiction is much more than ideologized narration, for it has proven that art can be created by incorporating and reacting to a sociopolitical and historical reality. *A festa, Sargento Getúlio, Essa terra, Sangue de Coca-Cola, A hora da estrela, Maíra, Mad Maria, Não verás país nenhum,* and *Galvez, Imperador do Acre* are responsive works that transcend a purely ideological reading. It is the aesthetically transcendent nature of these works that makes them of such interest to both the Brazilian and foreign reader.

While achieving distinction both individually and collectively, contemporary Brazilian writers have benefited from, contributed to, and expanded existing literary traditions. It is hoped that the preceding studies have added to an understanding of the significant Brazilian contribution to the international modern narrative.

NOTES

[1] Jacques Ehrmann, *Literature and Revolution* (Boston: Beacon Press, 1967), p. 5. In this same regard, Mario Vargas Llosa has stated, "Politics and literature have always been strongly united in the history of Latin America, beginning in the age of the conquistadors. Literature developed in a political atmosphere out of political conflicts." Latin American Festival, Bonn, Germany, summer of 1986 from a broadcast of the Voice of America (Portuguese broadcast, 13 July 1986).

[2] Jorge Amado, *Tocaia Grande: A face obscura* (Rio de Janeiro: Editora Record, 1986), p. 15.

[3] João Ubaldo Ribeiro has been praised by critics like *Newsweek*'s acerbic Peter Prescott, "A Good Barbarian," *Newsweek* 30 Jan. 1978, p. 78. Osvaldo Soriano, one of Argentina's foremost writers places Ubaldo Ribeiro on a par with writers like Borges, Hemingway, García Márquez, and Milan Kundera. In an interview with Allesandra Liccio, *Belfagor* 37, no. 2 (March 1982) p. 170, she calls *Sergeant Getúlio* a masterpiece, "autore di um capolavoro."

[4] This point is polemically controversial. It addresses the fact that critics like Hernán Vidal conclude that the so-called "boom" in Spanish American literature was caused in part by foreign perception. David William Foster offers a variant to this position by suggesting that the "boom" was to an extent the calculated appeal by certain writers and their agents to potential foreign interest. These extra-literary concerns are an inevitable and interesting sidebar to any discussion of the state and merit of Brazilian fiction and its relationship to Spanish American literature. See Hernán Vidal, *Literatura hispanoamericana e ideología liberal: surgimiento y crisis* (Takoma Park, MD: Hispamérica, 1976); and David William Foster, *Alternate Voices* (Columbia: University of Missouri Press, 1985), p. xxi. See also Charles Newman, *The Post-Modern Aura: The Art of Fiction in an Age of Inflation* (Evanston: Northwestern University Press, 1985). For a discussion of the comparative state of literary criticism in the Hispanic and Luso-Brazilian fields see Ronald W. Souza, "Canonical Questions," *I&E: Ideologies and Literature* 6 (1978): 102–06. See also Roberto Reis, "Hei de convencer,": 120–27.

SELECT
BIBLIOGRAPHY

Abdulla, Adnan K. *Catharsis in Literature* (Bloomington: Indiana University Press, 1985).

Alegría, Fernando. "Antiliteratura," *América Latina en su literatura*, ed. César Fernández Moreno (Mexico City: Siglo XXI, 1972), pp. 243–58.

Alter, Robert. *The Art of Biblical Narrative* (New York: Basic Books, 1980).

———. "The New American Novel," *Commentary*, vol. 60, no. 5 (Nov. 1975): 44–51.

Amado, Jorge, *Tocaia Grande: A face obscura* (Rio de Janeiro: Record, 1986). Published in English as *Showdown*, trans. Gregory Rabassa (New York: Bantam Books, 1988).

Andrade, Oswald de. *Obras completas II* (Rio de Janeiro: Civilização Brasileira, 1971). Published in English as *Seraphim Grosse Pointe*, trans. Kenneth D. Jackson and Albert Bork (Austin: New Latin Quarter Editions, 1979).

Ângelo, Ivan. *A festa* (São Paulo: Summus, 1978). Published in English as *The Celebration*, trans. Thomas Colchie (New York: Avon, 1982).

———. *A casa de vidro* (São Paulo: Cultura, 1980). Published in English as *The Tower of Glass*, trans. Ellen Watson (New York: Avon, 1986).

Antônio, João. *Abraçado ao meu rancor* (Rio de Janeiro: Guanabara, 1986).

Arbex, Luis. "Brazil," *International Film Guide 1986*, ed. Peter Cowie (London: The Tantivy Press, 1985).

Arlett, Robert. "Daniel Martin and the Contemporary Epic Novel," *Modern Fiction Studies* 31 (1985), 173–86.

Ausubel, Nathan. *Pictorial History of the Jewish People* (New York: Crown Press, 1984).

Baden, Nancy T. "Clarice Lispector," *A Dictionary of Contemporary Brazilian Authors*, eds. David William Foster and Roberto Reis (Tempe: Arizona State University, Center for Latin American Studies, 1981), pp. 73–74.

Baker, Robert A., and Michael Nietzel. *Private Eyes: One Hundred and One Knights* (Bowling Green, Ohio: Bowling Green State University Press, 1985).

Barth, John. "The Literature of Exhaustion," *On Contemporary Literature*, ed. Richard Kostelanetz (New York: Avon, 1969), pp. 622–75.

Beagle, Peter S. *The Garden of Earthly Delights* (New York: Rosebud Books, 1982).

Bellow, Saul. *Herzog* (New York: Fawcett, 1965).

Berger, Harold L. *Science Fiction and the New Dark Age* (Bowling Green, Ohio: Popular Press, 1976).

Blehl, S. J., and Vincent Ferrer. "Literature and Religious Belief," *Mansions of the Spirit*, ed. George A. Panichas (New York: Hawthorn Books, 1967).

Bletter, Diana Katcher. "Rio de Janeiro," *The Jewish Traveler*, ed. Alan M. Tigay (Garden City, NY: Doubleday, 1987).

Bloch, Robert. *This Crowded Earth* (New York: Ballantine, 1968).

Boyers, Robert. *Atrocity and Amnesia: The Political Novel since 1945* (New York: Oxford University Press, 1985).

Bosi, Alfredo. *O conto brasileiro contemporâneo.* (São Paulo: Cultrix, 1975).

Brandão, Ignácio de Loyola. *O beijo não vem da boca* (São Paulo: Global, 1985).

———. *Não verás país nenhum* (São Paulo: Global, 1985). Published in English as *And Still the Earth*, trans. Ellen Watson (New York: Avon, 1982).

———. *Zero* (Rio de Janeiro: Codecri, 1982), p. 86. Published in English as *Zero*, trans. Ellen Watson (New York: Avon, 1983).

Brasil, Assis. *Clarice Lispector, ensaio* (Rio de Janeiro: Simões, 1969).

Bruner, Jerome S. "Myth and Identity," *Myth and Mythmaking*, ed. Henry A. Murray (Boston: Beacon, 1960).

Brushwood, John. "Recent Translations of Latin American Fiction," *The Missouri Review* 5, no. 2 (1981–82).

Burke, Kenneth. "The Criticism of Criticism," *Accent* 15 (1955): 292.

Cagidemetrio, Alide. "The Real Thing," *Critical Angles*, ed. Marc Chénetier (Edwardsville and Carbondale: Southern Illinois University Press, 1986).

Callado, Antônio. *Bar Don Juan* (Rio de Janeiro: Civilazação Brasileira, 1982). Published in English as *Don Juan's Bar*, trans. Barbara Shelby (New York: Alfred Knopf, 1972).

———. *Quarup* (Rio de Janeiro: Civilização Brasileira, 1982). Published in English as *Quarup*, trans. Barbara Shelby (New York: Alfred Knopf, 1970).

Campbell, Joseph. *The Hero with a Thousand Faces* (Princeton: Princeton University Press, 1968).

———. "The Historical Development of Mythology," *Myth and Mythmaking*, ed. Henry A. Murray (Boston: Beacon Press, 1968), pp. 19–45.

———. "The Need for New Myths," *Time* 17 Jan. 1972, p. 51.

Campos, Haroldo de. "Serafim: um grande não-livro," *Obras completas*, II, Oswaldo de Andrade, pp. 99–127. Published in English as "Seraphim a Great Nonbook," *Seraphin Grosse Point*, trans. Kenneth G. Jackson and Albert G. Bork, pp. 113–131.

Carneiro, Maria Luiza Tucci. *O anti-semitismo na era Vargas* (Rio de Janeiro: Brasiliene, 1988).

Cawelti, John G. *Adventure, Mystery, and Romance* (Chicago: University of Chicago Press, 1976).

Chamberlain, Bobby J. "Murilo Rubião," *A Dictionary of Contemporary Brazilian Authors*, eds. D. W. Foster and Roberto Reis (Tempe: Arizona State University, Center for Latin American Studies, 1982), p. 131.

Chambers, Ian. *Popular Culture* (London: Methuen, 1986).

Chénetier, Marc. *Critical Angles: European Views of Contemporary American Literature* (Edwardsville and Carbondale: Southern Illinois University Press, 1986).

Cohn, Keith. *Film and Fiction* (New Haven: Yale University Press, 1979).

Coover, Robert. *A Night at the Movies: Or You Must Remember This* (New York: Simon & Schuster, 1987).

Costa, Flávio Moreira da. *O desastronauta: OK, Jack Kerouac, nós estamos te esperando em Copacabana* (Rio de Janeiro: Expressão e Cultura, 1971).

———. *Malvedeza durão* (Rio de Janeiro: Record, 1981).

Coutinho, Edilberto. *Maracanã, adeus* (Rio de Janeiro: Olympio, 1982).

Culler, Jonathan D. *On Deconstruction* (Ithaca, New York: Cornell University Press, 1982).

Däniken, Erich von. *Chariots of the Gods? Unsolved Mysteries of the Past* (New York: Putnam, 1969).

Denser, Márcia. *Diana Caçadora* (São Paulo: Global, 1986).

DiAntonio, Aaron. "The Genesis and Demise of the Jewish Agricultural Movement," unpublished paper submitted for A–25, Harvard College, 3–26–85.

DiAntonio, Robert. "Myth as a Unifying Force in 'O crime do professor de matemática,'" *Luso-Brazilian Review*, XXII, 2(1985) pp.27–32.

————. "The Passage from Myth to Anti-Myth in Antônio de Alcântara Machado's 'Gaetaninho'," *Annali Instituto Universitario Orientale*, Napoli, *Sezione Romanza* 28, 2 (1986) pp. 151–56.

————, and Aaron DiAntonio. "Jewish Brazilian Writing," *Jewish Spectator* 53, no. 1 (Spring, 1988) pp. 53–55.

————. Rev. of *Bufo & Spallanzani*, by Rubem Fonseca, *Chasqui* 17, no. 1 (May, 1988): 126.

————. Rev. of *The Land*, by Antônio Torres, *World Literature Today* 62, no. 2 (Spring, 1988): p. 260.

————. "'Nation' Traces Mystical Reality." Rev. of *The Strange Nation of Rafael Mendes*, by Moacyr Scliar. *The Kansas City Star* 14 Feb. 1988, p. 11E.

————. "Surprising Passion in Lispector's Final Novel." Rev. of *The Hour of the Star*, by Clarice Lispector. *The St. Louis Post-Dispatch* 23 Feb. 1988, p. 5D.

Dillistone, F. W. *The Novelist and the Passion Story* (New York: Sheed & Ward, 1960).

Dostoyesvsky, Fyodor. *Notes from Underground*, trans. Andrew R. MacAndrews (New York: Signet, 1961).

Drummond, Roberto. *Hitler manda lembranças* (Rio de Janeiro: Nova Fronteira, 1984).

————. *A morte de D. J. em Paris* (São Paulo: Ática, 1983).

————. *Sangue de Coca-Cola* (Rio de Janeiro: Nova Fronteira, 1985).

Dzialovsky, Francisco. *O terceiro testamento* (Rio de Janeiro: Anima, 1988).

Eagleton, Terry. *Literary Theory* (Minneapolis: University of Minnesota Press, 1983).

Ehrmann, Jacques. *Literature and Revolution* (Boston: Beacon Press, 1967).

Eliade, Mircea. *Ordeal by Labyrinth*, trans. Derek Cotman (Chicago: University of Chicago Press, 1978).

————. "The Yearning for Paradise in Primitive Tradition," *Myth and Mythmaking*, ed. Henry A. Murray (Boston: Beacon, 1960).

Eliot, T. S. *The Waste Land and Other Poems* (New York: Harvest, 1962).

Ellison, Fred P. *Brazil's New Novel: Four Northeastern Masters* (Berkley: The University of California Press, 1954).

Ellmann, Richard. *The Modern Tradition* (New York: Oxford, 1965).

Fitz, Earl E. "Bibliografia de y sobre Clarice Lispector," *Revista Iberoamericana*, 50, 126 (1984), 293–304.

————. *Clarice Lispector* (Boston: Twayne, 1985).

Fonseca, Rubem. *Bufo & Spallanzani* (Rio de Janeiro: Francisco Alves, 1985).

————. *A grande arte* (Rio de Janeiro: Francisco Alves, 1984). Published in English as *High Art*, trans. Ellen Watson (New York: Harper & Row, 1986).

————. *Lúcia McCartney*. (Rio de Janeiro: Olivé, 1969).

Foster, David William. *Alternate Voices* (Columbia: University of Missouri Press, 1985).

———. "Major Figures in the Brazilian Short Story," *The Latin American Short Story*, ed. Margaret Sayers Peden (Boston: G.K. Hall,1983).

Foster, David William, and Virginia Ramos Foster, eds. *Modern Latin American Literature*, (New York: Unger, 1975), vol. 1.

Foster, David William, and Roberto Reis, eds. *A Dictionary of Contemporary Brazilian Authors*. (Tempe: Arizona State University, Center for Latin American Studies, 1982).

Freud, Sigmund. *A General Introduction to Psychoanalysis*, trans. Joan Riviera (New York: Washington Square Press, 1968).

Freud, Anna. *The Ego and the Mechanisms of Defense*, trans. Cecil Barnes (New York: The Hogarth Press, 1973).

Friedman, Bruce Jay, ed. *Black Humor* (New York: Bantam, 1965).

Gass, William H. "Philosophy and Form of Fiction," *Fiction and the Figures of Life* (New York: Knopf, 1970).

Garcia, Irineu. "*Maíra*, ofício litúrgico de Darcy Ribeiro," *JL-Jornal de Letras, Artes e Idéias*, no 2, (1981).

Gilman, Richard. "The Idea of the Avant-Garde," *Writers and Politics*, eds. Edith Kurzweiland and William Phillips (Boston: Routledge & Kegan Paul, 1983).

Glicksberg, Charles I. *The Ironic Vision in Modern Literature* (The Hague: Martinue Nijhoff, 1969).

———. *The Self in Modern Literature* (University Park, PA: Pennsylvania State University Press, 1969).

———. *The Tragic Vision in Twentieth-Century Literature* (Edwardsville and Carbondale: Southern Illinois University Press, 1962).

Gomes, Dias, and Ferreira Gullar. *Dr. Getúlio, sua vida e sua glória* (Rio de Janeiro: Civilização Brasileira, 1968).

Habery, David T. *Three Sad Races: Racial Identity & National Consciousness in Brazilian Literature* (Cambridge: Cambridge University Press, 1983).

Hamilton, Edith. *Mythology* (New York: Mentor Book, 1953).

Harris, Charles B. *Contemporary American Novelists of the Absurd* (New Haven: College & University Press, 1971).

Hassan, Ihab H. "The Character of Post-War Fiction in America," *On Contemporary Literature*, ed. Richard Kostelanetz (New York: Avon, 1969).

Hendin, Josephine. "Experimental Fiction," *Harvard Guide to Contemporary Writing*, ed. Daniel Hoffman (Cambridge, MA: Belknap Press, 1979).

Herskovitz, Melville Jean. "Magic," *The Standard Dictionary of Folklore, Mythology and Legend*, ed. Maria Leach (New York: Funk & Wagnalls, 1975).

SELECT BIBLIOGRAPHY

Hoggart, Richard. *Speaking to Each Other*, Vol II: *About Literature* (New York: Chatto & Windus, 1970).

Hohlfeldt, Antônio. *Conto brasileiro contemporâneo* (Porto Alegre, Mercado Aberto, 1981).

Howe, Irving. *Literary Modernism* (New York: Fawcett, 1967).

Isaacson, José, and Santiago E. Kovadloff, eds. *Comunidades judías de Latinoamérica* (Buenos Aires: Editorial Candelabro, 1970).

Iser, Wolfgang. "The Reading Process: A Phenomenological Approach," trans. Catherine Macksey and Richard Macksey, *Reader-Response Criticism*, ed. Jane Tompkins (Baltimore: The Johns Hopkins University Press, 1985).

Jackson, Neil. "Christa Wolf," *Contemporary Foreign Language Writers*, eds. James Vinson and Daniel Kirkpatrick (New York: St. Martin's Press, 1984).

Jobes, Gertrude. *Dictionary of Mythology, Folklore and Symbols* (New York: The Scarecrow Press, 1962).

Johnson, Randal, and Robert Stam. *Brazilian Cinema* (Rutherford, NJ: Fairleigh Dickinson University Press, 1982).

Jozef, Bella. "La recuperación de la palabra poética," *Revista Iberoamericana*, vol. 50, no. 126 (1984).

Jung, Carl Gustav. *Psychological Reflections*, ed. Jolande Jacobi (New York: Harper, 1961).

Kadir, Djelal. "The Survival of Theory and the Surviving Fictions of Latin America," *Modern Fiction Studies* 32 (1986).

Kanfer, Stefan. "Macho Days on the Cacoa Frontier," a review of *Showdown* by Jorge Amado. *Time* magazine 15 February 1988: p. 92.

Kepp, Michael. "Armed Clashes Mark Brazil's Land Reform: Wealthy Landowners Hire Private Armies of Guards," *The St. Louis Post-Dispatch* 5 July 1986, p. B–1.

Klinkowitz, Jerome. *Literary Disruptions* (Urbana: University of Illinois Press, 1975).

Kostelanetz, Richard. "Contemporary Literature," *On Contemporary Literature*, ed. Richard Kostelanetz (New York: Avon Books, 1969), p. xxvi.

Kutnik, Jerzy. *The Novel as Performance: The Fiction of Ronald Sukenick and Raymond Federman* (Edwardsville and Carbondale: Southern Illinois Press, 1986).

Lambert, Francis. "Latin America since Independence," *The Cambridge Encyclopedia of Latin America*, ed. Simon Colleir (Cambridge: Cambridge University Press, 1985).

Leach, Maria. *The Standard Dictionary of Folklore, Mythology and Legend* (New York: Funk & Wagnalls, 1972).

Levi, Primo. *The Periodic Table*, trans. Raymond Rosenthal (New York: Schocken Books, 1984).

Lindstrom, Naomi. "Clarice Lispector: Articulating Woman's Experience," *Chasqui*, vol. 8, no. 1 (1978), pp. 43–52.

Lispector, Clarice. *A hora da estrela* (Rio de Janeiro: Nova Fonteira, 1984). Published in English as *The Hour of the Star*, trans. Giovanni Pontiero (Manchester, England: Carcanet, 1986).

———. *Laços de família* (Rio de Janeiro: Nova Fronteira, 1983). Published in English as *Family Ties*, trans. Giovanni Pontiero (Austin: The University of Texas Press, 1972).

———. *A legião estrangeira* (Rio de Janeiro: Editora do Autor, 1964). The English translation is *The Foreign Legion*, trans. Giovanni Pontiero (Manchester, England: Carcanet, 1986).

Lobo, Luiza. "Women Writers in Brazil Today," *World Literature Today* 61 (1986): 49–54.

Lowe, Elizabeth. *The City in Brazilian Literature* (Rutherford, NJ: Fairleigh Dickinson University Press, 1982).

———. "Cries and Whispers: Answers to the Politics of Repression in Contemporary Brazilian Women's Fiction," *Occasional Papers in Women's Studies* (Miami: Florida International University Press, 1986).

Lucas, Fábio. "Aspectos culturais da literatura brasileira," *O caráter social da literatura brasileira* (Rio de Janeiro: Paz e Terra, 1970). Published in English as "Cultural Aspects of Brazilian Literature," trans. Alexandrino E. Severino, *TriQuarterly*, ed. José Donoso 13/14 Fall/Winter, 1968/69.

Machado, Janete Gaspar. *Constantes ficcionais em romances dos anos 70* (Florianópolis: Ed. da USSC, 1981).

Mattos, Cyro de, and Hélio Pólvora. *Antologia de contos brasileiros de bichos* (Rio de Janeiro: Block Editores, 1970).

Mazzaro, Jerome. *Postmodern American Poetry* (Urbana: University of Illinois Press, 1980).

McHale, Brian. *Postmodernist Fiction* (New York: Methuen, 1987).

Métraux, Alfred. "Tree of Life," *The Standard Dictionary of Folklore, Mythology and Legend*, ed. Maria Leach (New York: Funk & Wagnalls, 1972), p. 1123.

Miller, Jim. "Listening to Foreign Voices," *Newsweek* 26 Sept. 1983, p. 88.

Moisés, Carlos Felipe. "Crazy Galvez & Mad Maria," *Escrita: Revista de Literatura* 8, no. 32 (1983).

Moisés, Massaud, and José Paulo Paes. *Pequeno dicionário de literatura brasileira* (São Paulo: Cultrix, 1980).

Momaday, N. Scott. *House Made of Dawn* (New York: Signet, 1969).

Morante, Elsa. *Arturo's Island*, trans. Isabel Quigly (New York: Knopf, 1959).

Newman, Charles. *The Post-Modern Aura: The Art of Fiction in an Age of Inflation* (Evanston: Northwestern University Press, 1985).

Nunes, Benedito. *O mundo de Clarice Lispector* (Manaus: Edições do Govêrno do Estado, 1966).

Nunes, Maria Luisa. "Narrative Modes in Clarice Lispector's *Laços de família*: The Rendering of Consciousness," *Luso-Brazilian Review* 14, 12 (1977), 174–84.

Ortega y Gasset, José. *The Dehumanization of Art* (Garden City, NY: Doubleday Anchor Books, 1956), pp. 45–58.

——. *Man and Crisis*, trans. Mildred Adams (London: Allen & Unwin, 1959).

Palls, Terry L. "The Miracle of the Ordinary: Literary Epiphany in Virginia Woolf and Clarice Lispector," *Luso-Brazilian Review* XXI, 1 (1984), 63–78.

Panichas, George A., ed. *The Politics of Twentieth-Century Novelists* (New York: Hawthorn Books, Inc., 1971).

Patai, Daphne. *Myth and Ideology in Contemporary Brazilian Fiction* (Rutherford, NJ: Associated University Presses, 1983).

Paul, Steve. "Bawdy in Brazil," a review of *Showdown* by Jorge Amado. *The Kansas City Star* 14 February 1988: 1 E.

Pellegrini, Domingos. *Paixões*. (São Paulo: Ática, 1984).

Pereira, Paulo. "Silviano Santiago: crítica e invenção," *Jornal de Letras*, no. 419, Oct. 1986.

Perez, Gilbert. "These Days in the Holocene," *The Hudson Review* 33 (1980), 587–88.

Portella, Eduardo. "O grito do silêncio," *A hora da estrela*, Clarice Lispector (Rio de Janeiro: Nova Fronteira, 1984), pp. 9–13.

Prescott, Peter. "A Good Barbarian," *Newsweek* 30 Jan. 1978, p. 78.

——. *Never in Doubt* (New York: Arbor House, 1986).

Pynchon, Thomas. "Is It O.K. to Be a Luddite?" *New York Times Book Review* 28 Oct. 1984.

Raymond, Michael W. "Tai-Me, Christ, and the Machine: Affirmation through Mythic Pluralism in *House Made of Dawn*," *Studies in American Fiction*, XI, 1 (spring, 1983), 71.

Reis, Roberto. "Hei de convencer," *I&E: Ideologies and Literature* 6 (1978) 120–27.

Rey, Marcos. *Esta noite ou nunca* (São Paulo: Ática, 1985).

Ribeiro, Darcy. *Maíra* (Lisbon: Dom Quixote, 1983). Published in English as *Maíra*, trans. Thomas Colchie (New York: Aventura, 1984).

Ribeiro, João Ubaldo. *Sargento Getulio* (Rio de Janeiro: Nova Fronteira, 1982). Published in English as *Sergeant Getulio*, trans. João Ubaldo Ribeiro (New York: Avon, 1984).

——. *Viva o povo brasileiro* (Rio de Janeiro: Nova Fronteira, 1985).

Rodriguez Monegal, Emir. "The Contemporary Brazilian Novel," *Fiction in Several Languages*, ed. Henri Peyre (Boston: Beacon Press, 1968).

———. "Writing Fiction Under the Censor's Eye," *World Literature Today* 53 (1979): 19–22.

Rubião, Murilo. *O pirotécnico Zacarias* (São Paulo: Ática, 1974). Published in English as *The Ex-Magician and Other Stories*, trans. Thomas Colchie (New York: Avon, 1979).

Sá, Jorge de. "Sugestões de aproveitamento didático de *Maracanã, Adeus*," Edilberto Coutinho, *Maracanã, Adeus* (Rio de Janeiro: José Olympio Editora, 1980).

Sachar, Howard M. *Diaspora: An Inquiry into the Contemporary Jewish World* (New York: Harper & Row, 1985).

Saltzman, Arthur M. *The Fiction of William Gass* (Edwardsville and Carbondale, IL: Southern Illinois University Press, 1986).

Sant'Anna, Sérgio. *O concerto de João Gilberto no Rio de Janeiro* (São Paulo: Ática, 1982).

———. *Confissões de Ralfo* (Rio de Janeiro: Civilização Brasileira, 1975).

Santiago, Silviano. *Stella Manhattan* (Rio de Janeiro: Nova Fronteira, 1985).

Sayers, Raymond S. Rev. of *The Ex-Magician and Other Stories* by Murilo Rubião, *World Literature Today* 54, no. 2 (1980), 264.

Schwartz, Howard, and Anthony Rudolf. *Voices Within the Ark* (New York: Avon, 1980).

Schwartz, Roberto. "Obra muriliana do fantástico como máscara," *Suplemento literário de Minas Gerais*, 15 March 1975, p. 14.

Scliar, Moacyr. *O centaur no jardim* (Porto Alegre: L & PM Editores, 1983). Published in English as *The Centaur in the Garden*, trans. Margaret A. Neves (New York: Ballantine, 1984).

———. *Os deuses de Raquel.* (Porto Alegre: L & PM Editores, 1978). Published in English as *The Gods of Raquel*, trans. Eloah P. Giacomelli (New York: Ballantine, 1986).

———. *A festa no castelo* (Porto Alegre: L & PM Editores, 1982).

———. *A guerra no Bom Fim.* (Porto Alegre: L & PM Editores, 1982).

Severino, Alexandrino E. "Major Trends in the Development of the Brazilian Short Story," *Studies in Short Fiction* 8, no. 1 (1971): 199–208.

Shechner, Mark. "Jewish Writers," *The Harvard Guide to Contemporary American Writing*, ed. Daniel Hoffman (Cambridge: Belknap Press, 1979).

Silverman, Malcolm. *Moderna ficção brasileira* (Rio de Janeiro: Civilização Brasileira, 1978).

———. *Moderna ficção brasileira 2* (Rio de Janeiro: Civilização Brasileira, 1981).

———. *O novo conto brasileiro* (Rio de Janeiro: Nova Fronteira, 1985).

———. Review of *Esta noite ou nunca* by Marcos Rey, *World Literature Today* 60, no. 2 (1986): 296–97.

Singer, Isaac Bashevis. *The Death of Methuselah* (New York: Farrar, Straus & Giroux, 1988).

Slater, Candace. *Stories on a String: The Brazilian Literatura de Cordel* (Los Angeles: The University of California Press, 1982)

Souza, Márcio. *A condolência* (Rio de Janeiro: Marco Zero, 1984).

———. *Galvez, Imperador do Acre* (Rio de Janeiro: Marco Zero, 1983). Published in English as *The Emperor of the Amazon*, trans. Thomas Colchie (New York: Avon, 1980).

———. *Mad Maria* (Rio de Janeiro: Civilização Brasileira, 1983). Published in English as *Mad Maria*, trans. Thomas Colchie (New York: Avon, 1985).

Souza, Ronald W. "Canonical Questions," *Ideologies and Literature* 6 (1978): 102–06.

Stepan, Alfred. "War on the People," *New York Times* 23 Nov. 1986, natl. edition.

Stevik, Philip. *Alternate Pleasures: Postrealist Fiction and Tradition* (Urbana: Univ. of Illinois Press, 1981).

Suckenick, Ronald. *Blown Away* (Los Angeles: Sun & Moon Press, 1986).

———. *In Form: Digressions on the Art of Fiction* (Edwardsville and Carbondale: Southern Illinois University Press, 1985).

Suvin, Darko. *Metamorphoses of Science Fiction* (New Haven: Yale University Press, 1979).

Sypher, Wylie. *Loss of the Self in Modern Literature and Art* (New York: Vintage Books, 1964).

Telles, Lygia Fagundes. *As meninas* (Rio de Janeiro: José Olympio, 1982). Published in English as *The Girl in the Photograph*, trans. Margret A. Neves (New York: Avon, 1982).

Thurston, SJ, Herbert, ed. *Butler's Lives of the Saints* (New York: P. J. Kennedy and Sons, 1956), pp. 184–87.

Tompkins, Jane. "An Introduction to Reader-Response Criticism," *Reader-Response Criticism*, ed. Jane Tompkins (Baltimore: The Johns Hopkins University Press, 1985).

Toole, John Kennedy. *A Confederacy of Dunces* (New York: Grove Press, 1981).

Torres, Antônio. *Essa terra*. trans. Margaret A. Neves (São Paulo: Ática, 1976). Published in English as *The Land* (London: Readers International, 1987).

Trinner, Joseph F. "Native Americans and the American Mix in N. Scott Momaday's *House Made of Dawn*," *Indiana Social Studies Quarterly* 28 (1975), 88–89.

Updike, John. *The Centaur* (New York: Bantam, 1963).

Vidal, Hernán. *Literatura hispanoamericana e ideología liberal: surgimiento y crisis* (Tacoma Park, MD: Hispamérica, 1976).

Viera, Nelson H. "Hitler and Mengele in Brasil: The Testimony of Roberto Drummond," *Modern Fiction Studies* 32, no.3 (1986): 427–37.

Vilela, Luiz. *Entre amigos* (São Paulo: Ática, 1983).

———. *O inferno é aqui mesmo* (São Paulo: Ática, 1979).

Vincent, John. *João Guimarães Rosa* (Boston: Twayne, 1978).

Vonnegut, Jr., Kurt. *Breakfast of Champions* (New York: Dell Publishing Co., Inc., 1973).

Waugh, Patricia. *Metafiction: The Theory and Practice of Self-Conscious Fiction* (New York: Methuen, 1984).

Wellek, René, and Austin Warren. *Theory of Literature* (New York: Harcourt, Brace and World, 1956).

Wheelock, Carter. "Borges, Cortázar, and the Aesthetic of the Vacant Mind," *International Fiction Review* 12, no. 1 (1985), pp. 3–10.

White, John J. *Mythology in the Modern Novel* (Princeton: Princeton University Press, 1971).

Wilson, Robert N. *The Writer as Social Seer* (Chapel Hill: University of North Carolina Press, 1979).

Wiznitzer, Arnold. *Jews in Colonial Brazil* (Morningside Heights, NY: Columbia University Press, 1960).

Wood, Michael. "In the Latino Americano Mirror," *The New York Review of Books* 28, 16 (Oct. 22, 1981), p. 53–57.

Zilberman, Regina. *Do mito ao romance* (Porto Alegre: Chronos, 1977).

Ziolkowski, Theodore. *Fictional Transfigurations of Jesus* (Princeton: Princeton University Press, 1972).

Zipes, Jack. "Mass Degradation of Humanity and Massive Contradictions in Bradbury's Vision of America in *Fahrenheit 451*," *No Place Else*, ed. Eric Rabkin (Edwardsville and Carbondale, IL: Southern Illinois University Press, 1983).

INDEX

217

218

INDEX

Paul, Steve, 179
Pereira, Teresinha Alvez, 57n4
Perez, Gilbert, 110n4
Piñon, Nelida, 183
playgiarism, 156
Pólvora, Hélio, 134
Pontiero, Giovanni, 162, 168
Portella, Eduardo, 168
post-modernist narrative, 161, 202
post-structuralist perspective, 164
prefiguration, 16–17, 57–58n8, 59n21, 66, 68, 73; techniques of, 42–44
Prescott, Peter S., 46, 195
Quarup, 7, 9, 77n8
racial myths, 7, 31–32
Raymond, Michael W., 74
reader, as participant, 15–26, 121, 155–61, 164, 168–71
reader identification, 93
reader-response theory, 34
reading process, phenomenological theory of, 168
reality, fragmentation of, 62
redemption, 43, 60n11
Rey, Marcos. *See* Esta noite ou nunca
Ribeiro, Darcy. *See* Maíra
Ribeiro, João Ubaldo, 59–60n9; *See also* Sargento Getúlio, Viva o povo brasileiro
Rodríguez Monegal, Emir, 12, 56n6, 140
Romance Novo (The New Novel), 34, 56–57n6
Rosa João Guimarães. *See* Grande Sertão: Veredas
Rubião, Murilo, 186
Sá, Jorge de, 63
Sachar, Howard M., 115
Saltzman, Arthur M., 158
Sangue de Coca-Cola (Coca-Cola Blood), 3–4, 63, 92–93, 157–58
Sant'Anna, Sérgio. *See* O concerto de João Gilberto no Rio de Janeiro, Confissões de Ralfo
Santiago, Silviano. *See* Stella Manhattan
Sargento Getúlio (Sergeant Getúlio), 135
Sartrean tenets, 57n3
satire, 110n9, 140
Sayers, Raymond S., 188
Scholes, Robert, 195
Schwartz, Howard, 129–30n9
Schwartz, Jorge, 189
science fiction, 135–36
Scliar, Moacyr, 139. *See also* A estranha

nacão de Rafael Mendes, A festa no castelo, O centauro no jardim
Seriphim Grosse Point, 79
Shechner, Mark, 113
short fiction, 62–63
Silverman, Malcolm, 176
Singer, Isaac Bashevis, 113
Slater, Candace, 156
sociopolitical narrative, 202
Soriano, Osvaldo, 204n3
Souza, Márcio, 85, 96, 155. *See also* A condolência, Galvez, Imperador do Acre, Mad Maria, O ordem do dia
Stella Manhattan, 5, 181–82
Stevik, Philip, 156
Sukenick, Ronald, 157–58
Suvin, Darko, 139
symbology, 37–38, 68, 154n8; in *A hora da estrela*, 167; of the hyacinth, 42–43
symbols of vegetation, as structuring principle, 151–52
Sypher, Wylie, 107
Tapajós, Renato. *See* Em camara lenta
Telles, Lygia Fagundes. *See* As meninas
Tenda dos milagres (Tent of Miracles), 157
Tereza Batista, Cansada de querra (Teresa Batista, Home from the War), 157
This Crowded Earth, 147
Tobit, book of, 28–29n6
Tocaia Grande: a face obscura (Showdown), 179–80, 203
Tompkins, Jane P., 164
Toro de San Marcos, 58n13
Torres, Antônio. *See* Essa terra
Trinner, Joseph F., 67
Updike, John, 88, 121–22
Vargas, Getúlio, 2. *See also* Estado Novo
Vargas Llosa, Mario, 204n1
Veríssimo, Érico, 46
Vidal, Hernán, 204n4
Vilela, Luiz. *See* Entre amigos
Vincent, Jon S., 47
Viva o povo brasileiro, 6
Vonnegut, Kurt, Jr., 81
Warren, Austin, 134
Wellek, René, 134
Wheelock, Carter, 199n21
White, John J., 17, 28–29n6, 38, 57–58n8, 66, 121
Wiznitzer, Arnold, 114